Historical Studies VIII

HISTORICAL STUDIES

Papers read before the Irish Conference of Historians

VIII

DUBLIN

27–30 May 1969

R. COBB
T. SCHIEDER
W. WALLACE
J. KUDRNA
O. MacDONAGH
L. DE PAOR
D. BETHELL
H. HAMMERSTEIN
J. BOSSY
D. McCARTNEY
J. LEE

Edited by T. D. WILLIAMS

GILL and MACMILLAN

First published 1971 by
Gill and Macmillan Ltd
Dublin 1
and in London through association with
Macmillan and Co. Ltd

7171 0503 2

Printed and bound in the Republic of Ireland by
the Book Division of Smurfit Print and Packaging Limited, Dublin.

Contents

Introduction

The Irish Committee of Historical Sciences, founded in March 1938 to provide for the representation of Irish historical interests on the Comité International des Sciences Historiques, has held a conference of historians annually since 1939, to transact routine business and to hear papers on historical subjects. Before 1953 a paper on an Irish subject was usually read by an Irish historian. In July 1953 a larger conference was held which lasted for three days. The subjects were not confined any longer to Irish history and the speakers included visiting scholars. It was decided that in future a conference of this kind should be held every second year.

The second biennial conference was held in Dublin in 1955, and the papers read at the conference were published under the title 'Historical Studies: papers read before the Second Irish Conference of Historians'. This was to be the first of a continuing series. Since 1955 the conference has been circulating among all the university colleges of Ireland and in 1965 a second cycle began. The conference has been deliberately kept small in size, but the attendance includes a considerable number of historians from outside Ireland.

There has been some inconsistency in the use of the terms 'Conference of Irish Historians' and 'Irish Conference of Historians'. The committee wishes it to be understood that the former term should apply to the annual single-session conferences held since 1939, and the latter to the biennial, multi-session conferences inaugurated in 1953. It has also been decided that the standing title of the published series shall in future be 'Historical Studies: papers read before the Irish Conference of Historians.' The following is a complete list of the volumes already published and of the conferences to which they refer:

Historical Studies: papers read before the
Irish Conference of Historians

vol.	conference	editor	date of publication
I	Trinity College and University College, Dublin, 11–13 July 1955	T. D. Williams	1958

II	Queen's University, Belfast, 22–4 May 1957	Michael Roberts	1959
III	University College, Cork, 27–9 May 1959	James Hogan	1961
IV	University College, Galway, 25–7 May 1961	G. A. Hayes-McCoy	1963
V	Magee University College, Londonderry, 30 May–1 June 1963	J. L. McCracken	1965
VI	Trinity College, Dublin, 2–5 June 1965	T. W. Moody	1968
VII	The Queen's University, Belfast, 24–7 May 1967	J. C. Beckett	1969
VIII	University College, Dublin, 27–30 May 1969	T. D. Williams	1971

The present volume comprises eight of the eleven papers read at the Ninth Irish Conference of Historians, organised by the Irish Committee of Historical Sciences, held at University College, Dublin, between 27 and 30 May, 1969. One paper was read at the previous conference at the Queen's University, Belfast, and two papers not read at the conference, have been substituted in place of papers read by the same authors at the conference.

The committee wishes to express its gratitude to University College, Dublin for its hospitality and for the grant that has made this publication possible.

T. D. Williams

University College, Dublin
June 1970

PART I: GENERAL HISTORY

The French Revolution and Private Life*

Richard Cobb

Revolutionary regimes and revolutionary periods put an extra premium on political and moral orthodoxy and on collective identity. This is no doubt always so in political and public life, but it is much more so in the exceptional circumstances of a revolutionary dictatorship and in a regime that places overall emphasis on indivisibility expressed in the steely concept of unanimity. If individuality had been allowed a certain amount of personal expression in the early years of the Revolution—and it could not be said that such an extreme eccentric as Jean-Paul Marat was the product of a conveyor-belt of properly moulded revolutionists—in the course of Robespierre's Red Summer of 1794, the revolutionary, in his public image, was subjected increasingly to the dictates of a universal model.

One cannot imagine Robespierre ever having a private life: every waking minute was given to the Republic of Virtue and, no doubt, his sleep too was likewise devoted to the Supreme Being and to means of securing a unanimity as harmonious as the Music of the Spheres. His sleep was certainly untroubled by indigestion, for he ate of carefully prepared dishes in moderation, or by the fumes of alcohol, for he never went beyond the half-bottle, and sex seems to have been confined to the organisation of Sunday School treats devoted to the glorification of maidenhood and, very discreetly and under careful wrappings, of motherhood. Robespierre, in fact, did not have any private life, at least during the last year of his political existence; and his main quarrel with his unfortunate sister, Charlotte, was that she did have one, that she was conducting a love affair with an unsuitable colleague of her brother's, a man not at all virtuous under any count. Robespierre, who had had the advantage of having been an orphan from a very early age, must have often regretted the bad luck that had saddled him with a sister of human proportions and endowed with human failings, for his brother Augustin was but a

* This paper, completely revised and greatly enlarged, now forms part of two chapters of a book to be published by Oxford University Press in 1972. The present text should not, therefore, be regarded as definitive.

projection of himself, and was even given the privilege of dying with himself (whereas the wretched Charlotte was further condemned to live on for many years and to survive the saintly pair through long periods of Vice, Debauchery and lack of unanimity).

Indeed, it might be argued that the real reason for Danton's execution was that he *had* a private life, and one that stuck out a mile. He made no bones about it, was quite prepared to state that he thought his recently-acquired sixteen-year-old wife a more important priority than saving the Republic. Of Robespierre's eleven colleagues, there would be little to be said—for little is known—in this respect. Their addresses are in the *Almanach National* of the year II,[1] a fact that was ascertained by Admirat when he wanted to shoot and/or stab one of them (but he went to the wrong address, was found lurking in the corridor, with a revolver in one hand and a dagger in the other—an ambidexterous would-be murderer who, when the *garde* arrived, attempted to take refuge in a staircase lavatory). A number of them stayed in hotels within walking distance of the Committees and the Convention, so that even their addresses reveal nothing other than that they wanted to reside as close as possible to their public life.

The only member of the Committee who had had an identifiable private life was Hérault de Séchelles, who had a prolonged love affair with two sisters, who were also foreigners; he was executed in the spring of 1794, as was the former monk, Chabot, who had married a girl who was rich, Jewish and Austrian—a hat-trick, in fact, in the very worst priorities attainable in revolutionary terms. Billaud-Varennes was to reserve his private life for deportation, when, in French Guiana, he set himself up in a Crusoe-like existence, with a beautiful and dark savage girl whom he taught to dress and for whom he constructed a hut of straw and palm leaves. But he was the only member of the great Committee in any way to conform to the standards set by the *abbé* Prévost. They were rather a dull, anonymous, terribly over-worked lot. The members of the Revolutionary Government had little time for anything else; they even tended to have their meals brought in by a nearby *traiteur*; and these they put down quickly, amidst scattered bundles of papers, some of which still bear wine stains. When it was a matter of preparing a big political trial and of sending a number of their former colleagues to the guillotine, they would convoke their equally faceless opposite numbers from the other Committee, work out the official hand-out through the night, taking a few hours' sleep on chairs or sofas. It was a superhuman and round-the-clock sort of government that left no

[1] *Almanach national de France, l'an deuxième de la République une et indivisible,* à Paris, de l'Imprimerie de Testu, rue Hautefeuille, no 14.

room for enjoyment and little even for sleep. It was hardly surprising—but it is reassuring—that it lasted only a year.

Historians of individuality, not to say of crankiness and of the extremes of eccentricity, will be much better off with the Counter-Revolution. For here at least there is no bleak concept of unanimity, no standard model, no striving after an indivisibility that would engulf all personal *traits* in the regimented prissiness of the Republic of Virtues. There were as many Counter-Revolutions as there were counter-revolutionaries; and, as these latter were so often thrown on their own devices, whether to continue the struggle in the rocky fastnesses of south-central France, or to eke out uncomfortable livelihoods in unlikely employments in unpleasant parts of Europe, or even in America, their commitment took the most extreme forms of personal self-expression. The counter-revolutionary had to fight largely on his own, in his own area and, left to his own devices, his personality was much more important than whatever confused positive programme he might enunciate; and he had the advantage, in terms of individual commitment, of proposing solutions that were almost entirely negative, destructive and simple in the extreme. He and his motley following knew what they were *against*; they shared identifiable and named hate-figures; and they were agreed how they were to deal with these.

The Revolutionary Government bureaucratised death in the pursuit of political virtue; death was not given names, it might embrace 90 per cent of the male population of France over the age of fourteen.[2] The Counter-Revolution went for individuals and it had to make do with small, loosely-knit bodies of armed men, concerned with individual vengeance and with decentralised lynching and exemplary murder. By the summer of 1794, the Revolutionary Government had taken to killing by stealth; but a counter-revolutionary murder had to be as public as possible, in order for its message to get home—hence, for instance, the advantage of a lynching on a bridge or on the main square, or the hanging of a southern farmer on the cypress tree at the entrance to his recently-purchased farm—a former *bien national*.

[2] It has often been argued that the terrible Law of 22 Prairial, year II, was designed to try unobtrusively and to dispose of with the minimum of fuss such members of the Convention as might appear dangerous to the Committees of government. But, in fact, its provisions were far wider than this, for, by introducing extensive moral definitions of what constituted an 'enemy of the people', the law could expose any individual convicted of some slight moral failing—ill-treating his father, political indifference, calling in question official statements, immoral conduct—to the risk of outlawry and to the death sentence. By the law, citizenship was given a moral content; it followed that citizens who lacked Virtue were in fact non-citizens, beings politically dead, and who could thus be physically eliminated as well as an operation of moral regeneration.

The Counter-Revolution's methods were anarchical, violent and highly personalised; and its leaders were amateur enthusiasts whose activities reflected their generally strong sense of individuality. All were motivated above all by the military virtues of personal honour, family pride, physical courage; most of them were lacking in any form of common-sense. Some found an outlet in secret inks, in the exciting and flattering paraphernalia of conspiracy; others favoured week-end *sorties* in which individual terrorists would be the quarry. And the counter-revolutionary was released from the stultifying burden of *public* life in France: he could only act by stealth, his political activity was but an extension of his private life, of his family circle. Many *sabreurs* had brothers, parents or cousins to avenge, and they often accompanied a killing with such comments, addressed to the victim, as *prend ça pour mon frère, et encore ça pour mon père*. It was also an extension of those wider obligations of employment, patronage, kinship and regional loyalties and antipathies. When, in the south-east, the Counter-Revolution expressed itself in the crudest, physical terms of the local murder gang—Company of Jesus, Company of Jehu, Company of the Sun—it owed its relative success or failure to the influence of local squires, to their ability to express themselves in terms of physical audacity and verbal incitement, to their hold over their tenants, and to those who, for a variety of reasons, were drawn to the wild ways and to individual acts of bloodshed and violence.

A *sortie* of a southern murder gang began in the *auberge* and ended in the *château*, with long pauses between killings in other wayside inns or urban wine-shops of the kind frequented by men from a single locality or from an identifiable trade. So the ranks of the counter-revolutionary squire could be expected to draw upon those who habitually lived on the border of crime and violence: the poacher, the former smuggler, the horse-dealer, the carter, the carrier, the river-worker (especially the *flotteur,* though he might equally be attracted to the violent ranks of the Ultra-Revolution), the old-clothes' merchant, the junk merchant, the blacksmith, the sailor, the docker, the hair-dresser, the former servant, the ex-soldier (especially, no doubt, such regiments as those of Auvergne, Royal-Piémont and the household troops), the fencing-master, the inn-keeper, the lock-smith, the counterfeiter, the jeweller, the engraver, the *notaire,* the former *parlementaire*. Indeed, in such a *negative* polarisation, the appeal would extend far beyond class or condition, sometimes to include virtually a whole community which, as the results of the accidents of geography and of the political history of the Revolution, had collectively invested in the defeat of the Republic (or of all the Republics) and in the prolongation of any form of violent anarchy that might weaken the existing regime in Paris.[3]

In short, the Counter-Revolution became a way of life, the expression of an individual mentality and the affirmation of a strongly-held sense of regional loyalty, most clearly expressed in the form of hostility to Paris. In this, it was able to unite ancient history, genealogical knowledge (genealogy was an obsession with many counter-revolutionary squires, especially in proud Languedoc or Provence, in the Vivarais, the Velay and the Forez) and historical memory with present political facts. The Counter-Revolution had the *past* on its side, and this mattered, especially in the rural and regional context, and at a time when the *present* was either Robespierre, Thermidorian class selfishness or Directorial incoherence, military rule and courts-martial, and the *gendarmerie mobile*. The Counter-Revolution, in the conditions of 1795 to 1802 or so, for these were the years in which it made itself physically most effective, at least in the Rhône valley, would have an undoubted pull on all those who, for one reason or another, had never loved the *sergent de la maréchaussée* and did not love any better his successor, the *sergent de la gendarmerie nationale*.[4] From 1795 to 1799, at least, such was the extent of its control over

[3] The Counter-Revolution tended to keep to the hills, occasionally descending into the plains on some marauding mission of pillage or vengeance. Its strongholds were the semi-fortified hill villages of the Massif-Central and the Luberan, of the Ardèche, the Lozère and the Aveyron; and so, in practical terms, the Counter-Revolution often expressed itself as the collective vengeance of the mountaineer on the republican plainsman. But, in the Rhône valley at least, it also possessed its urban strongholds. The facts of geography were aided, in this respect, by the accidents of revolutionary history. A town that had been rejected as *chef-lieu* by the *comité de division*, was likely to feel unsympathetic to the new regime, especially if, under the Civil Constitution, it lost its diocese and its ecclesiastical courts as well. It would have been surprising if Lyon, deprived of its very name, cut off from its hinterland to the west, and reduced to the rump of a Department, following its surrender in October 1793, could have felt any sympathy for the Republic of the year II and for rule from Paris.

On the subject of the first White Terror, or Counter-Terror in the Rhône valley and the Midi, see R. C. Cobb, *The Police and the People: French Popular Protest, 1789–1820*, Oxford, Clarendon Press, 1970, part II, section on the White Terror. See also my *A Second Identity: Essays on France and French History*, Oxford University Press, 1969, 'The White Terror', 192. On the subject of the counter-revolutionary, see Jacqueline Chaumié, *Le réseau d'Antraigues et la Contre-Révolution, 1791–1793*, Paris, 1965, and my 'The Comte d'Antraigues and the Counter-Revolutionary Mentality', *op. cit.*, 177. On the subject of the second White Terror, that of 1815, see Gwynne Lewis, *The White Terror in the Department of the Gard*, unpublished D.Phil. thesis, to be published by the Clarendon Press.

[4] Of 82 persons cited as having taken part in the various Lyon prison massacres, or in individual acts of murder committed in the city between the years III and VIII, 13 were engaged in various occupations concerned with the river traffic (*marinier, crocheteur, portefaix, ouvrier sur le port*, etc.); 8 were in the drink trade (*marchand de vin, aubergiste, cabaretier*, etc.). There were half-a-dozen hairdressers and as many tailors, cutters and silk-workers, the latter inevitably numerous in this city. There were a few carters, two or three deserters, five lawyers (*notaire, homme de loi*, etc.) and the usual range of shop-keepers and craftsmen. Perhaps the most distinctive feature of

life in the south-east, it might appear to have the *future* on its side as well, for, there, it constituted an effective counter-government.

The appeal might come from many different and conflicting sources. The womanisers, at both the top and bottom levels of society, might feel the pull in that direction. The type of lady who offered rewards in the form of the *repos du guerrier* and who admired the military virtues of a prickly sense of honour and of ability to kill would be more drawn to Christ and King than to the collective *trompette guerrière* of a depersonalised Sovereign People. It was the *squiress* who sent the squire out on such violent and dangerous missions, much as it was the *Marquise* who shamed the *Marquis* into emigration and enlistment in the *armée des Princes*.[5] At the other end of the scale, there is a Greek choir of raucous feminine incitement, provoking, stimulating, accompanying the more spectacular activities of the murder gangs; while, at the end of the foray, once the men have slaked their thirst and satisfied appetites stimulated by brutal and battering lynchings, there will be women of the lowest condition: prostitutes, seamstresses, *revendeuses,*[6] *brodeuses, crieuses, repasseuses, blanchisseuses, bouquetières,* etc.—the proletariate of female urban employment and seasonal labour, awaiting the returning heroes, at an inn frequented by *habitués* (innkeepers were deeply committed to the politics of exaggeration and violence, whether of the Counter-Revolution or of the Ultra-Revolution), or in some discreet house in a *faubourg* (Vaise, la Guillotière),[7] or in a gambling

the Lyon *assommeurs* was the large proportion of river-workers. Elsewhere, for instance in the Paris Sections bordering on the Seine, the river-workers had gravitated towards the politics of *sans-culotte* militancy. Of the few assassins about whom there is any information in Marseille, there is again a significant proportion of porters and hair-dressers. One of the alleged leaders of the *Compagnie du Soleil* had a wine shop on the port. [*A.N.* BB 18 692 (Rhône) and BB 18 172 Bouches-du-Rhône, Ministère de la Justice.]

[5] *A Second Identity*, *op. cit.*, 64, essay on Restif de la Bretonne, *Les Nuits de Paris*. See also his *Tableaux de la Vie ou les Moeurs du XVIIIme siècle*, '. . . Je n'ai jamais pu supporter que dans les tems de chevalerie, des Belles excitâssent aux combats sanglans; ni que du nôtre elles encouragent les guerriers et les chasseurs . . .'

[6] On this profession, see *Monsieur Nicolas*, *op. cit.*, V, 2481, '. . . Je vendis secrètement quelques chemises, pour payer Bonne . . . Mais je m'étais adressé à une Revendeuse de la rue de Versailles-Saint-Victor, et j'eus ainsi l'occasion de connaître cette engeance maudite. La première m'offrit 12 francs de ce que je mettais en vente: 4 chemises valaient au moins 48 alors [en 1759]; je crus pouvoir en demander 24. La Femme sortit, et une autre la remplaça: celle-ci m'offrit 9 livres du tout. Je me recriai. Une troisième ne m'en donna que 6 et je fus obligé de les abandonner à 7. Les trois misérables allèrent ensuite partager le bénéfice . . .'

[7] On the location of crime in the Lyon *faubourgs*, see *A.N.* BB 18 685–92 (Ministère de la Justice, Rhône, ans III à XII). See, for instance, *A.N.* BB 18 687 (commissaire près le tribunal correctionnel de Lyon, à celui du Département, 11 Pluviôse an VIII): '. . . Il est certain que les brigands auteurs de ces délits passent fréquemment dans le faubourg de Vaize, et ce qu'il y a d'étonnant, c'est que les malfaiteurs mangeant dans les cabarets, auberges ou cafés de ce canton, le juge de paix ait trouvé si peu de renseignemens sur leur compte . . . La terreur est dans ce canton . . .' See

establishment, or in a house of ill-fame,[8] ready to congratulate them, to hear a first-hand account of their operations and to drink to their prowess, to the death of the Republic, of republicans, *mathevons,* puritans, law-makers, law-enforcers and to the success of their next outing.

The Counter-Revolution would not have amounted to very much without its women and without its boisterous, noisy and quite open round of pleasures; and this is what the Revolution, at least in its robespierriste phase, had so much lacked. For the Revolution in fact lasted only *five* years and the Jacobin dictatorship only *eighteen months*, whereas the Counter-Revolution, in one form or another, always highly fragmented and regionalistic, always closely identified with local loyalties and antipathies, lasted nearly *twelve* years. So important is it to have pleasure, women, drink, gambling, romance and boastfulness on one's side. Christ and King was not an empty formula; it had quite a lot to offer. *On pouvait s'installer dans la Contre-Révolution.*

Nor was this all, by any means; for pleasure-seekers could find their way through any regime, even the pleasure-hating one of the Incorruptible. The anarchical Terror of the autumn of 1793 had as much to offer as the White Terror of 1795 to 1802 (or the Counter-Terror, as it has sometimes, and most aptly, been described) to the simple, resourceful man out for a good time, concerned with the satisfaction of the baser needs and with any occasion for self-dramatisation. Indeed, both Terrors were likely to appeal to the same sort of people, at least at ground-level activism; and, sometimes, the same sort of people, even the same people, served both, in succession.

The Counter-Revolution was, however, much more closely identified with crime, and with the criminally-inclined, than had been any of the forms of the republican Terror.[9] For one thing, it

also, juge de paix du canton de Tournus, au Ministre, 15 Ventôse an VIII (*ibid.* BB 18 687): '. . . Il a été trouvé . . . une carte sur laquelle se trouvait une adresse au c. Guillon, jardinier en Vaise, rue Gorge de Loup . . . j'ai appris que sa maison étoit depuis longtems soupçonnée être le repaire de leur bande et le dépôt de leurs vols . . .'

[8] *A.N.* BB 18 687 (le commissaire près le tribunal correctionnel à celui du Département, 10 Prairial an VIII): '. . . Dans l'intérieur de la ville, et dans ses faubourgs, les maisons de prostitution n'y recèlent pas seulement des filles sans vertu, mais le plus souvent des objets volés et les auteurs des crimes. Les maisons de jeu leur servent encore de point de réunion, c'est là même qu'ils redrutent, en offrant au joueur malheureux qu'ils ont dépouillé les moyens de regagner ce qu'ils ont perdu en s'associant à eux . . .'

[9] This did not, of course, prevent ingenious and resourceful men from using characteristic institutions of the Terror for their own criminal purposes, especially in the chaotic conditions of the autumn and early winter of 1793. All that was often needed to carry out requisitions in food-stuffs or precious metals was a tricolor sash, a piece of paper with a suitable heading, the ready and, preferably, loud use of the phrase *Au nom de la loi*, and a great deal of impudence. There are many instances, up and down the country, of false *armées révolutionnaires*, constituted by bandits,

offered, for a time, an escape and a refuge, as well as a sort of respectability, to desperate men who were on the run. A person who had but recently escaped from *la chaîne*[10] could find comradeship, food and drink, the admiration of a certain kind of woman and an opportunity to display his physical strength and daring within the semi-secret confines of a royalist murder gang. His enlistment would give new meaning to his persecution by a society of *gendarmes*, judges (not that he had much to fear from the judiciary, at least in the Midi), and administrators, jumped-up property-holders and *parvenus*.

With the invisible passport of the password, he could move from town to town, from village to village, from inn to inn, from trade to trade, as along the lines of an escape network of the 1940s. There would at each stage be someone to take him in, to take care of him, to keep him fed and warm and to send him on his way with a verbal introduction to the next staging-post and with a word of encouragement.[11] Fraternity was on all the battle flags of the Republic, but it was a reality with the Counter-Revolution; it was forced upon it as a means of survival. The Counter-Revolution organised its travel better, because it had constantly to be on the move and so prepare its hidden posting-houses and stopping-places, what could be called, in modern slang, its *clandés*.[12] A *perruquier* from the South, who had

terrorising farmers and carrying out requisitions ostensibly for the benefit of the Republic. Several of them operated north and east of Lyon. See my *Les armées révolutionnaires: instruments de la Terreur dans les départements*, 2 vols., Paris–The Hague, 1961 and 1963, 217 (239).

[10] '. . . Quelle existence peuvent avoir des hommes flétris et qui fuient la chaîne? Ils craignent de se livrer paisiblement au travail . . . ils n'ont donc plus de ressources que dans le vagabondage, et ces hommes, condamnés souvent pour simples vols, deviennent assassins, parce que le crime va toujours par gradation, et que ne pouvant plus rôder pour des escroqueries, ils sont forcés de ne paroître que la nuit et d'employer la violence. Et ce qui les favorise, c'est qu'ils reviennent toujours en nombre des bagnes, qu'ils forment bandes et s'associent . . .' (*A.N.* BB 18 687, commissaire près le tribunal correctionnel, à celui du Département, 10 Prairial an VII).

[11] See for instance *Arch. Vaucluse* 3 L 28* (agent national du district d'Avignon au juge de paix de Pujant, 29 Nivôse an III, on the subject of the murder of seven persons near Tavel): '. . . J'ai découvert que led. Olivier Paten restoit à Avignon en Germinal an II . . . et qu'il est actuellement à Montpellier avec sa femme. C'est un homme de 40 à 45 ans, il a un bras plus court que l'autre, c'est une espèce de marchand du Piedmont ou du Dauphiné . . . Je te dirai encore qu'il y a une espèce de compagnie ou société de ces espèces de gens qui sous prétexte de commerce volent et assassinent tant qu'ils peuvent . . . Je te dirai encore qu'à Nîmes il y a un nommé Barbien, aubergiste, qui a été longtems lié avec eux . . .'

[12] For a modern instance of a chain of *clandés*, see Albertine Sarrazin, *L'Astralague*. Mlle Sarrazin was brought up in reform schools, was later involved in organised crime, received several prison sentences and eventually married a former long-service prisoner. She wrote several autobiographical novels, largely concerned with life in women's prisons and with the constant preoccupation with escape, and died in her early thirties. Her novels are moving, compassionate, humorous and endowed with a generous warmth.

been engaged in highway robbery and who was travelling under a series of identities and with a pocketful of passports, as he moved from Marseille to Avignon, from there to Valence, thence to Vienna and Grenoble, Lyon, Chalon, Dijon, Auxerre, Paris and Rouen, being careful to avoid very small towns, would seek out each time another *perruquier*.[13] It was easier still for all those who travelled for their business: horse-dealers, river-workers, carriers and carters, commercial travellers (*courtiers en soie,* who so often needed to go from Lyon to Paris, and who were so difficult to bring to trial—they were always absent *pour leurs affaires*—proved most effective links in the network of the murder gangs), jugglers and street musicians, people who worked in fairs, told fortunes, itinerant magicians, wrestlers, artificial savages and so on, for they had an excuse to be anywhere at any time. In the course of years, they could have worked out the most elaborate chains of complicity and clandestinity, with close contacts with *logeurs* known to be safe, with girls who did not work for the police, with receivers, old-clothes' merchants, locksmiths and junk merchants who were members of the confraternity, and whose help would frequently be required.[14] The Counter-Revolution, like crime, tended to move by water; but it had its own private itineraries, it travelled too along deep, high-hedged tracks. It had its own ferries and its own ferrymen, its many hidden *points de chute*, in large, shuttered houses on the fringe of towns, in the *faubourgs* just outside the city limits, beyond the jurisdiction of the more zealous urban magistrates and the enquiring *commissaires* of Sections

[13] *A.N.* BB 18 688 (interrogatoire de Luc-Etienne Marloi, 38 ans, perruquier, natif de Marseille, devant le juge de paix du premier canton de Lyon, 15 Prairial an XI). (He had been convicted of taking part in an attack on a stage-coach in the Bouches-du-Rhône, in the course of which General Bonaparte had lost all his luggage). '. . . "A quelle époque avez-vous déposé les armes?" R. "Il y a environ trois ans que j'ai remis les armes entre les mains de la municipalité d'Auriol." D. "Depuis ce tems dans quel lieu avez-vous été domicilié?" R. "Depuis cette époque, je n'ai point eu de domicile fixe, parce qu'on m'avoit fait craindre que je serais arrêté, je me suis d'abord caché chez un nommé Simon, ménager entre Salon et Grand (?) et j'y suis resté environ . . . 9 mois, après quoi je suis venu à Gardane où j'ai demeuré environ 6 mois chez le nommé André Porcel, ménager, demeurant à une petite distance de Gardane, après ce tems j'allai à Auriol . . . Saint-Hillaire me remit le passeport sous le nom de Jean-Baptiste Étienne, avec ce passeport je me rendis à Lyon où je suis resté . . . 17 mois, savoir 10 mois et demi chez un nommé Lacroix, perruquier au local de l'ancienne douane, et les autres 6 mois chez un nommé Pichon, autre perruquier, demeurant place des Célestins . . ."' The leader of the gang, Alexis Maurin, 33, accounts thus for his movements in the course of the three years following the highway robbery: '. . . J'ai été tour à tour Lyon, Paris, Rouen, l'été dernier, j'ai été à Avignon . . . j'ai porté le nom de Jean-Baptiste Étienne et que j'ai été connu pendant 3 mois sous ce nom au faubourg de la Guillotière à Lyon . . .' They were both guillotined on a public square in Aix on 19 Brumaire year XII.

[14] On the chains of complicity, see *The Police and the People*, part II, the *bandes*.

—spacious houses with large walled gardens, and many exits.[15]

It had, above all, its great *Capital*, a city proud in its tradition of resistance to Paris (or to Versailles), in its independence of authority and, more recently, in its daily feats of violence. This was *Lyon*, after 1793, and any time up to 1803, the twin centre of Counter-Revolution and crime. It was a town ideally organised for escape, for robbery, for hiding and for murder, in whatever cause. During these years, *any* murder could be passed off as an act of political vengeance and as a blow for the absent King, so much had the jacobin and terrorist minority been detested in the city.[16] Nature had provided two rivers, both deep, one fast-flowing; man had provided a score of bridges and several kilometres of quays. It is not known just how

[15] The counter-revolutionary could rely on a chain of welcoming houses and inns on the south to north axis, from Marseille to Lyon; there were reliable refuges for him, along his route, in such places as Arles, Beaucaire, Tarascon, Avignon, Montélimar, Pont-Saint-Esprit. He would then have to move out of the Rhône valley, to seek refuge in the Ardèche. From there, he could proceed, in comparative safety, to localities in the south of the Loire. South of Lyon, Condrieu, Saint-Genis Laval and la Mulatière could offer every guarantee; north of the city, Vaize, Neuville, l'Ile-Barbe, the monts du Beaujolais, Chalon—but Mâon was to be avoided. He could also enjoy comparative impunity on the steep, twisting roads from Lyon to Montbrison, Boën and Le Puy, but he would be well advised to avoid the Paris highroad from Lyon to Roanne. His communications were less protected east of Lyon, in the direction of Grenoble. There was a constant coming and going between Lyon and Marseille, between Lyon and Chalon, between Avignon and Nîmes, between Marseille and Nîmes. But, beyond Nîmes, westwards, communications appear to have been less well assured. The Right Bank of the Rhône offered excellent cover, almost everywhere between Lyon and Avignon.

Condrieu being an important river port on the Rhône, its inhabitants, mostly *mariniers*, tended to gravitate towards Lyon, quai des Céslestins—the principal port on the Saône, as well as to Chalon-sur-Saône. [*Arch. Rhône* 12 L 4*, registre de l'administration cantonale de Condrieu, Brumaire-Frimaire an VII: '. . . Pierre Four, dit *Coque*, voiturier sur le Rhône, domicilié au port de Condrieu . . . déclare qu'il entend à l'avenir habiter la commune de Lyon, quartier du port du temple . . .' (Déclaration du 9 Brumaire an VII) '. . . Jean-Jacques Chabert, tonnelier, domicilié à Condrieu, déclare vouloir transférer son domicile à Chalon-sur-Saône . . . Etienne Vialet, gendre à Rousset, domicilié à Condrieu, déclare aussi avoir fixé son domicile à Lyon, cour des Célestins, chez Jacques Rousset, son beau-père . . . Le Citoyen Louis Chevalier, fils à Michel Chevalier, domicilié au grand port de Condrieu déclare que depuis son mariage il a fixé son domicile dans la commune des Roches, domicile de son beau-père . . .' Such declarations of change of address are interesting as indicating the network of family relationships linking the river workers of this port with Lyon and other ports on the Saône.]

[16] A number of the murders committed in or near Lyon during these years were undoubtedly of a private nature. A pregnant woman was assassinated on 21 Messidor year VIII by two deserters, Pierre Quinet and Charles Schreder, who were later executed. (*A.N.* BB 18 687). She was the wife of a stone-mason, who had just drawn her husband's pay; she was killed in her house, rue Belle-Cordière. On 10 Prairial of the same year, the *commissaire général* informed the Minister: '. . . Il y a quelques jours qu'un particulier a été assassiné à Lyon, et l'on en donne pour motif qu'il étoit juif, qu'on lui avoit présenté à acheter des marchandises volées, qu'il avoit refusé et que l'on craignoit son témoignage. Telle est du moins l'une des versions répandues dans le public . . .' (*Ibid.*, BB 18 687). On 30 Brumaire year IX, a building contractor was murdered in la Croix-Rousse by a group of stone-masons, following a dispute

many people were thus tipped into the Rhône or the Saône, their bodies often to re-emerge as far down as Valence, between the end of 1794 and the early years of the Empire—it would run certainly into four figures. What is fairly certain is that few were supporters of Christ and King, that most had, in one form or another, been involved in the repressive bureaucracy of the year II.[17]

Indeed, Lyon was such a good place to murder people that people came from a long way off to do it. The provincial specialisations of the inns and eating-houses helped; *Au rendez-vous des Ardéchois* meant what it said (and still does). It was reasonable for an avenger from Montbrison or from Feurs to look out for a former terrorist from his town in a lodging-house called *l'hôtel des Foréziens*, or in the horse market or in a café near it, so many Foréziens being *maquignons* or blacksmiths. A Mâconnais ex-terrorist, on a two-day visit to Lyon for his business, was recognised and murdered by another Mâconnais while crossing the pont la Feuillée. The localisation within the city of people of specified provincial origin, as well as the specialisation of certain trades by people from certain villages, in Lyon conditions at least, greatly aided the counter-revolutionary and the law-breaker.[18]

Furthermore, the city was on the very edge of its bizarre, amputated Department. A five minute walk across the pont de la Guillotière would bring the man on the run into the Isère and to a *faubourg* notorious for its violence and its anarchy and for the number of its carters' inns. *La Guille* was an ancient and respected centre of crime; it was also on the route between the *bagne* of Toulon and that of Rochefort. The manacles, balls and hand-cuffs of those condemned to the galleys who went through the place, in both directions, twice a year had a habit of falling off or of breaking, while in la Guillotière, as if they had been children's toys. And much the same thing tended to happen on the other side of Lyon, at its northern exit, on

over wages. The murderers were said to have been unemployed labourers from Saint-Etienne who, with the approach of autumn, had been thrown out of work. This might be described then as a 'social crime'; it certainly had no political undertones. (*Ibid.*, BB 18 687). On 18 Nivôse year IX, a gambler was stabbed to death on leaving the gaming house. A second murder took place in similar circumstances on 27 Nivôse. On 29 Ventôse, a 60-year-old widow was stabbed to death in her house, with thirteen knife wounds and her throat cut. (*Ibid.*, BB 18 688). On 21 Prairial, a man who had escaped from the galleys was killed by the Montessuy brothers, likewise *évadés des fers*, following a dispute over stolen goods. Nearly all these crimes were, however, given a political interpretation by public opinion.

[17] For an estimate of the figures of those murdered in Lyon and its faubourgs between the year III and the year XII, see *The Police and the People*, *op. cit.*, 'The White Terror'.

[18] This was particularly true of the Foréziens, who tended to crowd together in the quartier Saint-Paul, on the side of the Saône nearest to the Département de la Loire, or on the quays the far side of the river. The Dauphinois were especially numerous in la Guillotière, on the highroad from the east. River workers kept to la Mulatière, and to the port des Célestins. Roannais were numerous in Vaise.

the road to Paris in the *faubourg* of Vaize, which further specialised in the organisation of attacks on the Paris-Lyon mail coach. A slightly longer walk would take the law-breaker into the Ain.[19]

The city itself was almost equally well organised for clandestinity, escape and unobtrusive murder. The network of *traboules* enabled the criminal or the assassin to move under ground, cutting through high blocks of ochre-coloured seven-storey houses, without ever emerging at street level, almost from one end of the peninsula to the other. After the long siege of 1793, the town was partly in ruins, its walls down, its forts dismantled and uproofed, many of its houses falling down and a multitude of locks and keys, of every size, displayed on the junk-markets of the quays.[20] Many bodies were found, their throats slit, among the ruins of the old fortifications. The extraordinary steep streets of la Croix-Rousse, la Grande-Côte, Vaize and Fourvière offered a further invitation to argument and violence, following the multiplicity of accidents to persons and properties provoked by run-way hand-carts and barrows.[21] Finally, Lyon possessed the almost unique privilege of having no *concierges*, no portresses, and few *cochers de fiacre* (defeated by the gradients), the usual auxiliaries of the political and criminal police and the most profitable source of information about both residents and strangers

[19] '. . . Cette ville . . . doit plus particulièrement fixer l'attention du Gouvernement . . . par . . . la situation d'une ville placée à l'extrémité du Département et limitrophe de ceux de l'Isère et de l'Ain, à tel point, que dans moins d'un quart d'heure, le coupable échappe à l'action de la police, en passant rapidement d'une jurisdiction dans une autre . . .' (*A.N.* BB 18 687, commissaire près le tribunal correctionnel, au juge tribunal criminel de Lyon, 30 Brumaire an IX).

[20] '. . . Il ne faut pas confondre cette Ville, dans l'état où elle se trouve, avec plusieurs autres. Ses clôtures ont été abbatues, et les brigans peuvent par tous les points rentrer pendant la nuit dans leur repaire, ou en sortir. Il existe même des ouvertures qui conduisent dans les caves des anciens bastions démolis qui servent de retraite aux effets volés, ou aux cadavres des assassinés ou aux assassins. Cette circonstance doit rendre la police extrêmement difficile à Lyon . . .' The body of the Director of the hospice, who had been murdered by one of the inmates, in the year IX, remained in the cellar of the building for a month without being discovered. (*A.N.* BB 18 687, commissaire près le tribunal correctionnel à celui du département, 10 Prairial an VIII). See also: '. . . Il s'est opéré dans cette commune une quantité majeure de démolitions . . . il s'est vendu à cette occasion, ou volé, beaucoup de serrures et des clefs superflues. Ces objets ont été achetés par des marchands de vieux fers qui les revendent au premier venu; le malfaiteur n'a qu'à prendre l'empreinte de la serrure d'un domicile, il est moralement sûr de trouver chez ces marchands en détail plusieurs clefs assorties . . .' (*Ibid.*, BB 18 687, commissaire près les tribunaux du Rhône, au Ministre de la Justice, 18 Nivôse an VIII).

[21] See, for instance, *A.N.* BB 18 688 (le général divisionnaire Duchesne, commandant la 19me division militaire, au Ministre de la Justice, 15 Pluviôse an X) '. . . Un assassinat horrible s'est commis dans la ville de Lyon le 10 du pt. sur la personne d'un père de famille; ce délit s'est fait en plein jour, dans une rue passagère, et les prévenus, arrêtés en flagrant délit, sont trois carabiniers de la 21me brigade . . . L'individu tué conduisoit une voiture à bras qui dans une pente rapide [à Vaize] heurta l'un des militaires; celui-ci donna un soufflet au conducteur de la voiture qui le frappa à son tour, alors il fut percé d'un coup de sabre et mourut'.

(in Paris, the Terror would have been powerless without them). It was difficult therefore to establish the comings and goings of inmates, the arrival or departure of unfamiliar faces, the postmarks on letters received, the size and shape of parcels carried out furtively at night or brazenly at midday, chance remarks murmured or shouted in the night, the usual stock-in-trade of the concierge, that unpleasant female animal in Paris.

The Lyonnais were lucky in many ways; furthermore, they knew they were, and tended to stick to their city; we do not find many of them in Paris.[22] If they moved, it was more likely to be southwards, to Marseille, following the course of the Rhône, just as the Auxerrois, the inhabitants of Vermenton and those who lived by the lac des Settons in the Morvan, tended to be orientated, via the Cure and the Seine, to Paris and its wood ports.[23]

They were secretive people; their town contained many secret places, underground passages, concealed doors, cellar rooms papered in old rose or scarlet and crammed with gold plate, comfortable houses enclosed by high walls, plane trees and cypresses, large enough and discreet enough to contain a team of counterfeiters[24] (one of the unofficial local industries and a further activity in which Counter-Revolution and crime could feed upon one another's skills and aims),

[22] Restif, returning on foot to Paris in 1759, comes up with two Lyonnaises, a middle-aged woman and her alleged daughter, on the road through Burgundy. The so-called mother intends to sell the girl to a *matrulle* of the Palais-Royal; Restif contrives to separate them, the older woman continues on her way, the girl, whom Restif cannot marry, says she will return to Lyon. (*Monsieur Nicolas*, *op. cit.*, V, 2440). Lyonnais in Paris tended to be *crocheteurs* or sedan-chair carriers.

[23] '. . . Elle sourit, comme pour se moquer de mon adieu éternel, en allant à Paris, à 45 lieues et dont, au moyen de la rivière, notre Ville n'est qu'un Fauxbourg . . .' (*Ibid.*, IV, 1808.)

[24] There is a graphic description of such a house, and of such company, in an account given by Galle, a Lyon engraver, to the *commissaire de police* of la Croix-Rousse, 29 Prairial year IV: '. . . qu'un jour, revenant des Brotteaux, il est accosté par deux citoyens très bien vêtus qui lui disent le bien connoître, qu'ils ont quelque chose à lui communiquer et le conduisent chez Michaud, aux Brotteaux, où il y avoit un goûter tout prêt, des vins étrangers, etc. Il déclare étre sorti de là un peu pris de vin, de là il fut conduit à un appartement tenant à un jardin qui qu'il croit être rue Bourgneuf, maison du cheval verd, c'est l'appartement le plus reculé dans ladite maison. Il se trouva pareillement dans led. appartement un souper tout prêt et des femmes que l'on qualifioit de madame une telle etc., mais qu'il a bien reconnu ces dames pour les avoir vues chez la Dervieux, tenant maison publique de filles, qu'il a été retenu dans cet endroit deux jours à faire ce qu'on appelle la ribotte et qu'ensuite, toujours entouré des mêmes personnages, il a été conduit à la Croix Rousse, Grande Rue du Faubourg, dans une maison qui est située près d'un café, dans cette maison il a remarqué qu'il y avoit une branlière, que l'on y danse ordinairement le dimanche et que les particuliers dont il est question y occupent une chambre, que c'est un traiteur qui est reputé l'homme le plus fort dans lad. commune, qui est venu le servir à table; de cette maison, il a été conduit à l'Isle-Barbe [an island on the Saône six kilometres north of Lyon] à côté de l'église dans une maison assez vaste, il y a une belle treille à l'entrée, là il a été conduit dans une chambre où on lui a dit *n'ayez pas peur*, et de suite il a vu garnir le plateau de la cheminée d'une quantité de pistolets

chapels of strange cults down dark alley-ways, deep, narrow streets lacking in lighting, an icy wind to blow out the lantern of the passing night watch, a constant coming and going over the twenty-odd bridges and footbridges,[25] on the ferries and along the quays, a peninsular bottleneck through which all going from East to West would be forced to pass, a young wine constantly, cheaply and plentifully available (Lyon's 'third river'), a language rich in threats and in incitement, an availability of weapons of all descriptions[26] (Lyon, although it in no way belonged to an alien Midi, was sufficiently far south to be in stiletto and stabbing country) and a habit of carrying them resulting in the nick-name of a heavy stick as a *juge-de-paix,* the prevalence of drunkenness, gambling and whoring, the beauty of the local women. These were the ingredients of a mentality, of a way of life, and, in the exceptional and terribly violent circumstances of the revolutionary period, of intransigent, vengeful political commitment.

In Lyon, perhaps more than anywhere, the borders between private life and political militancy were less apparent, running into one another in a city in which people lived on top of one another, in a crowded peninsula, and in which they sought air and breathing space on the broader confines of the long, double waterfront. Thus counter-revolutionary commitment could be dictated as much by

que sortoient de leurs poches ceux qui alloient et venoient dans cet endroit, on lui a proposé de faire une gravure pour faire un timbre sec, pour servir à la fabrication de fausses promesses de mandat, il lui a été offert en même tems une grande quantité d'outils propres à la gravure, des loupes etc., il a vu qu'on affectoit de lui faire voir beaucoup et pour le rassurer, on lui a offert cent louis d'or. Il a été retenu dans cet endroit 8 jours . . . il a vu paroître à peu près cent visages différens, toujours bonne table . . . il a bien reconnu le nommé Laurencin pour un des chefs, mais il n'a entendu nommer personne que par des sobriquets, on lui donnoit celui de Monsieur de la Canardière et il a cru s'apercevoir qu'effectivement on vouloit l'envoyer à l'eau, il a remarqué un grand bel homme . . . ayant ordinairement avec lui un chien danois moucheté . . . et un autre très gros homme gêné dans sa marche, qu'il croit monter très souvent à cheval, gravé de petite vérole, âgé d'environ 24 ans et il croit que son nom est Cuissieux, il est instruit que ceux qui sont dans le complot se rendent souvent au café du cheval blanc, rue Grenette, au premier étage . . .' (*A.N.* BB 18 685). The engraver, one feels, was very lucky to have survived, after acquiring such dangerous knowledge and having lived at close quarters with what was clearly a well organised gang. It was no doubt intended that he should justify his nickname and end up, like so many others, in the Saône.

[25] In Lyon, the commonest murder stations during the period of the first White Terror, from 1795 to 1802, were: the pont la Feuillé, the pont de l'Arsenal, the pont Saint-Vincent, the pont de pierre, the port du Temple, the quays, the two rivers, Vaize, la Mulatière (on the river), la Guillotière (on the river), les Brotteaux (on the river).

[26] '. . . Ce qui est véritablement effrayant, c'est l'audace des coupables, ce sont les instruments dont ils sont armés; ces crimes se commettent presqu'à la nuit tombante, dans les quartiers les plus fréquentés et avec des poignards extrêmemement dangereux. Par une suite de l'effroi général, les coupables échappent toujours et rarement on trouve des témoins à entendre contr'eux . . .' (commissaire général de police de Lyon, au Ministre, 10 Prairial an VIII, *A.N.* BB 18 687).

trade and by geography, as by the experience of an immediate and bitterly painful political past that called out for revenge. In Lyon, after 1793, there was no frontier between private vengeance and collective vengeance, while *any* murder was political. Here then is perhaps the extreme example of the inter-action of private life and of political intransigence.

There was, then, a fusion between the public and the private life of the counter-revolutionary. There existed too, no doubt, a continuity, a natural gradation between his pre-revolutionary existence and his political militancy and semi-criminal activity of the revolutionary period. It was normal for a former *faux-saunier* to enlist as a *sabreur*, for a smuggler to seek a new vocation as a counterfeiter or as a distributor of *faux assignats*. Many case histories illustrate the ease and naturalness of such transformations, in terms of individuals and of individual trades, while often emphasising, in an individual context, the enormous difficulty posed by the problem of establishing a given person's true identity, especially after five years of revolutionary upheaval.

A similar technique could be applied to the exploration of the emergence of a terrorist mentality and of revolutionary commitment, likewise over a period of years. Terrorists were not born overnight,[27] and as the average age of the committed militant was from 30 to 45, the key to his commitment must be sought, when such

[27] There is an admirable illustration of this theme in a recent biography of a middle-ranking terrorist: Claude Hohl, *Un agent du Comité de sûreté générale: Nicolas Guénot*, Paris, Bibliothèque nationale, 1968. The author proposes as his aim—and it is one that should be that of any specialist of the revolutionary period—'de remonter à un passé tout proche . . . et d'examiner . . . la structure rigide et désespérante des cadres [de l'ancienne société], la dureté générale des conditions de vie . . .' And of the pre-revolutionary career of his subject he writes: 'la période de sa vie qui précède la Terreur prend rétrospectivement l'allure d'un temps de préparation au rôle que cet individu allait tenir . . .' Nicolas Guénot furnishes a truly ideal case history, in this respect, his age, his condition, the area from which he came, *la montée à Paris*, and the bitter experience of a cruel and violent society all no doubt preparing him for his role as a zealous acolyte of Terror and repression. He was born in April 1754, in Voutenay, in the Yonne, on the edge of the Morvan. His father was a river worker, like most of the inhabitants of this large village. Guénot himself was naturally drawn to the trade of *flotteur*, the workers who floated the wood down the Cure and the Yonne into the Seine and the wood ports of Paris. It was hard and ill-paid work, grossly exploited by the big timber merchants of Vermenton and Auxerre. The *flotteurs* formed a wild, close-knit, violent corporation, orientated as much towards Paris as towards the Morvan and the Yonne. At 17, Guénot floated a train of wood to the Capital, where he remained, first of all as a *cocher de fiacre*, a trade on the borders of police informing and crime; it was no doubt at this stage that he formed his first contacts with the police. In 1776, he enlisted in the Gardes-Françaises, a corps notorious for its extreme brutality and predatory violence and its connections with procuring. He was the object of several lawsuits and one court-martial, all arising out of brawls in cafés. Discharged in 1783, he returned to Voutenay, was had up for poaching and threatening behaviour. Already before the Revolution, he had

evidence about people not given to writing up their personal recollections exists,[28] in a life of hardship, deprivation and brutality during the decade preceding the revolutionary outbreak.

I wish to stress here the urgency of returning to the biographical approach, while still taking into account the collective assumptions of a trade, of a certain province, or of a given town or quarter, when attempting to assess the sources of revolutionary militancy.[29] For the terrorists, like the counter-revolutionaries were extreme individual-

threatened to kill two inhabitants, both well-to-do farmers. He returned to Paris at the age of 30, taking up again the trade of *cocher de fiacre*. By 1791, he had earned the good graces of the *commissaire de police* of his Section by denouncing a manufacturer of false assignats; but, significantly, he did not denounce *all* those involved, warning some in advance so that they were able to escape arrest. In 1792, he became a gaoler at Sainte-Pélagie; but, soon afterwards, he was carrying out arrests and house searches as a deputy to the *commissaire*. His career as a political policeman was made. He was also concerned in the policing of furnished rooms and prostitution. In 1793, he was also given a *droit de regard* over the jugglers and professional strong men in the Champs-Elysées. In the year II, he denounced a number of wood merchants from his own village and was able to secure their arrests. He also went on terrorist missions in the Yonne and in the neighbourhood of Paris; on one of these, he carried out the arrest of the poet, André Chénier. At this time, he was an accredited agent of the Committee of General Security. But in the summer of 1794, he was arrested for peculation, and only regained his freedom after the fall of Robespierre. He continued in police work under the Thermidorian regime and the Directory. But in the year X, he was banished to his village. His reputation there, as an ex-terrorist and as a man of violence, was such that, for years, he had to live in the woods, sleeping out, and coming into the outskirts of the village in the middle of the night, to collect food put out for him by one of his vary rare friends. On one occasion, he was surrounded in a house, escaped to the roof, where he was shot at and severely wounded by the *garde nationale*. Later, he was employed as a farm hand by his elder brother, whom he tried to kill. He died a pauper in 1832. Guénot was a man of extraordinary violence, both verbal and physical; he was also utterly courageous and totally imprudent. He conducted before, during and after the Revolution a single-handed vendetta against all the powers-that-be of his village, including the *maire* and the wood merchants. He was married, had five children, but left his wife and family in Paris. He served the Terror with singleminded enthusiasm, but he was not above accepting bribes, and, throughout his career as a policeman, he maintained more than friendly contacts with sections of the underworld. Guénot was born in one of the most violent parts of France and was employed in one of the most brutal and violent corporations; he later served in the most undisciplined corps of the old army. There is no doubt that he enjoyed the Terror and the power that it gave him. He was scarcely literate, as his peculiar letters prove. There were many Guénots in the service of Terror and Repression in 1793–4; but, in his case at least, thanks to M. Hohl's exhaustive research, it is possible to see stage by stage, the formation of a terrorist mentality and of terrorist commitment during the hard years before the Revolution. His career is likewise a typical commentary on the theme, so dear to Restif de la Bretonne, of *la montée à Paris* and of *les dangers de la ville*. His life history might have come out of *Le Paysan Perverti* or *M. Nicolas*. What is more, Voutenay was only a few miles south of Restif's birthplace, Sacy; and Restif had many relatives engaged in *flottage* on the Yonne. M. Hohl's book is an example of what can be achieved in this vital sector of human history, the use of the *cas témoin*.

[28] Hohl, *op. cit.*, 9: '. . . Le journal intime de cette conscuence n'a pu être trouvé, il n'a jamais existé . . .'

[29] An even more impressive example of the biographical approach is Colin Lucas's unpublished D.Phil. thesis, *The Mission of Claude Javogues in the Department of the*

ists, and, even though they might express themselves in the language of collective orthodoxy, they spoke with their own loud voices and indeed, owed much of the ascendancy that they were able to exercise for a time over their fellow-citizens, in conditions of open assemblies to the strength of their vocal organs, dominating *à la force du poumon*. It was important to be able to shout others down, for this was how the so-called 'direct democracy' of the *sans-culottes* got its business done. One cannot conceive of a soft-voiced terrorist (no wonder the Thermidorians called the militants of the previous year *aboyeurs*!) nor of one who stuttered; such people would have had to seek outlet in the more subterranean channels of the bureaucracy of terror: informing and delation, the latter largely a woman's world.

The terrorist is a public man, thriving on self-dramatisation and immensely enjoying every minute of his public appearance.[30] Perhaps too it was the knowledge that it could not last that made him move so fast, shout so loud and emit such bloody threats.[31] Perhaps, also, he was a lonely man, a crank and an outsider, denied the comforts of marriage and the self-assurance of love and affection, and who threw himself into revolutionary activity, taking a nightly bath of collective fraternity, in order to forget that loneliness and to put off to as late as possible the return to an empty room and an empty bed. These are merely conjectures, but they need to be made.[32]

We have supped too well and too long of *les sans-culottes*, of *la sansculotterie*, of *le sans-culottisme*, until we have become sick and tired of the lot of them. We have seen them drilled, dressed by the right, marched up and down, and dismissed, responding with alacrity to the orders of their commanders writing of the Paris version of

Loire: a case history (to be published by the Clarendon Press). Javogues is above all a study in extreme drunkenness, verbal and physical violence, incoherence and utter temerity; and yet there is nothing to indicate, in his pre-revolutionary past, that he would become one of the most picturesque, and most feared, proconsuls of the Terror; and, after his recall, in the spring of 1794, he proved that he could restrain his violence and control his fearful tongue, when the occasion demanded. His principal acolyte, Lepalus, on the other hand, proves to be less of a riddle; he was an embittered, unsuccessful, mediocre man, for whom the Revolution represented the last chance of improving on a career that had never got out of the provincial rut and of making a name for himself beyond the limits of his visible horizon. Lepalus was successful at least in this, since he was to be tried, condemned to death and guillotined in Paris. There were undoubtedly many men of this kind in the middle ranks of the bureaucracy of Terror and repression. For such, the Revolution, especially in the conditions of 1793, could come as an undreamt-of chance to achieve something at last and to break out of the predictable frame of stultifying routine and mediocrity.

[30] R. C. Cobb, 'Quelques aspects de la mentalité révolutionnaire', in *Terreur et subsistances*, Paris, 1965.

[31] *The Police and the People*, *op. cit.*, part II.

[32] *A Second Identity*, *op. cit.*, 145–58, 'The beginnings of the revolutionary crisis in Paris'.

them in books ever shorter. It is altogether too well rehearsed, too much of a fairground piece; historians are so given to placing unsophisticated and primitive protesters inside a 'movement', as if they had been bought up by a football team, or were wearing coloured shirts, or were holding cards indicating that Citizen X was 'No. 3223 of the Paris *sans-culotte* movement'. They had no inkling that they were part of a 'movement'; they had never heard of the word, nor had anyone else before 1958.

Indeed, it would be difficult to imagine a more disparate group than the so-called *sans-culottes,* a mere *agglomérat* of negative attitudes and prejudices, of crude fears, of collective antipathies, of shared and accepted habits of violence and of violent solutions, of a range of personalities extending from the semi-literate Breton water-carrier, to the sophisticated, but embittered, former *clerc de procureur*. The *sans-culottes* are only definable collectively in terms of what they were against—and they were against an awful lot of people. Their careers as terrorist militants had been prepared long before the Revolution.

The Revolution itself was not all-embracing and totally invasive. There were many sectors of private life that must have escaped altogether. It is doubtful, for instance, that love marched readily to the dictates of the year II and that the General Will invaded the attic of the servant girl and the apprentice. The Terror might destroy the sleep of the unworthy with the 4 a.m. *visite domiciliaire* of the men with the arrest warrants; but many flats and the vast majority of the enormous number of furnished rooms on seventh floors were never visited. When they were, it was on the part of the *commissaire,* come to establish the facts of a suicide, of a murder, of a rape, of a theft, of a night flit, of desertion; *this* Terror, if it could be so called, owed little to the Revolution. It went on all the time, but with its seasonal ups and downs, the *commissaire* becoming more active in the autumn, when the lodging houses filled up with seasonal workers, back from the harvest, and with *filoux et voleurs,* drawn back to Paris by the return from the country estates of the well-to-do. It was a terror directed against regular crime, not against temporary political deviation.

Nor did sex respond to the dictates of the revolutionary war trumpet and to the rousseauite visions of a prissy Robespierre. Young people might walk hand in hand down avenues of poplars garlanded with flags and tricolor ribbons, listening to the massed choirs of revolutionary feast days, their hearts brimming with fraternity; but they did not live in revolutionary dormitories, and, once they had got home, they shut the door on the year II. The Terror, it is true, did artificially disturb the facts of love. There is plenty of evidence of a 25 per cent drop in conception rates, at least in the big cities, from 1793 to 1796, and there was an even steeper decline in marriages for the same period.[33] Doctors, when seeking to explain the disastrous increase in the death rates among the urban and rural poor during the period 1794 to 1796 refer to the anxieties, fatigues and weariness provoked by five years of revolutionising and by two years of extreme hardship.

Suicide, too, appears to march to the revolutionary overtures and to respond to public rather than to private pressures. In the year II, elderly aristocratic ladies of the Faubourg, abandoned by their children, and living on in the maids' attics of their former palaces requisitioned for the expanding needs of a revolutionary bureaucracy, committed suicide by throwing themselves out of high windows, after leaving notes for the *commissaire de police*, asking him to provide for a pet lap-dog or for a canary left behind from the general wreck of a way of life. But a great many others saw it out, as governesses in the families of the new rich, and putting to commercial use skills in embroidery and crochet-work acquired from the nuns. In 1795–6, suicide took a further toll, but this time of poor women, driven desperate by hunger and seeking an end for themselves and for their children in a conveniently placed Seine.

Prostitution and gambling were severely persecuted by the high-minded authorities of the year II, who also conducted a frontal attack on obscene literature. But there was no diminution to recruitment to prostitution, though the girls in that trade had little love for the Revolution, nor was there in the clientèle. It merely changed in character. The *Gardes-Françaises* had disappeared, but the police spies had not; the Princes had emigrated, but had been succeeded by middle-class customers and by the military.[34] Gambling went on unabated, much to the distress of the revolutionary authorities, who saw in it a major source of political indifference and absenteeism and a realm of purely private pleasure. The gamblers did not mind

[33] *Terreur et subsistances, op. cit.*, 'Disette et mortalité à Rouen en l'an III et en l'an IV'. See also *M. Nicolas*, IV, 1912: '. . . Aussi la conservation des Femelles est bien plus importante pour la population que celle des Mâles. Le genre humain, avec le système actuel des grandes armées et la monogamie chrétienne, doît décroître insensiblement, et décroît en effet . . . Tout cela est plus urgent et plus facile aujourd'hui, sous le régime républicain, où nous sommes forcés d'avoir des Armées plus nombreuses, et que nous avons rendu à la population les Religieuses décloîtrées et les Moines dépensionnés . . .' Restif looked forward, quite rightly as it turned out, to an eventual steep rise in the birth-rate as a long-term result of the political Revolution.

[34] The revolutionary authorities of the year II were not only puritanical in their attitude to prostitutes; they were also severely practical. Venereal diseases were an even greater source of weakness to the republican war effort than desertion and *insoumission*. Perhaps as many as one in five of all soldiers on leave in Paris was

whether they played with Kings and Queens and Knaves or with playing cards bearing the new revolutionary devices.[35] The *imagerie de Chartres* continued to prosper, the Old Saints' calendars continued to be published and read, there was no great change in the contents of the *bibliothèque de colportage*,[36] popular culture remained unaffected. *Cartouche* and *Mandrin* remained far more popular, familiar heroes, than the newly-established boys and girls who perished, holding the bridge, pierced with a thousand lances, or standing on burning decks. The Criminal Hero outlasted the Revolutionary Martyr.[37]

The important thing was the angle of vision, especially if one went down far enough. What would *la Fille de la Populace*, as described by Restif, know of the Revolution? For her, Authority had previously figured physically as the public execution on the Place de Grêve; Government and Power, as the chief magistrate, the *guet* and the Lieutenant Criminel.[38] The Revolution would merely mean a change in the geographical location of the place of punishment and the substitution of the instrument of death, the gibbet and the rack, by the guillotine. Authority would remain for her equally distant, equally fearful. And what would the Revolution mean to *la Fille de Manoeuvre,* whose only joys were the noisy dances in the week-end *guinguettes* and the nightly carters' balls in the *faubourgs*: or what would it mean to *l'Ouvrière*, whose language, in its crudity, remained unaffected by revolutionary puritanism, and whose conduct was governed by the wild standards of the *Soldats-aux-Gardes*?[39]

able thus to escape from the areas of military operations for as much as three months, spent being treated in Paris hospitals. It was not merely a figure of speech when the revolutionary *commissaires* spoke of the prostitutes as having *gangréné les défenseurs de la patrie*. See also, *The Police and the People*, *op. cit.*, part II, 'Paris prostitution'. See also *M. Nicolas*, IV, 1968: '. . . Je me suis déjà élevé contre les Puristes, ces tyrans du genre humain, ces infâmes Robespierres (sic), qui veulent que tout soit aussi triste et glacé que leur âme froide. C'est Robespierre qui faisait défendre par Chaumette, qu'il y eût des Prostituées, sans prendre les moyens qui contrebalançaient cette défense; car la Prostitution est naturelle . . .'

[35] See on the subject of gambling, *Terreur et subsistances*, *op. cit.*, 'Quelques aspects de la mentalité révolutionnaire'.

[36] Albert Souboul, *Paysans, sans-culottes et jacobins*, Paris, 1966, 203.

[37] See, for instance, Louis Sébastien Mercier, in *Le Nouveau Paris*, Paris 1797, on the subject of the popularity of the housebreaker and bandit, Poulaillier. See also Vidocq, *Les chauffeurs du Nord*, Paris 1841, a novel that is concerned with a *bande* that operated in the Nord in 1795 and 1796.

[38] '. . . Les Filles de la Populace . . . les Crieuses des rues, les marchandes ambulantes de poisson, de fruits, d'amadoue, de vieux chapeaux, etc. . . . Imaginez des êtres sans morale, sans idées, ni de l'honnêteté, ni de la religion, ni de la droiture, en un mot, d'aucune loi sociale . . . Rarement ces Filles sont corrigibles; elles naissent, meurent et vivent dans Paris . . . sans en avoir jamais eu plus d'idées que si elles étaient nées parmi les Hottentots . . . toute leur politique est à la Grêve, c'est là seulement qu'elles voient un acte de l'autorité publique; le Guet est pour elles tout le Gouvernement et le Commissaire est le seul Magistrat . . .' (Restif, *Tableaux*, *op. cit.*)

[39] '. . . Les Filles de Manoeuvres, c'est à dire des gens sans profession, qui travaillent à la journée; elles sont marchandes de fruits, filles-de-peine, blanchisseuses etc. . . .

The Revolution did nothing to alter masculine violence in relation to women, it brought no diminution to the repetitive *déclarations de grossesse* that form such a volume of the daily reports of the *commissaires de police*. Rape and seduction did not march to the new tunes of the year II, and a Revolution that formulated the Rights of Man never had even a passing thought for the virginity of women. Girls continued to be kicked in the stomach, beaten, stripped, whipped, tarred and feathered, dragged by the hair across the room, made love to on the tables of wine-shops, knocked about, their clothes torn, as joyfully, and with as much impunity as under the old regime.[40] The Revolution might have created a new man, but not as far as women were concerned. Revolutionary soldiers were no change, in this respect, from the brutal and violent *Gardes-Françaises*. A *sans-culotte* shopkeeper, a militant in his Section, perhaps one of the leaders of left-wing extremism (and thus qualifying for the attention of historians as a pre-socialist and as a person already groping his way towards *babouviste* solutions, so earning his place in the sixty-seventh Congress of Babouviste Studies), would not hesitate to break into the mezzanine bedroom of his female servant. For the country girl come up to Paris, nothing would have been changed; *la Paysanne Pervertie* of 1775 would remain *la Paysanne Pervertie* of 1794, though her chances of being eventually abducted by a duke would have been considerably diminished and the range of promotion open to her greatly narrowed. But, in 1795, dukes could be conveniently replaced by the Thermidorian new rich and by young generals.

Marguerite Barrois, a country girl from the east of France, arrived in Paris on 6 Thermidor year II, with a letter of introduction to a watchmaker from the same village as herself; on the night of 9 to 10

les individus qui composent [cette classe], voyant moins les autres classes, en sont moins commues d'ailleurs, comme elles ne sont pas mises en Demoiselles, et que leur vêtir tranche absolument, les petites Bourgeoises ne les jalousent pas . . .' (*ibid. Tableaux*). 'Les Ouvrières . . . les Couturières, les Tailleuses, les Brocheuses, les Gazières etc. La plupart de ces Infortunées gagnent si peu qu'il leur est presqu' impossible d'être sages . . . La plupart sont des Dévergondées, qui ne rougissent pas de tenir les propos les plus sales, qui fréquentent les Cabarets comme les Hommes, et les endroits pernicieux où l'on danse le soir, comme les tabagies du Port-au-bled . . . J'ai connu des Filles Brocheuses qui valaient moins que les Soldats-aux-Gardes, pour la retenue, la décence, la sobriété. la pudeur . . .' (*ibid.*)

[40] *Archives de la Préfecture de Police* A/A 61–2, 95–8, 187–8 (commissaires de police des Sections des Arcis, de la Butte-des-Moulins et du Muséum, ans II–IV). See also *M. Nicolas*, III, 1647. See also *Tableaux, op. cit.*: '[Le Vicomte dit] ". . . Je passois tout à l'heure par la petite rue Saint-Anastase; j'ai vu un mari et une femme enceinte qui se battaient! Le sujet de leur querelle était une fille de dix ans que la mère avait corrigée, et qui était allée se plaindre à son père, maître tonnelier. Cet homme est venu furieux se jeter sur sa femme . . . j'ai compris que c'était un homme brutal, fort violent, qui n'avait pas le coeur mauvais, et auquel l'éducation seule avait manqué"; "Je frémis", dit la Marquise, "et l'on nous parle des Hottentots", continue le Marquis, "dans la même ville, au seine d'une capitale policée; nous avons des Hottentots è notre porte . . ."'

Thermidor, she succumbed to the insistence of an apprentice who slept in a cupboard opposite her bedroom and was also from the same village, who employed as a clinching argument: 'Next winter, we will go back to our village and get married.' A month later, she was pregnant; she would remember the night of 9–10 Thermidor, but not for the reasons for which it is commemorated in history books.[41]

Restif, at frequent intervals in 1793–5, notes down, as he prints the immensely wordy *Monsieur Nicolas*, that such-and-such a date was the fortieth anniversary of a successful seduction. For him, 31 May 1793 is thus an occasion to recall an outing with Jeannette Rousseau or with Marianne Tangis that ended up in the hay-loft, and, in March–April 1794, at a time when the *hébertistes* are being arrested, he is harking back to a spring night in an island on the Yonne with Rose or Fanchette; on 10 June 1794, his mind is not on the terrible law of that day (22 Prairial an II) but on his dear Toinette, a servant girl from the Morvan, who had accorded him her favours and her affection forty years earlier;[42] a calendar far more reassuring than that of bloody *journées* marked by barricades and squares and forecourts strewn with the corpses of men who will no longer make love and of children who never will. 1789, for Restif, is the year he moved his lodgings, losing, as a result, all his favourite books.[43] In September 1796, his thoughts are still towards the past; he notes, that month, that the *curé* of Courgis is still alive, having survived the Revolution, despite a brief imprisonment in Auxerre.[44] Restif may have been a crank, a night bird and an extreme individualist, but he is as good a historian as Barère or Choudieu. He is informing at a different level;[45] he, not Barère, is the first historian to have understood the attraction

[41] *A.P.P.* A/A 187 (commissaire de police de la Section du Muséum, an III). See also *The Police and the People*, part III, 'Town and Country'.

[42] *M. Nicolas*, II, 1266, III, 1444, 1559, 1601. '. . . Elle est donc finie, cette terrible journée du 26 mars (1754)! elle est finie! elle roule dans le fleuve immense des temps —je la vois, je la vois encore . . . au bout de 40 années (jeudi, 3 avril 1794, à ma case) . . . je vois Colette . . . Colette, l'âme de ma vie . . .' In the revolutionary calendar, this was 14 Germinal year II. See also, on the subject of Toinette: '. . . Elle le verra, au bout de 40 ans (10 juin 1794) et cette lecture ne la flattera pas; elle lira la NOTE que je place ici . . .' This time, the recollection coincides with 22 Prairial year II, the date of the most sinister piece of legislation of the whole Terror.

[43] *M. Nicolas*, IV, 2120 '. . . Mon *Aristophane* s'est perdu, lors de mon déménagement pendant le cruel hiver 1788–9, de chez Pointcloud, procureur au parlement, rue des Bernardins, no 10. Ce scélérat . . . me donna congé dans le tems où j'étais embarrassé de toute l'édition des *Nuits de Paris* . . . Depuis sept ans (6 mars 1795) je ne puis rétablir l'ordre, parce que je suis logé plus étroitement! retrouver mes livres, mes pensées éparsees! . . .'

[44] *M. Nicolas*, V, 2455: '. . . Le Curé de Kourgis vit encore aujourd'hui 5 septembre 1796 (19 Fructidor), et l'Abbé Tomas est mort le 12 février 1786 . . .'

[45] An example that would have appealed to Restif—though, in fact it comes from his rival, Mercier (*Le Nouveau Paris*)—as illustrating the connection between private life and revolutionary events is the story of the *chien Luxembourg*. *Luxembourg* was a stray dog—apparently some sort of Great Dane—who, in 1788, had elected to set

of social exploration, through sexual experience. Jerphanion, in *Les hommes de bonne volonté,* would take the experiment a stage further, with a bed awaiting him and occupied by a national product, in every capital in Europe—a typically masculine fantasy.[46] But Restif's *Seigneurs-Populaires* were seeking happiness, not just the brief excitement of a change of milieu. There is no doubt that the Revolution, by greatly adding to the picaresque elements in eighteenth century life, and by enormously extending both the range and the depth of mobility, must have made such love matches much more possible.[47]

up his abode in the gardens of the Luxembourg Palace, where he rapidly became a well-known figure to the *bons bourgeois* and their families who frequented the terraces and avenues of this green space. He was fed regularly by old ladies from what was to become later in the Revolution, the Section du Luxembourg. As the Revolution progressed on its path of violence, the citizens of the quarter were in the habit of greeting one another, as if to reassure themselves that, despite the *journées* that every now and then brutally interrupted the course of Paris political history, life was still going on normally: *as-tu vu le chien Luxembourg ces derniers temps?* or *comment va Luxembourg? Luxembourg* seems to have been aware of his importance as a barometer of 'normalcy', for he put in an appearance on the terraces of the gardens on the occasion of the Champ de Mars, the *31 mai*, the *2 juin*, the *4 septembre* and the *9 Thermidor*. By the year II, he had, however, become a great deal thinner, and his friends noticed that his coat, previously very fine and glossy, was beginning to moult in patches, while his expression had become melancholy and his eyes bloodshot. Under Robespierre, he no longer jumped up, barking joyfully, to greet his friends. After Thermidor, his condition worsened; and, like so many bipeds during the terrible famine of 1795, he assumed skeletal shape, and was to be observed staggering unhappily under bushes, in the snow of that long, bitter winter. He was still about in the following summer. But by the autumn, he was no longer to be seen and was presumed to have hidden himself in some shrubbery and died, at the beginning of the Directory. After a few weeks, he was almost entirely forgotten, people no longer asked: *as-tu vu Luxembourg*? And the quarter had finally lost its most celebrated and reassuring inhabitant, and one who had succeeded, no doubt like other eccentrics, in living outside and parallel to the Revolution.

[46] '*Démophile*. Son Valet-de-Chambre lui dit alors—M. le duc, songez-vous que vous avez encore à vous rendre populaire dans le quartier le plus bourgeois de Paris! Si vous manquez la rue Saint-Denis, vous oubliez l'essentiel . . . *Democrate:* . . . on lui donna une petite chambre au grenier, un lit de sangle, un matelas, et un grand drap qu'il devait mettre en double. Il fit son lit . . .' (Restif, *Le Palais-Royal*). Restif is constantly obsessed by the possibility thus of securing personal happiness by moving down; he too indulges in the vision of the room over the sweet shop. Ten years earlier he had written, in *le Paysan:* '. . . Quel plaisir de pouvoir embrasser tous les états! Par mes habits, je m'élève aujourd'hui au niveau des Grands, et demain je descends et me confonds avec le plus bas des hommes . . . Je suis de toutes les classes; et je retrouve avec la grossière harangère mais jolie, des plaisirs au moins égaux à ceux que me procuraient la Marquise de XXXXX! . . .'

[47] This was as true of the *émigrés* as of those who stayed in France throughout the Revolution. Many of the *émigrés* not only discovered, under the stress of hardship, vocations and skills that had previously remained unsuspected, or that, for reasons of dignity, they had been unable to indulge—one became a celebrated London book-binder, another an antiquarian bookseller, others again entered the service of the Empress, or made fortunes in the United States—they also acquired foreign wives or mistresses and greatly extended the area, in terms of class and nationality, of their sexual experience and of their personal happiness. One of them married an Irish prostitute in London (Jean Vidalenc, *Les émigrés français, 1789–1825*, P.U.F., 1963).

In the general spectacle of carnage, violence, vengeance and intransigence, one would at least like to think that this was so.[48]

Death and birth did not wait upon the dictates of the Convention, though, as we have seen, the Terror might multiply the former and diminish the latter. And we have no knowledge of how the Republic of the year II may have appeared to little boys and girls of five, born with the Revolution, other than possibly as a good time, as a period of marvellous anarchical freedom, when they did not have to go to school, since most of the schools were closed. The little boy might have to learn to recite the Rights of Man rather than the *Pater*, and, if his parents beat him, he could always denounce them as bad republicans and might indeed well get a hearing. But his sister would still have to do her embroidery, run errands for her mother, eke out a few *sous* selling flowers on street corners, carrying love notes to wealthy ladies, or carrying bundles of fire-wood from house to house; and she was still in as great a danger as ever of being kidnapped, if she was pretty, neat, and well-dressed. The reports of the *commissaires* for the years II and III are full of detailed descriptions of lost children, last seen wearing a nankeen skirt in blue and white stripes, white stockings, buckle shoes, velvet bodice; and the same source reveals the sad, nightly haul of runaway children and adolescents, found sleeping in entrances to houses, under the arcades, or on the pavement, above the ovens of bakers, clinging together—often brother and sister—and come to the City in order to escape parental brutality or lack of love. The Revolution might make a cult of child martyrs; but it did not lighten the heavy hand of unloving parents.

The Revolution brought added prosperity to the pawnshop and to

[48] There is something extremely satisfying in this spectacle of the public events of a sanguinary and violent revolution being put to good purpose by private individuals to improve their own condition or to enrich their private lives. Thus we hear of a man condemned to two years' imprisonment for theft, by the Lyon tribunal, in the year II: '. . . Il avoit trouvé occasion de s'évader par l'effet des circonstances et mouvement populaire comme il le dit, ces circonstances sont celles où les assommeurs se promenoient dans cette ville et élargissoient des prisons ceux qui leur convenoient, ce Villard fut du nombre des élargis . . .' (*A.N.* BB 18 686, commissaire central, au Ministre, 21 Vendémiaire an V). There is another example, from this same source: 'Je viens d'apprendre', writes the *commissaire*, 5 Pluviôse an VI, 'qu'Astier a été condamné à la potence, l'on prétend qu'à force d'argent sa famille parvint à le faire évader des prisons où il étoit détenu et que de là il passa à Nice, où il exerça la profession de doreur et d'où il revint dans son pays dans le tourment de la Révolution. L'on assure que le crime qui lui a valu cette condamnation étoit l'assassinat d'une fille publique . . .' (*Ibid.* BB 18 686, le commissaire au Ministre, 5 Pluviôse an VI). No doubt things often worked out rather differently; Restif, in *les Tableaux*, quotes a very unhappy case: '. . . Rien de stable en ce monde. D'Angi, l'honnête, l'heureux D'Angi, qui n'avait d'autre crime que son bonheur, fut accusé, par des ennemis secrets, d'avoir accaparé. On se jetta sur sa maison, on la pille, on le saisit, on le massacre. Son beau-père, sa belle-mère périssent dans le tumulte—une épouse jusqu'alors heureuse ne peut supporter cet affreux malheur . . . elle laissa orphelines 6 créatures innocentes, qu'on eut l'inhumanité de conduire aux Enfans Trouvés . . .'

the junk, rag-and-bone and old clothes' merchants. It was a time of unheard of opportunity for necromancers, readers in cards, palmists and sorceresses. The revolutionary skies showered down *lettres d'or*, written in the hand of God; the waiting-room of a well-known magician, rue de Buci, was constantly crowded with people of all conditions. There seems to have been a very widespread escape into the dark lands of make-believe, legend and *Tarot*. It did at least offer an alternative to the all-embracing priorities of collective rejoicing, crowd enthusiasm and an increasingly strident unanimity. The palmist, like the juggler at the fair, the tight-rope walker, the sword-swallower, the professional savage, were beyond the reach of Robespierre (it is unlikely that he had ever had the time or the inclination to stop and look at them). And they still remained the popular favourites.

Of course, others were ruined, or had to look elsewhere. The fencing master sought employment with the *garde nationale*: there would always be something for that loud-mouthed, prickly man in the new, uncertain hierarchies of revolutionary honour. The governess often starved, no-one knows what became of the *chaisière* and the organist—one *Suisse* at least, but only one, ended up a General. Students, professors, *docteurs-ès-théologie* disappeared almost without a trace. For a decade, France subsisted without a single University, but the Schools of Medicine were maintained. Life must have become harder for the professional sponger, his livelihood undercut by rationing, civil marriage, civil death and by *le baptême républicain*, as well as by emigration, though it is likely that people of that adaptable profession were able to come back into their own after Thermidor. The old, the sick, the infirm, in 1795, were shivering in the stinking remains of the clothing that the *hospice* authorities had issued to them in 1789 (what then would *they* make of a Revolution that left them semi-clothed in the parsimonious uniforms of ancien régime ecclesiastical charity?).[49] Some of the mad seem to have been unaware that there had *been* a Revolution at all (two had got out, when the Bastille was pulled down, but they were both back behind bars, and chained to the wall, in Charenton, within ten days); Sade had not yet been sent there (he *enjoyed* the Revolution, though he must have had to cut down on his peculiar entertainments). Wandering madmen, dressed in skins, and muttering at street corners, confused the Revolution with the end of the world, while evoking the Wars of Religion of the sixteenth century. Children continued to beg in enormous numbers, though they temporarily abandoned church steps in favour of the forecourt of the Tuileries and the entrances to clubs. But babies continued to be left

[49] *The Police and the People*, part II, 'The Year IV'.

at night on church steps, even when the churches had become stables, powder-magazines and arsenals. Drunkenness was as much as ever a source of popular violence and ferocity,[50] while the Revolution multiplied the occasions for collective inebriation, adding its own commemorative dates to an already over-loaded Saints' calendar;[51] *décadi* were observed but so were Sundays. The calendar, more than anything else, defeated the Revolution and the revolutionaries.

Militancy was, in the long run, no match for the various pressures of home, family, meals, drink, billiards, gambling, sport and women. Organised collective militancy was an indoor affair (though, in the revolutionary summers, people like David attempted to bring it out of doors as well) and the meeting places were warm. It could last out the autumn and the winter, when the *assemblées* could prove a cheaper draw than the *cafés*. Fraternity probably meant an escape from loneliness. But the spring sun would do much to kill it, even in the urban context. And the summer, so favourable to the excesses of collective popular violence, would bring people out into the open, to play bowls on the quays or to watch the endless parade of elegance, debauchery, vice and crime offered by the Palais-Royal—the greatest, most varied of the open-air theatres, an arcaded promenade where all classes met, where the Revolution had begun with men on chairs and print-shops pouring out calls to arms, and where it ended, in 1795, in ostentatious luxury, extravagant clothing and the triumphant parading of the be-plumed prostitutes.[52] There was an almost universal revolt against austerity. As a spectacle—and a very bloody one—the mid-day lynchings and the dusk killings, the dinner-time murders of the White Terror, all acted out in the presence of a numerous audience, on the public square, on the bridge, or on the waterfront, at the gate into the village or on the square opposite the parish church, had much more to offer a primitive public, often

[50] People drank more as food became less abundant; drunkenness seems to have attained its maximum intensity in the conditions of the famine of the year III. But, already in the year II, an official enquiry reveals the immense number of wine-shops within the Paris city limits, and the almost universal practice followed by *cabaretiers* and *marchands de vin* of adulterating their 'wine' by mixing with it beetroot, pear juice, alum, tartar or other more noxious ingredients. (See 'Une enquête sur le vin en l'an II', R. C. Cobb, in *Annales historiques de la Révolution française*, No. 195).

[51] It also added to an already over-loaded memory, and so offered many further occasions for collective vengeance. In the south-east, at the height of the first White Terror, murder days might equally commemorate Saint-Bartholomew, Christmas, 15 August, or 9 Thermidor, or indeed all together. And there are other dates, representing past acts of violence, of a more local context, but commemorated with no less ferocity in places wrapped in on their own unhappy history like Nîmes, Arles, Beaucaire, Tarascon, Salon, Martigues, Avignon and, of course, Lyon.

[52] For a visual description of the Thermidorian and Directorial Palais-Royal, see the strange prints of Isabey (*A Second Identity*, 307, 'Republic of Vices').

composed largely of women and children, than the smoke-filled discussions of the rump of *sociétés populaires*. The White Terror, save for the victims and their families, was fun.

Of course, even the Republic of the year II was not a totalitarian regime. It might have the means to force open doors and to penetrate into bedrooms, at 4 a.m., in a frigid night made silent by the disappearance of the noisy carriages of the libertine and the gambler on his way home (nocturnal silence is one indication of an authoritarian, mysterious regime);[53] and it could create and impose a language repetitive in its orthodoxy.[54] But it could not enter people's minds, had little effect on personal conduct and completely failed to organise leisure, save in the occasional Sunday-school treat.[55] It could not extend to the submerged world of the very poor, and though it made wine worse, it did not make it any less plentiful. It did, for a time, create a new man—the militant of the year II—but he was too odd, too unpleasant, too silly, too impossible, to last.[56] It completely failed to create a new woman. It left the poor poorer. It drove out of existence some forms of crime, but created new ones. And, by greatly increasing mobility, releasing the poor countryman from the prison of rural poverty, setting the country girl on the road to the city, extending the scope and the variety of the marriage market, and offering, in an extending bureaucracy, many new alternative forms of employment, it added a much greater degree of variety to private life and gave to many former provincials the possibilities of a picaresque existence.[57] Far from the uniform, militarised Sparta of

[53] Mercier, in *le Nouveau Paris*, has created a verbal description of *les heures de Paris*, by day and by night, a pattern of work and leisure, the breathing of the great city, comparable to the extraordinary account of the flux and reflux of the working population in *Le six octobre* of Jules Romains. At 4 a.m. the carriages of the libertines and the gamblers come clattering over the cobbles, moving west or south, across the Seine, from the area of the Palais-Royal. The bourgeois, on the third floor, the artisan on the fourth, the apprentice on the seventh, half awakened, turn sleepily to their companions and make love; many Parisians, writes Mercier, were thus conceived in the early hours at a time when the tired libertine was heading for home.

[54] On the language of unanimity, see *The Police and the People*, part I, section II, 'L'Esprit public',

[55] There is little evidence to suggest that the *fête de l'Etre suprême* and the other republican feast days were widely followed by the population, while, even on the outskirts of Paris, Sunday continued to be celebrated in the summer of 1794.

[56] *M. Nicolas*, IV, 2137. '... Cette remarque est de 1784; je ne la ferois pas aujourd'hui 15 Auguste 1790—J'y ajoute aujourd'hui 18 mars 1795 (28 Ventôse an III) la remarque qu'on va trouver dans la page suivante sur la cruauté des *Jacobins*. Qu'en conclure? Que toute tyrannie est insupportable, et celle des *Sans-culottes* encore plus que celle des Princes, qui n'oppriment pas tout, parce qu'ils ne connoissent pas tout; au lieu que les nombreux Tyrans Sans-culottes voient partout; ils sont méchans, jaloux de leurs égaux, ivres du pouvoir d'être oppresseurs, pouvoir qu'ils ne croient jamais porter assez loin, insolens et injustes comme tous les ignorans, tous les hommes sans éducation, cruels comme l'est quiconque qui fut longtems avili . . .'

[57] Especially in the numerous positions in an extensive bureaucracy of Occupation, in posts that were semi-civilian and semi-military. See *The Police and the People*, part II, 'Exile'.

Saint-Just's dreadful *Institutions*, the Revolution, in its final and conclusive stage, with the advent of Thermidorian individualism, social inequality and anarchical vice, had greatly reduced the disciplines of public life, destroyed many of the old collective taboos, fragmented the family and given limitless scope to the resourceful, the unscrupulous and the semi-criminal.[58] The indifferent had sat out the storm and had survived, as they had thought all along that they would succeed in doing, if they remained unnoticed and unobtrusive. They had always felt, however obscurely, that the Terror was too unnatural a state of affairs to last.

The Revolution added unexpected, baffling new chapters to individual existences, placing new men in new places, strange men in strange jobs, shaking individual lives into unfamiliar patterns, while failing even to reach a great many of the fringe elements of French society. It had not been defeated by private life, but private life had passed it by. The ultimate insult perhaps to a Revolution that had sought to be universal and to change the face of the world was that it should have been exploited, in terms of local politics and of village polarisations, in the interests of private vendettas and of personal vengeance. People went into the Revolution for what they could get out of it. It was a national lottery, the full complexity and mystery of which can only be hinted at in the endless variety of individual lives and of individual experiences.

[58] Despite endless paper checks, the Terror was never able to catch up with the elusive problem of identity. Mobility and mobilisation made it much easier for many with a past to set themselves up in places where they were not known and, often, to embark on highly successful revolutionary careers, sometimes as noisy demagogues. There were many of these 'parachutists', who, in the conditions of 1793 and the year II, suddenly appeared in a *commune* and, by the strength of their vocal cords or the extravagance of their proposals, soon obtained a hearing, and even an ascendancy over a *société* or a municipality. An operation of this type was so common as to have been described in current political slang as *se refaire une virginité républicaine*. This at least, unlike that of Marguerite Barrois, was a virginity that could be lost and regained any number of times. It was much the same with identities. The Lyon authorities, over a period of three years, were hard put to it to establish the identity of a man who first of all described himself as Louis Beau, *doreur sur métaux*, native of Rouen, parish of Saint-Maclou, born in August 1770. When enquiries revealed that there was no such person, Beau said his real name was Claude Cavaillon Pinaud, that he had been born in the village of Novaleize (Mont-Blanc) in 1770, leaving the place in 1793, at the age of 23. This time, he is taken to Novaleize by the *gendarmerie*. We learn from their report that 'il n'a pas su indiquer les noms des villages avoisinans Novaleize, ni les voisins de son prétendu père, ni le nom du Pasteur qui étoit à Novaleize lors de son départ, ni son signalement; il ne se souvient pas s'il y avoit des maisons en face de l'église, il ne se rappelle ni le nombre des cabarets, ni le nom des cabaretiers de l'endroit . . . il ne connoissoit point le nom du hameau où demeuroient ses prétendus père et mère; il ne se rappelle point les noms de ses parrain et marraine . . .' (*A.N.* BB 18 68, rapport de la gendarmerie de Lyon du 3 Fructidor an VIII). As he could not remember the number of cafés in the place, it was reasonable to suppose, as the Lyon authorities rightly did, that he had never been there! But, without an identity, he could not be tried, although he was certainly a deserter, and probably a burglar and a murderer and the accomplice of a bandit who had been executed in Grenoble. The methods of the *gendarmerie*, on this occasion, are very revealing.

The German Kaiserreich from 1871 as a Nation-State

Theodor Schieder

The Kaiserreich as it developed after 1871 was a very complicated historical creation. It was brought into being by the most powerful of the German states and it was dominated by the same state. The name of the new Reich was that of the Reich of the Middle Ages, with the Kaiser as the representative of authority. Its organisation was that of a federation of principalities and free cities. Within the federation the normal governmental functions enjoyed by a present-day federal nation were extremely limited. And yet it is possible, at least in my opinion, to describe the historical significance of the Kaiserreich most accurately by referring to it as a 'nation-state'.

With this observation our task is not made any easier, and it leads us into a very difficult historical problem. This problem centres around the unity of the historical and political conceptions of a nation as it appeared to the different European nations; this was also the point around which the greatest of political conflicts developed. Like all European nations whose birth can be traced to the nineteenth or early twentieth centuries, the Germans declared themselves to be a nation-state. In other words, they justified their existence as a nation from their will to be united and from the political form which they adopted, but they did not share the same opinion about the implications of what they were attempting to create. Their effort can best be understood from the unity of will or political confession around which the citizens of the nation united, as in France; or to name the other extreme, it can be explained as the organisation of a group having a common language. This had been the old German conception of a nation.

No absolute contrast between the concept of a nation in western political thought and the ethnic and linguistic nationalism of Herder is to be found. Western European nations, with the exception of Switzerland, were strongly affected by the drive towards linguistic and ethnic assimilation. On the other hand, in the cultural and ethnic nations of middle and eastern Europe every group appreciated the importance of the state as goal and medium for its national policies. Any attempt to make a clear differentiation between the two notions is doomed to failure.

Instead one must turn to the real historical phenomena and try to extract from them the conception of a modern nation-state. This method will form the foundation of the ensuing discussion, which will be centred around three basic questions: firstly the personification of the national consciousness, secondly the political form of national entity in the Kaiserreich and lastly the symbols of its sovereignty and its political organisation.

Let us begin with the first question. The German Reich after 1871 was a creation of the Prussian state which, under the leadership of Bismarck, developed a common interest with the national movement of the middle class. Although this combination never led to full harmony, it was based on a secure foundation of common convictions. At Frankfurt the followers of Hegel, who formed the moderate Liberal Party, had already shown their willingness to found a national entity, but only if it were a strong one. For them the idea of nationalism was of less importance than the building of a strong nation-state. For the representatives of the Kleindeutsch, or little Germany, school the alliance of the national party with Prussia was not an act of emergency, but one of necessity. Prussia was looked on as an ideological centre; it also represented protestantism, with which they associated the intellectual and moral development of the nation.

As far as Prussian aims were concerned this movement proved to be the right ally, but only after the suspicions stemming from the revolution of 1848 had been dispelled, together with the hostility towards the party which after 1860 represented the main opposition in the Prussian constitutional conflict. Bismarck's principles of power-politics provided the method for overcoming these suspicions. He created the alliance between Prussia and the Kleindeutsch element and, as Jacob Burckhardt stated, cut off the German revolution from the top.

But in contrast to the era of Prussian reforms and the revolution of 1848–9, there was now a strong authoritanian state of the type which had existed under Frederick the Great. National liberalism met it as an unequal partner. Through the political power structure and the constitutional compromises made between 1867 and 1871, liberal constitutionalism and, in a wider sense, the national liberalism of German intellectuals were brought within bounds. Their limits were tightened by two almost simultaneous developments. The upheaval in social structures as a result of increasing industrialisation gave rise to a new class which had not participated previously in national development. The middle class lost its uniform social structure and began to diversify in the new industrial society. In this way it lost its common political desires and also its intellectual relationship with the traditional educational patterns of the early nineteenth century. Secondly, the national entity began its existence at a time when the intellectual content of national liberalism was exhausted and Hegel had lost his position of leadership among German intellectuals.

So it was that the state, the social movement and the cultural spirit separated immediately after the foundation of the Reich in 1871. Since then the question of the ideal content of the Reich has not been left untouched. The nation-state became the authoritative power in the fields of politics and social life, even for those who worked against it. But it was closely bound to several minor areas of intellectual life, namely, law and the social sciences, the most important of the latter group being history.

It must be granted that no single intellectual and historical observation is sufficient to get to the root of the problem. The question which the social historian must ask is who, or what group, represented the nation-state. The situation is easily explained if we look at the relative strength of the parties in the Reichstag and their position in relation to the policies of the Reich. In this way it is possible to clarify the shift of opinion from national liberalism, Bismarck's most important ally during the years in which the Reich was founded, to the conservative groups. Bismarck was instrumental in splintering the National Liberal Party in the later 1870s, but the reason for the break-up lay still deeper.

One of the most astonishing occurrences in the history of the nation between 1871 and 1914 was the full acceptance of the policies of the Reich by the conservative upper-class from the Prussian regions east of the Elbe. This development began with the founding of the German Conservative Party in 1876 and ended with the identification of the concepts 'national' and 'conservative', an equation that had been unthought of in the 1870s, but which became common practice after the collapse of 1918. It had a series of explanations. At various times the interests of agriculture had much in common with those of heavy industry, as was demonstrated in the transition to protective tariffs in the late 1870s. There was also the common encouragement of imperialist policies in the era immediately after Bismarck's fall, in which the links between the concept of a powerful state of Prussian-conservative origin and the economic expansionism of the middle class proved to be enduring.

On the other side, but in line with the fusion of Prussian conservatism with the policies of the Reich, a gradual rapprochement took place between the Reich and those groups which had stood outside, or in opposition to it in the first decades of its existence. For example the Catholics who had originally been politically organised in the Centre Party in favour of a greater Germany and to some extent the socialist workers contained their demands within the boundaries of practical solutions. These altered according to the merits of each case, but never led to any fundamental changes. This policy can already be noted in the Centre Party when the Kulturkampf was being played down, and after the turn of the century; it can be observed among the Social Democrats, although in the case of this latter group, it was only fully manifested for the first time in 1914.

In order to give a complete account of this development some discussion of the situation in 1871 is required. We must investigate the groups who favoured the Prussian Kleindeutsch solution and those groups which stood in opposition to it. Here we meet three different forms of opposition.

First, there were those groups which had been defeated in 1866–71 and which, in some way, defended the German past with all its traditions against the new authority and order. Thus it was that the defeated representatives of the political solution which sought a greater German 'Universal' Reich[1] formed an alliance with Austria. These representatives included the followers of dynastic patriotism, such as could be found in the Welfen and the Bavarian Patriot Party. These groups would never have got any popular influence if they had not found the support of catholicism, which represented the authority of a universal opposition to the ideas of the time, that is to say, to liberalism and nationalism. They represented the resistance of one particular political tradition to the new national power state. They also expressed the indignation felt over the loss of the universal European heritage by the exclusion of Austria from the Reich. This combination was the basis for a great intellectual and political alliance which gave these different groups the strength which they lacked individually.

The second opposition group was the result of the revolutionary social upheaval into which the young Reich found itself cast shortly after its foundation. The working class lacked the educational traditions of the middle class and saw the young nation-state as an outsider. It brought an independent class consciousness into a society with a middle-class feudal structure. In its neglected position it moved through class consciousness towards the idea of the class struggle. The Grossdeutsch, or greater Germany, Catholic opposition, with its inheritance of a super-national conception of the Reich,

[1] In this context the term 'Universal' is used as meaning a political entity which does not have to be justified in nationalist terms.

might challenge the Kleindeutsch national state but both were confronted by the socialists with their own programme of international class solidarity. According to Naumann, it took middle-class liberalism almost three decades to recognise the invincibility of the Socialist Party. Naumann acknowledged the need to recognise the working class as a real power in national politics. After the encroachments of the so-called 'revisionists' and the strengthening of the trade unions, the Social Democrats proved, contrary to popular belief, that they were determined not to overthrow the nation by revolutionary means, but to change it structurally from within. This was a social, historical and political occurrence of no less significance than the alliance of conservative Prussian leadership with the policies of the Reich.

The third opposition group in the Reich was made up of foreign nationals, non-Germans who lived within its boundaries. It is not possible, as in the case of the Social Democrats, to measure their impact on the Reich, but they stood in close relation to the main stream of thought of the nation-state, especially in regard to the principle of national self-determination. Since the withdrawal of Austria, which left the Kleindeutsch political entity under the leadership of Prussia, the problem of non-German nationals within the Reich was no longer so acute. This issue, which had been central to the decisions of the Assembly in Frankfurt Paul's Church, receded into the background.

The German nation-state, however, did see itself pitted against non-German nationals to the north-west and the east, in north Schleswig, in Alsace-Lorraine and in the Prussian eastern provinces where linguistic, ethnic or political differences existed. The problems of nationality within the Reich were not relics of a super-national past before 1806, but a result of the process of national unification itself. In the eastern parts of Prussia, the Polish question became an issue of national policy. The roots of the problem were in the checks and balance system of the Congress of Vienna, and the difficulties became more acute after the incorporation of these regions into the North German Confederation. The Alsace-Lorraine problem in the west arose out of the war with France in 1870–71, and that of Schleswig stemmed from the war with Denmark in 1864 and the Peace of Prague concluded after the war with Austria in 1866.

The contrasts between the concepts of the nation-state and its effects were most marked in Alsace-Lorraine. Its return to the Reich in 1870–71 was the cause for celebration in Germany, as a sign of the bond between the concepts of 'Nation' and 'Reich'. The claim to cession of this area to Germany was based historically on the homecoming of the 'avulsa imperii' and on the principle of ethnic nationality. Nowhere in European history were the two basic concepts of nationalism, subjective and objective, so closely linked as they were in this instance. The German-speaking Alsatians however, protested against the German claim of cession in the French National Assembly at Bordeaux. This protest was repeated by the first representatives of Alsace-Lorraine to be seated in the Reichstag in 1874.

In addition, the representatives of the Poles in the Prussian eastern provinces demanded the exclusion of the Polish areas under Prussian authority from the new German nation-state. In the Reichstag debate on 1 April 1871, the representatives of both sides met face to face. Bismarck tried to impose the principle of the nation-state, which bound Alsace to France, on the Poles. 'The gentlemen', he said, 'belong to no other state and to no other people than to those of Prussia, to which I count myself'. But he could not get them to forget that the Prussia of which he spoke was now incorporated into the German Reich. 'We shall', countered a Polish representative, 'remain under Prussian rule so long as God wills, but we shall not become a part of the German Reich'. Another Polish representative resorted to the defence of the historic and ethnic concepts of nationality and cited Alsace as an example; he heartily welcomed the victory of the principles of nationalism in Alsace and German Lorraine. So it was that the same basic arguments were used by both sides, but without reaching a compromise. As a result the nation-state was faced with negative results on several of its boundaries. This was not a negation of principle, as was made by the defenders of the super-national entity or international politics, but a search for a consequential application of these principles. The Danes, the Alsatians and the Poles wanted to belong to a nation-state other than the German one.

It was precisely this problem which set limits for German policy and caused abruptness of decision and action. The nationalists, both the Germans and the minority groups, became more and more estranged. It is indeed questionable whether this situation had remained unchanged since the beginning of the Reich. The possibilities that alternative political directions might have been taken require closer consideration.

The first point to be considered is the peculiar notion which Bismarck, founder of the Reich, had of the principle of the nation-state. For him it was only a means to an end, to the historical national principle as personified by Prussia and which was to reinforce and lead the way to its victory in domestic and foreign affairs. It was for this reason that he could cut short national reforms at the point where the interests of Prussia dictated, and not proceed further with them as the wider principles of nationalism required. The Reich was created to fit the needs of Prussian hegemony. The southern German states had little interest in unification; both in the North German annexation of 1866 and in the foundation of the Reich in 1870 special rights were guaranteed to them. On the outer circumference of the newly created Reich lay the unimpeachable sovereignty of the Austrian monarchy.

The second possibility that a basically different policy of nationalism might have emerged must be sought in the intellectual traditions of German liberalism. The liberals had a split conception of nationalism, influenced as it was by both Herder and Hegel. Nationalism in the Hegelian sense could be explained as the fullness which the state attained as the reality of ethnic ideas. For Herder the state embodied the principles of spirit and culture, which find their realisation in language.

In 1869, the Prussian statistician and follower of Herder, Richard Bockh, argued that language forms the common intellectual foundation for the construction of a unified society. The suppression of language would be equivalent to the destruction of the spirit of a people. For this reason the compulsory use of a foreign language and national assimilation were contrary to the principles of nature. The principle of nationalism is sufficiently realised, according to Bockh, when freedom of speech is established without altering national boundaries. Attention must be given to the intellectual self-determination of every people in their mother tongue, even when this people live within the boundaries of another nation. So it was that Bockh required reciprocal assurances of the observance of the right of self-determination from the Danish and German nationals in north Schleswig. These promises were to be protected by all powers which had bound themselves to the observance of the status quo in that region. The rights of the Poles he saw as a responsibility resting on the German government.

The idea of national and cultural tolerance, which had earlier found expression in the Constitution of the Frankfurt National Assembly in 1849 (Article 188) was no longer relevant to the national liberal conception of the nation. The nation-state, at least at its highest level, was no longer understood as the balancing power, but as the creator of a unified entity which could employ force for its own preservation. It was also seen as the creator of a common national language for use within its boundaries. Prussian Germany found itself in the same position as Hungary and Russia in the 1860s, once it had to create a national language. The theories of liberalism were then altered to justify the destruction of other nationalities within the Reich, and even to demand their destruction, as the writings of the liberal publicist Constantine Rössler and the works of Heinrich von Treitschke testify.

Linguistic and national policies in Prussian Germany responded to these challenges, as was demonstrated by the laws enacted during and after the 1870s and their practical application. The basic tenor of liberal and conservative language policy in Germany was the claim of the nation-state to secure the German language as the official language of the state. The non-German languages within the Reich were granted limited rights in local affairs, but never obtained equality with German. Their usage was limited to non-official spheres as vernacular languages. Behind this policy stood the belief and the will to make German the only official language in the Reich. Every healthy people, as was said in a contemporary essay dealing with language policies, must desire that its vernacular language become the official language of the nation and vice-versa. The implication was that the nation should be changed into an entity with a single common language. This was carrying the thought of Bismarck's time one step further; the total incorporation of the Poles into the Reich and into Prussian Germany was to be accomplished by complete assimilation of language.

This policy, no matter how offensive it might have been, was carried through with a very defensive strategy. The superiority of the Poles in the social and political spheres was apparent; it was the result of the expansion of what was sometimes called their 'community within the Prussian state'. The German opposition took up a far more militant nationalistic policy. In addition to the efforts to bring about linguistic and cultural assimilation, the attempted germanisation of the lands through the colonisation laws (Ansiedlgesetz) of 1886 commenced. And yet, no matter how unified the language policies of Prussian Germany might have appeared at first glance, the tendencies were very divergent. The differences between the tolerant liberalism of Bockh and the followers of a strict assimilation in the sense of Rössler and Treitschke continued to be effective in an indirect way.

After the turn of the century, the situation became even more explosive. The discussion now centred around the value of German as the exclusive language within the nation-state and the use of more radical means for its recognition as such. The official sphere, in which German was used exclusively was expanded and it was demanded that all assemblies which conducted their debates in other languages be abolished. This requirement was based on the Prussian Official Correspondence Language Law (Geschäftssprachengesetz) of 1876, which was the only German language law in operation until that time. It stated that only when assemblies agreed to use German would the police administer their decisions.

Leading lawyers of this period used the occasion to view the nation-state as a legal conception with all its consequences. In 1902 the Bonn constitutional lawyer and Prussian crown syndic, Philip Zorn, wrote an essay on the official German language, in which he expounded and developed the theory of the language laws of the nation, Zorn used as an argument the common legal principle that the silence of the German and Prussian constitutions on the question of language rested on the assumption that in Prussia and in the Reich, German was the only official language. Although the language of private life was left open by the state, everything which fell within the public sphere, be it in the state or the political community generally, was to be dominated by the German language. In this way, the full value of the national language was to be attained in the Reich. The language policies became the self-verification of the national entity and at the same time one of its most effective weapons for the suppression of the political activity of other linguistic groups within its boundaries. It is notable, however, that the tolerant decisions of Prussia's highest administrative court hindered the effective implementation of this policy, and with permanent consequences.

Let us turn to some of the results. The language policy of the German nation-state, with Prussia as its political centre, was intended to secure for German the most extensive use in the official life of the nation. This intention was extended by the more radical defenders of national German policies to the full assertion of German as the only language within the Reich. This meant the full assimilation of non-German languages, especially through the schools. The historian and publicist Hans Delbrück called attention to the failure of this policy in 1894. The intensity with which the Poles were taught German, while at the same time the Germans were discouraged from learning Polish, had led the Poles to become bilingual, thereby giving them an economic advantage over the Germans. The dilemma of national politics was that the effort to terminate language conflict within the Reich created instead a powerful opposition. The Reich was structurally weakened by attempting to fight this opposition by legal means, a contest which its social structure was not strong enough to bear. The Polish community in the Prussian state became an antibody within the nation, a symptom of the disturbance caused by the intrusion of foreign material.

The domestic polices of the Kaiserreich had always carried with them a sense of the incompleteness of national unity and this might in part explain the haste and exaggeration with which it acted. It was not simply the question of nationality as such which grew out of this awareness. To a greater extent issues of nationality constantly impinged on domestic crises as, for example, in the Kulturkampf, the social questions and the political differences with the agricultural community east of the Elbe.

We must also consider to what extent a sense of incompleteness in the nation affected foreign affairs. Is it possible to describe the era of the Kaiserreich as a continuation of the policies of greater Germany and of irredentism in some form? Is it possible to draw an unbroken line of greater German policies from the Frankfurt National Assembly of 1848 to the national imperialism of the Hitler regime after 1938? Under Hitler the German Reich of 1871 was viewed as an amputated national entity with a limited character of its own. A national consciousness, impressed by the idea of a German Reich or the 'Reichsnation' which after 1871 had yielded to Bismarck's policies of restraint within its own boundaries, would lack all moderation during Hitler's years in power. Still more, it appeared that unlimited nationalism disclosed peculiar changes in the consciousness of the nation.

In the 1880s, and more fully in the 1890s, a new type of impulsive nationalism developed. It can be characterised as an aggressive national movement running parallel to the consolidated conception of imperial Germany. It possessed no common bond with the old greater Germany movement or with the earlier conception of a nation. The idea of an unfinished national entity was, therefore, no longer represented in the sense of the old principles of nationalism, but in the sense of the new, symbolised by an imperialist policy stemming from notions of national prestige. The development of national consciousness had come late for Germany, which lagged behind the leading nations of Europe in this respect. Only by expressing this consciousness could Germany preserve its existence as a nation.

The peculiar mixture of popular, national and imperialist aims was, according to Hannah Arendt, characteristic of this era. It found its most influential exponent in the Pan-German Movement. On the occasion of the foundation of this organisation in 1891, its basic principles were stated as seeking to maintain and support the endeavours of Germans in all nations, especially where German-speaking people had to fight for the assertion of their individuality. Another principle was to coordinate all German movements in the world to achieve these aims. The German imperialism of this era was therefore not simply the political expression of dynamic economic and industrial expansion, but was firmly rooted in nationalism. The national entity was no longer to be realised within the continental confines of the German people, but in terms of national political prestige involving Germans in the entire world. Thus there developed in Germany an atmosphere similar to the one prevailing in most other European nations of that era.

It was undeniably a great historical achievement that the German nation-state of 1871 had given Germans an effective, though limited, arena in which to formulate their national destiny. In the nationalist tendencies of the Pan-German Movement the restrictions disappeared. In its expansionism, as Hannah Arendt said, the Pan-German movement crossed all geographic boundaries of a definite national community and in doing so became limitless. The moderating factors behind Bismarck's foundation of the Reich passed into history. It became evident that official German policy had not always kept pace with the changing attitudes of public opinion. It stood on the shaky foundation of an undefined national atmosphere, unsure, often helpless and still more often inconsistent in its decisions.

The last task remaining for us is to analyse the national policies of the Reich through its use of symbols and its political form. For the historian of the Middle Ages the doctrine of the symbols of authority has already been developed into a branch of historical science, but for the modern historian a systematic method of research is lacking. The degree to which the modern nation had created a political style and symbol of its own was amazing. It had been influenced by the French Revolution and at several points by the American one. In the U.S.A. the Constitution is not only viewed as a code of political norms and values, but is also honoured as a symbol. Its integrity has been preserved by its elasticity, despite the difficulties encountered in its practical applications, and also by its ability to achieve national integration. The French Revolution pointed the way for the use of symbols in a democracy. These included the national anthem; the national holidays, which were introduced in Article 12 of the Constitution of 1791; the national flag, the tricolour, which ended the use of heraldic symbols; and, lastly, the national monuments, with which the nineteenth century had been so fully blessed. These symbols are and should be a lasting stimulus to excite national consciousness. They should also generate a feeling of national unity, just as similar feelings were evoked by the symbolism of the princely states, personified by the baroque with its large self-representation, or by the demonstrations of power in the military monarchies such as Prussia.

In examining the German Reich after 1871 with the above criteria, a deep and growing schism can be noted between the 'national democratic' and the 'national monarchic' elements, and this explains more satisfactorily the problems of the national flag and national holidays. The new Reich created for itself a tricolour, which was not the tricolour of the revolution of 1848, but one in which the colours of hegemonical Prussia dominated. The colours, black-red-gold, represented not so much the German democratic tradition as the continuation of the greater Germany movement outside the boundaries of the Reich. But the new flag's power as a symbol of integration began to grow only after the creation of the German fleet. It was first declared to be the national flag by proclamation of the Kaiser in 1892. Its incorporation in the constitution of 1871 had been entirely a measure of expediency: provision for its use had been made in the section concerning the navy and merchant marine, but it was applicable only to these two groups. Nor did the Kaiserreich possess a national anthem. The 'Deutschland' hymn of Hofmann von Fallersleben was first designated as the national anthem by the Reich's President, Friedrich Ebert, in 1922.

The official policy of restraint also applied to national holidays. The celebration of 'Sedan Day' was inaugurated by the spontaneous action of nationalist circles under the leadership of Pastor von Bodelschwingh, in spite of the opposition of many people, the most notable of whom were the Grand Duke of Baden, Field Marshal Moltke and later Bishop von Ketteler. In 1871, and in the years that followed, this celebration became a test of strength between the so-called 'friends of the Reich' and its enemies. It was for this reason that Theodor Mommsen suggested doing away with it. It had much significance for national consciousness, but failed to heal the schism in the nation which had developed after the Kulturkampf and the ensuing anti-socialist laws.

These points are important in an inquiry into the problem of the German nation-state, and the question of the legal position of the Kaiser is central to the discussion. Medieval concepts common in the thought-patterns of the German national movement of the late nineteenth century were carried over from older national concepts of the early nineteenth century. During the debates of the Constitutional Assembly which met in Frankfurt and in the resulting Constitutional Draft of 1849 the concept of a hereditary dynasty (Erbkaisertum) was asserted. This was coupled with the decision to make Prussia the central authority in a federation of monarchs, which was precisely the connection sought by Bismarck. Not only did he understand much more clearly than the followers of liberal national policies the fascination which the title of Kaiser had for southern Germans, but he also saw in it the embodiment of centralisation. He felt that the title of Kaiser was appropriate, and would make Prussian hegemony in the monarchical federation tolerable to the sceptical princes in the south.

It is widely known how strong was the aversion of King Wilhelm of Prussia and of a wide circle with a Prussian conservative tradition towards the title of Kaiser. Less is known of the antipathy in the ranks of the national liberals. It can best be understood in the context of the great scientific and political debates in the decade preceding the founding of the Reich. The topic of the discussions between Heinrich von Sybel and Julius Ficker was the politics of the medieval Kaisers. Although the bulk of the debate was carried on by these two men, most of the intellectuals of the nation participated. It might seem ironic that the same men who had deprived the Kaiser and the Reich of the Middle Ages of all significance were now trying to build a new Reich with a new conception of the Kaiser.

'I fear', wrote the historian Max Duncker, 'the pomp and ceremony that will accompany the new Reich. I fear also the greater Germany that sticks in it and would prefer to leave the person of the Kaiser and Emperor-King to the Austrians . . .' When the names 'Kaiser' and 'Reich' were finally anchored to the constitution, the majority of national liberals attempted to deny their continuity with the Holy Roman Empire and instead sought to interpret the old names in terms of nationalism. Hardly any explanation of the legal position of the Kaiser was advanced in which the bond of the new to the old dignity was not emphatically denied, although the Kaiser himself implied the existence of just such a link in his proclamation of 18 January 1871. 'This alleged historical connection', according to a famous lawyer, 'between the new and old empires is just as unbelievable as any alleged connection between the Kaiser dignity of the Middle Ages and the Caesars of the Roman Empire. The Old Reich and its Kaiser are dead, and God should allow them no favourable resurrection, because they don't deserve it and they would be disastrous for us'.

Finally, what was the meaning of the Kaiser for the German nation-state? What were the results of the resumption of the old name in the light of new political, social and international conditions? The legal position of the Kaiser in the Reich was complicated by divergent interpretations of the constitution. It is for this reason that we cannot understand his legal position by using the standard maxims of constitutional law applicable in the nineteenth century. There was general agreement that the Kaiser was neither the sovereign monarch of the Reich, nor was he its president. 'He cannot be an official as a president of a republic, because he does not possess sovereignty', wrote the constitutional lawyer Paul Laband in summing up the position of the Kaiser in the Reich. On the other hand, the Kaiser could not simply be classified as one of the many links in a chain of a collective sovereignty of princes and free-cities, whose exectuive body was the Federal Council (Bundesrat). He was granted more privileges, which stemmed in part from his position as the holder of the federation's presidency. Furthermore, his position as commander-in-chief of the armed forces gave him an authoritative position similar to that of a monarch. As it was, the Kaiser named and dismissed the Reich's chancellors, just like a sovereign monarch, even if this function was carried out in the name of the Reich and the federation's presidency.

This complicated system of a federation of monarchs with a monarch as its head was an object of discussion among lawyers of that day. It was understood as little in the political life of Germany as in other countries. Because of its complications it is tempting to put aside all constitutional hurdles and picture the Kaiser simply as the Reich's monarch, 'the visible symbol of the national unity of Germany', as Paul Laband wrote in 1907 in an essay on the historical development of the Reich's Constitution. He added that in the naive conception of the people there was no German Reich without the Kaiser, and that no clause in the constitution could take this belief from them. They pictured a Reich without a Kaiser as a political body without a head!

> Everything that glows in the heart of the nation with regard to the sacred feelings of love for the fatherland, which moves the people to a patriotic self-denial and a will to self-sacrifice in favour of the nation, which stimulates the national pride and gives the population an undeniable confidence in the order of things, with an uplifting of objective legal observations and the winning of character, is a deep-seated love and adoration of the Kaiser as the head and leader of the people. The people may cheer and rejoice with the Kaiser, but there is no reason for the federation's presidency to build a portal to their honour.

These sentences, written in the years of the so-called personal government of Wilhelm II preceding the 'Daily Telegraph Affair' almost constitute an abdication of the constitutional system in favour of the popular voice. It showed the danger of a constitutional order in which the boundaries were not clearly defined. Nothing stood between the Kaiser as the symbol of the nation and the Kaiser as the absolute authority of the Reich.

It was precisely this which must have been disastrous for a monarch like Wilhelm II. He set himself above the legal basis of his authority and never bothered to consider the consequences of his actions. He is said to have boasted of never having read the constitution or ever having known its content. Few political realities were met in the practice of personal rule in the reign of Wilhelm II, and the fiction of personal rule could only prosper in an unbalanced constitutional system. Wilhelm II, without a doubt, acted on the impossible assumption that the Kaiser alone, as the traditional symbol of authority, could preserve the nation. He seemed, at least at the beginning of his reign, to be changing the structure of the Reich with the help of the working class; just as he later expanded the conception of the Reich into the conception of a world empire. This took place without deeper reflection and with a frightening dilettantism, and it became more pronounced after 1908 when the excitement which accompanied the 'Daily Telegraph crisis' provoked a disastrous fluctuation between his unlimited self-estimation and his deep lack of self-confidence.

The nation was temporarily able to withstand the Kaiser's self-elevation but it was ultimately to contribute to its self-destruction, as the critical weeks of 1908 showed. In spite of the many declarations of Byzantine admiration, mixed with a growing criticism which was both alarming and indignant, the Kaiser was doomed. Even the will to change drastically the course of constitutional politics waned at an early date.

Neither constitutionally nor in the sphere of social policies was the harmony between nation and Kaiser, as personified by Wilhelm II, to be realised again. The underlying reasons were not only the person of the last Kaiser, but also the contrasting developments in the political and social spheres. This divisive process was observed by Friedrich Naumann in his essay 'Democracy and Empire', published in 1900. His was the most important intellectual attempt to save the Kaiser for the changing national entity. He touched on the plebiscitary element of the German Empire, on what was called Caesarism under Napoleon III and tried to change the Kaiser from being the leader of an agrarian and feudal society into the leader of a new industrial one. It is revealing that this great contemporary analysis of the social problems of the nation came to an end and was incorporated into the wider issues of world politics, industrial expansion and Caesarian dictatorship. Within the nation almost everything must have seemed like a great Utopia. But the persistence of major problems was undeniable. The Kaiser, no longer the symbol but the holder of political authority in the nation, and the industrial revolution, the strongest socio-economic force in the nation, became closely involved with each other. Their coordination, however, was in no way successful, particularly as regards such necessary constitutional adjustments as the parliamentary reform of the Reich's constitution or the reform of the Prussian franchise.

The Reich was supported as a nation-state by wider groups than had previously been the case. This came about before the life and death struggle of the nation. The socialist workers merged imperceptibly into the nation, and the Catholic components of the population worked through their political representatives, the Centre Party.

Those who lived in Prussia had found in the conception of the Reich a point with which they could defeat Prussia. In his magnificent survey of the Reich and the nation after 1871, published after the first world war, Friedrich Meinecke believed that he could speak of symptoms of improvement which were beginning to show themselves under the cover of official policies. 'The re-examination of the old programmes, that relearning of the old and the addition of new knowledge was noticeable in all quarters. While the parties showed themselves hard and ungiving in the one sphere, they stretched their thinking many times to try and comprehend all developments'. But internal balance was still lacking in the nation. National consciousness swung between the limitations of the nation-state and the Reichs-nation on the one side, and an aimless, distant, expansive nationalism on the other. Between those two extremes the foreign policy of the Reich found its way to destruction in the first world war.

An Appraisal of Edvard Beneš as a Statesman

William V. Wallace

Throughout his adult life Edvard Beneš was an intensely political being; virtually everything else took second place to politics. From the age of thirty-two, when he had his first taste of office, until he died at the age of sixty-four he was always in the public eye. He became secretary general of the Czechoslovak National Council when it was established in Paris in 1916; he was then successively foreign minister of Czechoslovakia from 1918 to 1935 and president from 1935 until after the Munich Agreement in 1938; he became president of the Czechoslovak government-in-exile when it was set up in London in 1939, and he returned home to serve as president of the liberated state from 1945 until a few months before his death in 1948. During his long career Czechoslovakia came into existence, was destroyed and re-created, and finally in 1948 fell under Soviet domination. It was a period of great events for the Czechoslovak people. But it was also a period of traumatic history for Europe and the world. Versailles and Munich witnessed the decline and fall of the Old Europe. The Russian liberation of Prague in 1945 and the Communist seizure of power there three years later were in turn symptom and confirmation of the cold war between the Soviet Union and the United States. If politics were in Beneš' heart, Beneš was also at the heart of politics in Czechoslovakia, in Europe and occasionally in the world at large.

It is odd that for a man of such far-reaching importance there is no up-to-date biography in English. The period of the second world war produced one or two, journalistic but not unsatisfactory in their way.[1] The English-speaking public had a guilt complex about Munich and—the reverse of the coin—Beneš was a kind of hero. Beneš was also on hand in the war years to provide biographical material simply in the course of conversation. By contrast, the events

[1] e.g., C. Mackenzie, *Dr Beneš*, London, 1946.

of 1948 in Czechoslovakia seemed to be Russia's crime or Beneš' mistake, and he died out of touch with the west. There was neither interest nor accessible material.

It is equally odd perhaps that there is no good biography of Beneš in Czech. Many tributes and assessments were made in the heyday of the first republic.[2] But nothing could be published under the Nazis; the immediate post-war years were a time of distraction and uncertainty; and most of the twenty years from his death until the brief freedoms of 1968 were dominated by official hostility to him as a representative of the old bourgeois society.[3]

Of course, a daunting problem for possible biographers of Beneš both inside and outside Czechoslovakia is the sheer chronological and spatial range of the man. What makes him historically interesting makes him biographically forbidding. The intricacies of thirty years of Czechoslovak politics, the subtleties and complications of European diplomacy in the period between the wars, the nuances of Russo-American relations in the period from 1941 onwards are life-time studies in themselves. There are also gaps in the sources. The Czechoslovak archives have been made available to historians in a somewhat haphazard way. The German archives are fairly full, but the French are only slightly less sealed than the Russian, and the American are available for a period just slightly more recent than the British. Witnesses have died, or have been eliminated. For western scholars, too, there is the language problem. But despite all these problems, the time has probably arrived at least to begin re-appraising Beneš the statesman. There are enough original sources and serious monographs making use of them to make a start possible.

A basic source for the study of Beneš is what he wrote about himself. He produced one volume of memoirs on his contribution to the founding of the Czechoslovak state during the first world war, and another on the actions he took during the second world war to re-establish Czechoslovakia at the end of it. Both were published in his life-time.[4] He also left behind him an incomplete volume on the Munich crisis. Fragments of this were published in London in 1955 and a larger portion in Prague in 1968.[5] In general, of course, memoirs are a hazardous source of history. Recollections are fallible;

[2] e.g., A. Hartl (ed.), *Edvard Beneš: filosof a státník* (*Edvard Beneš: philosopher and statesman*), Praha, 1937.

[3] e.g., V. Král, *O Masarykově a Benešově kontrarevoluční protisovětské politice* (*Concerning Masaryk's and Beneš's counter-revolutionary anti-soviet policy*), Praha, 1953.

[4] E. Beneš, *My War Memoirs* (London, 1928), trans. by P. Selver; E. Beneš, *Memoirs of Dr E. Beneš: From Munich to New War and New Victory*, London, 1954, trans. by G. Lias.

[5] E. Beneš, *Mnichovské dny* (*Munich Days*), London, 1955; E. Beneš, *Mnichovské dny*, Praha, 1968.

and the desire to defend the past or shape the future can play a decisive role in altering the record. But Beneš' memoirs are both reliable and revealing. He was so wholly absorbed in his activities that he had less opportunity than most to forget the ins and outs, and his politics were so consistent and so continuous that, even if his memoirs had been politically motivated (which for the most part they were not), they would still be accurate representations of the man. What is missing, however, is the account he might have written, had he been spared, of his post-1945 presidency and in particular of his part in the crisis of February 1948. But here there survives in skeletal form the Beneš story as recalled by his most intimate official.[6] Beneš' political tracts and official statements are to be found in considerable numbers.[7] His foreign policy views, and others' references to them, are liberally scattered among the published diplomatic papers. There are also various interesting collections of Czechoslovak materials; two volumes on the period 1939–45, for example, appeared quite recently.[8] The sum of available sources is growing steadily.

The volume of historical research directly or indirectly concerning Beneš is also accumulating steadily. His political activities as an emigré in the first world war have just been set in reasonable perspective by a Czechoslovak historian.[9] His contribution at the Peace Conference in 1919 to the actual shaping of Czechoslovakia's frontiers has been thoroughly investigated by an American historian.[10] Czechoslovak historians have also been carefully, if a little one-sidedly, investigating his activities and achievements in the twenties and thirties.[11] The weight of the literature on Munich is oppressive, though Beneš himself is still sparsely treated.[12] His efforts to steer Czechoslovakia through the conflict of ideologies in the forties met with rival interpretations from Czechoslovak writers at home and abroad in the fifties.[13] But in the years leading up to 1968 these differences narrowed and more reasoned interpretations of the man

[6] J. Smutný, *Únorovy převrat 1948* (*The February Coup 1948*), London, 1955–57.
[7] e.g., E. Beneš, *Bohemia's Case for Independence*, London, 1917; E. Beneš, *Šest let exilu a druhé světové války* (*Six Years of Exile and of the Second World War*), Praha, 1946.
[8] L. Otáhalová and M. Červinková (eds.), *Dokumenty z historie československé politiky 1939–43* (*Documents from the history of Czechoslovak politics 1939–43*), I and II, Praha, 1966.
[9] K. Pichlík, *Zahraniční odboj 1914–18, bez legend* (*The Struggle abroad 1914–18, without legends*), Praha, 1968.
[10] D. Perman, *The Shaping of the Czechoslovak State*, Leiden, 1962.
[11] e.g., A. Gajanová, *ČSR a středoevropská politika velmocí 1918–38* (*Czechoslovakia and the Central European policies of the great powers 1918–38*), Praha, 1967, and R. Kvaček, *Nad Evropou zataženo* (*Europe overcast*), Praha, 1966.
[12] But see M. Lvová, *Mnichov a Edvard Beneš* (*Munich and Edvard Beneš*), Praha, 1968.
[13] e.g., Z. Fierlinger, *Zrada československé buržoasie a jejích spojenců* (*The treason of the Czechoslovak bourgeoisie and their allies*), Praha, 1951, and J. Korbel, *The Communist Subversion of Czechoslovakia 1938–48*, Princeton, 1959.

began to come from young communist historians in particular.[14] It may not be too long before a major biography is a feasible project.

Beneš was born into an age of nationalist excitement. By 1884, the year of his birth, Germany and Italy were well-established states. Rumania had chipped its way to independence. Bulgaria was about to defy the great powers and unite its separate halves into an autonomous whole. Within the Habsburg empire, Hungary had won near-equality of status with Austria. The Czechs, to a greater extent perhaps than the other subject peoples, had resurrected their written language and created a new literature; they had built a national theatre and discovered their national composers; they had produced one political party to boycott the Austrian government and they were in the course of finding others to challenge Vienna on a whole range of national questions. Bohemia was also a province where industry was developing rapidly out of a well-to-do agriculture and where in due course it was natural for the tenth child of a prosperous small farmer to go to Prague for his schooling and to continue on to university both there and abroad. It was no more possible for the young man to escape the questing minds at work in his universities than it was for him to be unaware of the aspirations of his country relatives and his fellow citizens in Prague to be on equal terms with the Germans of their province.

A wandering postgraduate who could finance himself by his journalistic activities and win a doctorate from the University of Dijon in 1908 at the age of twenty-four and another from the University of Prague a year later was hardly likely to remain unmoved by the inequity and inefficiency of Austro-Hungarian rule. In the course of his travels Beneš formed a strong attachment to France and what he subsequently called the 'tradition of the great revolution'. He acquired great respect for England and its search for a 'harmonious human individuality'. As he wrote in his memoirs,

> I returned from abroad strengthened in my original opposition to our political and social conditions. In comparison with England and France, and with western Europe in general, Austria-Hungary, disorganised by its welter of nationalities, struck me as the prototype of the reactionary, militaristic and bureaucratic character of Germany, but without its administrative and financial order, without its inner strength and influence. I had felt repelled by Germany, but the Habsburg empire repelled me more. The traditional anti-Austrian training of a Czech had caused all these feelings to take systematic shape from my youth onwards; I was instinctively a social and national malcontent when I left home. After some time, in 1907 and 1908, believing almost fanatically in the

[14] e.g., J. Belda et al., *Na rozhraní dvou epoch* (*At the watershed of two epochs*), Praha, 1948.

strength and influence of democratic principles, I expected that a change and a regeneration would result from universal suffrage in Austria. Nevertheless, I returned a convinced radical and revolutionary, even though my early training and the hardships of life had taught me at home before the war to suppress passions and sentiments, to master them by means of the intellect and to preserve a political calm and balance.[15]

Circumstances combined with intellectual training to set him inescapably against Austria-Hungary.

These early attitudes remained with him for life. He never lost his early love for France or his admiration for England. To some extent this was his undoing in the negotiations that led to Munich. 'I expected with certainty', he maintained later,

that neither France, which was our ally, nor Great Britain, which had taken so much responsibility upon itself through the Runciman mission, would negotiate about us between themselves—and especially with Germany—without consulting us and obtaining our agreement . . . All this I had the right to expect of the democratic powers.[16]

Even after Munich he was convinced that France and Britain would be 'forced to go to war in spite of the Munich treason—or rather because of it'.[17]

His antipathy towards Austria-Hungary did not die with the break-up of the empire in 1918. In 1920 and again in 1921 he made it quite clear that he would regard a Habsburg restoration in Hungary as an immediate *casus belli.*[18] But his real *bête noire* was Pan-Germanism in whatever guise. The reasoned brief he published in 1917 on *Bohemia's Case for Independence* devoted an entire chapter to the 'Pan-German Plan'; this was 'the dream of making Germany a world-power' and it was 'essentially founded on the crushing of Serbia, the humiliation of Italy, and the complete annihilation of the national aspirations and hopes of the oppressed nations of Austria-Hungary, above all of the Czech-Slovaks'.[19] The lectures he gave in the University of Chicago in the spring of 1939 and published as *Democracy Today and Tomorrow* elaborated the case against Pan-Germanism, strengthening it by reference to Nazi racialist theories:

This movement put forward two political theses even before the war: the gradual unification of all Germans, and, as a consequence of this unification, the great world-wide expansion of this eighty-million nation, first in central and eastern Europe, then in the near east and

[15] Beneš, *My War Memoirs*, *op. cit.*, 18.
[16] Beneš, *Mnichovské dny*, *op. cit.*, 252–53.
[17] Beneš, *Memoirs of Dr E. Beneš*, *op. cit.*, 52.
[18] V. Olivová, 'Československá zahraniční politika a pokus o restauraci Habsburků v roce 1921' (Czechoslovak foreign policy and the attempt at a restoration of the Habsburgs in 1921), *Československý časopis historický*, VIII, Praha, 1959, 680 and 690.
[19] Beneš, *Bohemia's Case for Independence*, *op. cit.*, 45 and 51.

north Africa—and then in the whole pre-war world. The present national socialist Pan-Germanism differs in some points from this pre-war prototype. It had its origin, first of all, in its theory of race.[20]

When at the end of the second world war he arranged—as humanely as possible—the transfer of the Sudeten Germans to Germany, it was to destroy completely a Pan-German weapon. 'A great and fateful chapter in our national history', he later wrote, 'one which had so often moulded our whole destiny—and which at least twice might have caused the destruction of our nation—was thus finally closed.'[21]

Nevertheless Beneš' attitude was never irrationally anti-German. He regretted the necessity of expelling the Sudetens. 'I recognise your tragic situation', he said to one of them,

and I am deeply grieved about it. But such things happen to nations through the fault of their leaders and by the chain of historical events . . . That was why I made those superhuman efforts during Munich for a real agreement with our Germans and with Germany as a whole. But in what kind of situation have we been since 1938?[22]

Nor in 1908 had Beneš reached the pitch of feeling he claimed in his post-1918 memoirs. Czechoslovak nationalism was too sophisticated and successful a phenomenon for that, and Beneš himself too rational and realistic.

As one Czechoslovak historian has recently suggested, the Czechs were already by the turn of the nineteenth century a 'nation without a state'. They felt and acted like a nation; all they lacked was the independent political apparatus of a state. 'Not only in the economic and social fields, but also in the various branches of science and art Czech society was an integral part of the broad European whole and participated in a series of progressive advances'.[23] Whether an independent state would be created or something short of that—or whether the situation would remain as it was—was a question to which only time could give an answer. Beneš might loathe Austria, but in 1908 even he was not prepared to advocate total independence. In his Dijon thesis of that year he suggested that the only solution to the Czech-German problem was the delimitation of nationally homogeneous areas and the acceptance of their autonomy within Austria-Hungary.[24] Like his most influential mentor, Tomáš Masaryk, he was a political realist and like Masaryk, he reached the point of decision only with the outbreak of war in 1914. Thinking

[20] Beneš, *Democracy Today and Tomorrow*, London, 1939, 159–60.
[21] Beneš, *Memoirs of Dr E. Beneš*, *op. cit.*, 223.
[22] *Ibid.*, 220.
[23] J. Kořalka, 'Národ bez státu' (Nation without a state), in *Naše živá i mrtvá minulost* (*Our living and dead past*), Praha, 1968, 136–57.
[24] Perman, *op. cit.*, 13–14.

about the Habsburg empire then he rapidly reached the conclusion that 'either it would come to an end through losing the war, or it would come to an end in a social upheaval and revolution after the war'.[25] The political realities had changed. There was now a chance to create a state for the nation.

During the war Beneš played a role second in importance only to Masaryk's. Indeed in the patient work of negotiation his contribution might be regarded as the greater, if the less glamorous. He developed vital links with the national movement at home and devoted endless hours to negotiations with foreign governments. As Masaryk put it to Karel Čapek somewhat later, 'without Beneš we should not have had our Republic'.[26] In the end Austria-Hungary was destroyed and Czechoslovakia founded. It was naturally a moment for idealistic pride. In his memoirs Beneš recalled how the war had gradually become 'an immense struggle for the successive democratisation of humanity', nationally and internationally:

In the life of each separate country this process was exhibited mainly by the democratic character which was imparted to the political institutions in all the new states, as well as in all the former absolutist or semi-democratic states . . . In international politics the democratising development of present-day society, accelerated by the war, was shown chiefly in the proclamation of the principle of national self-determination, the establishment of new national states in Europe, and a marked tendency towards decentralisation and autonomy in the case of heterogeneous states or empires.

The war had led to the happiest of outcomes; and he himself had contributed in an idealistic way:

I did not fulfil my national and human duty in the struggle for national independence because I regarded the collective entity of the nation as a factor which is self-sufficing and constitutes an end in itself. I fulfilled this duty simply because I regarded it as a dictate of humanity for every individual just as for every collective entity to live without unnecessary restrictions and to develop a national culture.[27]

Yet, a second world war and two post-war periods later, these claims have a hollow ring. Surely Beneš, political realist that he was, could not have deluded himself so, even in the twenties.

Certainly Beneš was not trying to deceive anyone else. Even if his memoirs were in small part both apologia and declaration of faith, he was too much a disciple of the policy Masaryk had proved rewarding to play false: 'propaganda must be honest—exaggeration is harmful

[25] Beneš, *My War Memoirs, op. cit.*, 22–23.
[26] Karel Čapek, *President Masaryk tells his Story*, London, 1934, 224.
[27] Beneš, *My War Memoirs, op. cit.*, 493–96.

and lies are worse'.[28] But in much the same way as Masaryk, he was really something of an idealist, though he used descriptions like 'critical realist' to camouflage the fact.[29] Before the war he had been exposed to French and British democratic ideals and during it he had, like everyone else, been over-exposed to the even headier variety emanating from the United States. At the end of the war it did seem as if all the autocratic empires had disappeared and been replaced by a series of democratic nations. Even the Ottoman empire in Asia had been broken up; Russia was in the midst of a revolution; and the Second Reich had given way to Weimar. A League of Nations, imperfect but an entirely new phenomenon, had come into existence. In this sense it was wholly natural for Beneš to believe sincerely that his ideals were sound and that he had managed to put them into practice.

But he did not really deceive himself. In his memoirs he was just as clear that 'the peace treaties did not strictly reproduce these principles'; and at the Peace Conference he was wholly realistic in his presentation of the Czechoslovak case. The situation in the wake of four centuries of Habsburg rule was confused in the extreme. There were no indisputable ethnic frontiers; such as there were bore little relation to strategic and economic frontiers. Beneš argued quite openly for the historic frontier, which was also ill-defined and was certainly in conflict even with vague ethnic lines. But he was realistic enough to appreciate that political viability was more important than an ethnic solution pushed to an unattainable extreme. He was also much more realistic—less chauvinist—than Karel Kramář, the prime minister and leader of the delegation. Beneš was always prepared to amend the historic frontier inwards. Notes of a meeting of the Council of Ten record his words:

> The Czech nation, after three hundred years of servitude and vicissitudes which had almost led to its extermination, felt that it must be prudent, reasonable and just to its neighbours; and that it must avoid provoking jealousy and renewed struggles which might again plunge it into similar danger. It was in this spirit that he wished to explain the territorial problem.[30]

Beneš' genuine idealism was more than a little tinged with political realism.

Of all foreign ministers after Versailles Beneš was probably the one who most ardently supported the League of Nations. For him

[28] T. G. Masaryk, *The Making of a State*, London, 1927, 90–91; cf. Beneš, *My War Memoirs*, *op. cit.*, 103–119.
[29] *Ibid.*, 20–22.
[30] Perman, *op. cit.*, 128–30.

the League was the guarantor of the democratic principle at both national and international levels: it was 'a medium for the democratisation of political and social life, and . . . especially a medium for the democratisation of all international relationships'. Here too he was undoubtedly an idealist. But for one thing, he had no alternative; he did not command a state with enough economic and military power to allow him to be cynical. For another he recognised the shortcomings of the League: 'international democracy and the democratisation of the world were and are in their turn the necessary conditions for the existence and real functioning of the League'.[31]

He later dated the decline of the League from 1924–25; but even before that he had begun to make good its deficiencies by means of alliances. He was fully aware of the weakness of Czechoslovakia and of the danger of revisionism. The Little Entente was intended to be his guarantee against Habsburg revisionism.[32] More important, his alliance with France in 1924 and conjointly with the Soviet Union in 1935 was intended to be his guarantee against German revisionism.[33] This again was Beneš the political realist. The Czechoslovaks were a tough people with a strong nationalist heart. Although they suffered from the slump of 1929 they had a comparatively rich economy. Although they could not necessarily count on the loyalty of their minorities they had an army which was both well trained and well equipped. But *vis-à-vis* Germany they were geographically exposed, particularly after the *Anschluss,* and in terms of manpower and industry they were outclassed. By early 1938, when Hitler turned aggressively against Czechoslovakia, Beneš no longer placed his trust in the League although he still spoke of his 'obligations based on the principles of the Covenant'.[34] For reasons both of idealism and of realism he was anxious, as even Eisenlohr, the German minister in Prague, concluded, to negotiate a 'good relationship with Germany'.[35] But above all he knew he had to depend on his allies. 'We will never abandon the western powers with whom we are linked by a common democracy' was how he put it in March. 'We hope they will not abandon us'.[36] It was a hard world, and Beneš knew it.

Just as his purpose once the first world war had broken out was to create an independent Czechoslovakia with western help, so his hope

[31] Beneš, *Democracy Today and Tomorrow*, *op. cit.*, 113–36.
[32] Gajanová, *op. cit.*, 69–81; P. S. Wandycz, *France and her Eastern Allies 1919–25*, Minneapolis, 1962, 193–201; cf. Beneš, *Memoirs of Dr Edvard Beneš*, *op. cit.*, 8–9.
[33] Gajanová, *op. cit.*, 145–57; Wandycz, *op. cit.*, 292–311; Kvaček, *op. cit.*, 66–94; cf. Beneš, *Memoirs of Dr Edvard Beneš*, *op. cit.*, 6–7.
[34] M. Curtis (ed.), *Documents on International Affairs 1938*, II, London, 1943, 118.
[35] *Documents on German Foreign Policy 1918–45*, Series D, II, London, 1950, no. 47 and nos. 34, 38 and 56.
[36] M. Curtis (ed.), *op. cit.*, 118.

as the second world war threatened was in the same way to preserve it. In September 1938 he signally failed. To retain western support he made concession after concession to German demands during a long and trying spring and summer. At Munich it was the western powers who forced him to accept the *de facto* destruction of Czechoslovak independence. After Munich, of course, he was criticised for betraying his ideals, for yielding to Franco-British pressure and for surrendering to German aggression. He was equally condemned for being unrealistic, for failing to spot treachery and for refusing to resort to arms. But in face of the virtual collusion of Germany, Britain and France he had no choice. Yet in a sense he made a choice and it was a wise one. To his generals who begged him to go to war with Germany he put it this way:

What you ask to do it is your duty to ask and to do, it is to the honour of the Czechoslovak army. You are right, our people wish to do what you ask, and it is noble that at this difficult moment the nation and the army feel this way and are so fully at one.

But . . . I cannot take into account only what the people and the army feel. I must look at the whole of our situation, internal and international, at all the elements in what is now happening, and at all the consequences which any steps we take might bring in their train. Above all, make no mistake, England and France would not join us if we went to war ourselves. According to the reports I have and according to what I see myself in France and in England, neither of these countries would go to war today on account of the Czech Germans and both would act towards us as if we were responsible for the war . . . It would be recklessness on my part at this moment if I were to think to lead the nation to slaughter in a war all on its own.

But remember what I say to you now . . . what is at present taking place is only the beginning of a great European tragedy. War—a great European war—will come . . . They do not want to fight in better circumstances now at our side; they will have to fight in worse and on our behalf.[37]

This was statesmanlike realism. He knew that Czechoslovakia would have to fight alone and that alone it would be defeated. Instead, he waited until the western powers had to fight. He lost the Czechoslovak nation its independence for some years; but he saved it from being exterminated and created the conditions for the ultimate restoration of its independence.

But Beneš was also criticised at the time for failing to utilise Soviet help. The criticism intensified during and after the war as the Soviet Union became more powerful and the Communist Party

[37] Beneš, *Mnichovské dny*, *op. cit.*, 340–42; cf. L. Krejčí, 'Obranyschopnost CSR 1938' (The defensibility of Czechoslovakia in 1938), *Odboj a revoluce: zpravy*, VI, 2, Praha, 1968, 14–41; and cf. Beneš, *Šest let exilu a druhé světové války*, *op. cit.*, 22–32.

took over the destiny of the Czechoslovak nation. Beneš had acted for anti-communist motives and with complete disregard for the reality of Soviet strength. It is of course wholly true that Beneš looked to the west for his ideals and for his alliances. He defined his philosophical outlook in his Chicago lectures in 1939:

as a democrat, I cannot accept communism in its fundamental political and philosophical theses . . . Communism in its philosophy and morality has certain similarities with democracy . . . [but] . . . In certain sections of its political practice it uses in a large degree the methods and means which the other authoritarian regimes use, and is, therefore, nearer to fascism and national socialism.[38]

His diplomatic attitude he made crystal clear to Newton, the British minister in Prague, in May 1938:

Czechoslovakia's relations with Russia had always been and would remain a secondary consideration, dependent on the attitude of France and Great Britain. Czechoslovakia's present connection with Russia was purely contingent on the Franco-Russian treaty, but if western Europe disinterested herself in Russia, Czechoslovakia would also be disinterested. His country . . . would always follow and be bound to western Europe and never to eastern Europe. Any connection with Russia would only be through western Europe and Czechoslovakia would refuse to be an instrument of Russian policy.

Beneš' attitude went back to the Russian revolution and even before. But it did not imply that he was anti-Soviet or failed to appreciate the potential value of Soviet assistance. As he added in his talk with Newton,

He was a westerner but did not wish to exclude Russia from Europe where she might be a useful make-weight against German pressure. Similarly he believed that France and England needed Russia as a balancing factor. An attempt to exclude Russia completely from Europe would . . . be disastrous and would only force her to make an agreement with Germany against the rest of Europe.[39]

His approach to the Soviet Union was based on a mixture of democratic principles and diplomatic hard-headedness.

However it was the hard-headedness that came to the surface in the month of Munich. As he later recalled in his memoirs, he had not wanted to accept Soviet help on its own for a number of reasons:

(*a*) The whole western world—directly or indirectly—would have believed that Hitler was right in his propaganda about Czechoslovakia being an instrument of Bolshevism in central Europe and would immediately have turned against us . . .

[38] Beneš, *Democracy Today and Tomorrow*, *op. cit.*, 180–83.
[39] *Documents on British Foreign Policy 1919–39*, Third Series, I, London, 1949, no. 229.

(*b*) . . . In view of the fact that 'through its war Czechoslovakia would have delivered itself into the hands of the Soviets', both western powers would have relieved themselves of the heavy responsibility for their whole policy of helping Germany against us . . .
(*c*) . . . I did not even exclude the possibility that reactionary circles in the western democracies would have gone so far as to render direct assistance to Germany against Russia.
(*d*) . . . In this special situation I was not quite sure about the attitude of some of our own reactionary circles . . . to have introduced disruption to our internal situation at this moment I regarded as tantamount to national catastrophe.[40]

If anything, Beneš' sympathies by this stage were pro-Soviet. He did not wish to invite the destruction of Czechoslovakia; but equally he did not wish to encourage the destruction of Russia.

Ultimately, Beneš was fully vindicated. There was a war. The western powers fought Germany and did so alongside the Soviet Union. It might even be said that Beneš saved the western powers and the Soviet Union from fighting the wrong war. At any rate, Czechoslovakia was resurrected in 1945. This time Beneš had the leading role. To some extent the job was easier than the first one of creating Czechoslovakia, though the guilt complex of the western powers made the going hard.[41] On the other hand, the Soviet Union represented a new factor. In the crucial period 1917–19 the Russian revolution had lent weight to Czechoslovak nationalism and the fear of Bolshevism had helped Czechoslovakia to win recognition from the western powers. In the period 1941–45 the Soviet Union undoubtedly assisted Czechoslovakia back to independence. But within three years Czechoslovakia had lost its independence once again—this time to the Soviet Union. On this score, too, Beneš came under fire. He should not have negotiated an alliance with Russia in 1943 and so given it a foothold in the country.[42] He should not have accepted the resignation of the so-called democratic ministers in February 1948 and so invited the Russians in for good.[43] At the same time, of course, he came under fire from the other side, for thinking of joining the Marshall Plan in 1947 and for resigning on the issue of the new Czechoslovak constitution in May 1948.[44]

It was ever the misfortune of moderates to be criticised by extremists; and Beneš had been under fire before. Up to a point he had no

[40] Beneš, *Mnichovské dny*, *op. cit.*, 318–21; cf. *Mnichov v dokumentech* (*Munich in documents*), II, Praha, 1958, no. 158.
[41] Beneš, *Memoirs of Dr Edvard Beneš*, *op. cit.*, 50–130; cf. R. H. Bruce Lockhart, *Comes the Reckoning*, London, 1947, 53–121.
[42] e.g., O. Friedman, *The Break-up of Czech Democracy*, London, 1950, 17–33.
[43] e.g., H. Ripka, *Czechoslovakia Enslaved*, London, 1950, 293–94.
[44] e.g., J. Veselý, *Kronika únorových dnů 1948*, Praha, 1958, 24–30 and 215–23.

choice in what he did. The Munich Agreement made the Czechoslovak people distrust the western powers more perhaps than Beneš himself did; the experience of German occupation was bitter. So in the course of the war he had little option but to find a better ally than he had had before. The war also raised the Soviet Union to great power status, so that Beneš would have had to come to terms even if it had been against his will. In 1943 his alliance with the Soviet Union made broad political sense.[45] That by 1945 his relations with Moscow had deteriorated was the consequence as much of western impotence as of Soviet aggrandisement; but now that Czechoslovakia was all but in Russia's exclusive sphere of influence, Beneš in his realistic way had to make the best of his alliance, and he did. For war also promoted both revolutionary attitudes and socialist feelings in Europe at large, and these affected Czechoslovak politics too. Beneš was not swept helplessly along in a fast current. He had encouraged revolution before, although circumstances had conspired to keep him in the realm of international politics. As foreign minister up to 1937 and as a crisis president from then on, he had had little time to spend on internal social questions. But in 1945 it was his provisional government, with only one-third communist membership, that nationalised two-thirds of Czechoslovak industry.[46] This was deliberate policy; it was Beneš the idealist—yet still Beneš the realist. In negotiating his alliance with Russia, 'although he had no sympathy with communism, he was from the first prepared to carry out wide measures of social reform which would make Czechoslovakia a half-way house between east and west'.[47] The Soviet Union could not be ignored; Czechoslovakia could only live after the war as before by consent of all the major powers, including the Soviet Union. But the corollary of this was that ultimately all the powers must agree. Part of Beneš' contribution to their agreement was his 'half-way house' policy of social reform. The other part was his continuing treaty with the Soviet Union. In his memoirs he put it this way:

> Our answer to the question, west or east, is to say deliberately and plainly —west and east. In this sense—and in this sense only—did I sign and approve the treaty with the Soviet Union of December 1943, intentionally and consciously linking it with the Anglo-Soviet treaty of May 1942.[48]

Inescapably, hopefully, not altogether unrealistically, he worked

[45] E. Táborský, 'Beneš and Stalin—Moscow, 1943 and 1945', *Journal of Central European Affairs*, XIII, Denver, Colorado, 1953–54, 154–81.
[46] R. R. Betts, *Central and South East Europe 1945–48*, London, 1950, 171–74.
[47] R. H. Bruce Lockhart, 'The Second Exile of Edvard Beneš', *Slavonic and East European Review*, XXVIII, London, 1949, 57.
[48] Beneš, *Memoirs of Dr Edvard Beneš, op. cit.*, 282.

towards continuing east-west co-existence as the one means of preserving Czechoslovak independence.

Beneš' attitude to the Marshall Plan, first to contemplate joining, then to withdraw, was wholly conditioned by this 'west and east' approach to Czechoslovakia's survival. But with the onset of the cold war, of which the Marshall Plan was a part, 'west and east' was an impossibility. Czechoslovakia found itself inevitably drawn into the Soviet bloc.[49] Beneš himself was ailing a little; overwork since his postgraduate days, strain in the first world war and heartbreak both before and during the second, had left their mark. But this was of little political consequence. The fact was that there was even less possibility in 1948 than there had been in 1938 for Beneš—or Czechoslovakia—to resist the will of the great powers. But he left his mark. It was symptomatic that in the last resort what he tried fundamentally to save in the Czechoslovak situation was the democratic principle. In February 1948 he accepted the resignation of the so-called democratic ministers because they were a governmental minority and left him, as he saw it, no constitutional alternative. And then in May 1948 he refused to sign the new communist constitution because it denied what he considered to be the democratic right of free election. 'I always was and I still am a democrat and a socialist', he wrote in his letter of resignation,

> I agree with those articles of the constitution which are to form a new basis for the economic construction of the state and for the socialist development of the future life of our national society. But I maintain that some articles of the constitution are of such a character that my conscience and convictions about democracy and my concepts of popular and civil rights prevent me from agreeing fully with them.[50]

The social and economic development of Czechoslovakia went forward after Beneš' death. But the suffering in human and cultural terms was great, and eventually even the social and economic development came to a near halt. It was then, in 1968, that the Czechoslovaks turned again to contemplate the ideals that Beneš had fought for and that had once created and once resurrected the nation. But external events again intervened. Yet perhaps others will learn what first the Austrians and then the Germans did not. Beneš' ideals made realistic politics.

[49] J. Šedivý, 'K některým otázkám československé zahraniční politiky a vlivu mezinárodní situace na vnitropolitický vyvoj ČSR v letech 1945–48' (Concerning some questions of Czechoslovak foreign policy and the influence of the international situation upon the internal development of Czechoslovakia in the years 1945–48), in *Československá revoluce v letech 1944–48* (*The Czechoslovak revolution in the years 1944–48*), Praha, 1966, 210–23.

[50] J. Smutný, *op. cit.*, V, 58–59.

The Methodological and Political Foundations of Czech Historiography in the Twentieth Century

Jaroslav Kudrna

In literary science and aesthetics, efforts to re-evaluate the legacy of the late nineteenth century are common. A certain confusion, however, existed until recent times in the case of the so-called Goll school of historiography. This school represented the predominant current in the historical thinking of the first Czechoslovak Republic. It was closely connected with some political ideas that came under criticism from different standpoints in the period immediately after 1948. This criticism gave birth to the idea that the Goll school was fatally one-sided. It is true that the oversimplified evaluation has been modified in various respects recently, but some of the original criticism is still repeated and is nowadays even supported by scientific arguments which try to demonstrate the limitations of the main aspects of the school's approach to history. It is now evident, however, that most of the ideas and achievements of the Goll school showed greater vitality than, for instance, those which have been characteristic of Czech historiography in the last twenty years. It is not without a certain irony that the Marxist school unconsciously reiterated some theses of German historiography that were formulated, amongst others, by Pfitzner, namely that the Goll school made important discoveries in source-research but failed in its methodological generalisations.

In the 1950s Marxist-orientated historiography argued that the Goll school was derived from western European historiography. More recently it has asserted that this school even retarded Czech historical thinking compared with the development of world historiography in the same period.

It cannot be denied that the objections raised against the Goll school are partly justified. The Goll school lacked, for instance, the capacity for self-reflection and analysis of its methodological foundations. With the exception of Goll's article on the methodological principles of historiography, no Czech historian can be mentioned who dedicated himself to the methodological problems of historiography. This fact was largely exploited by the German historians who discovered the Goll school shortly before the second world war. We may recall Pfitzner's article published in *Historische Zeitschrift* as a treatise of fundamental importance. Pfitzner tried to denigrate Czech historiography as a whole and to discredit it as a certain type of 'heimatkunde' (local and folklore history). Pfitzner maintained that Czech historiography was unoriginal in its methodological principles and that it did not contribute any new methodological principles to world historiography. Czech historiography was lagging behind German historical thinking. It was mainly indebted to the Historical Institute of Vienna and even if the Goll school had achieved any international reputation, this had only been possible through the aid of the Institute.

Let me now re-examine the methodological foundations of the Goll school. It is a widespread opinion among Czech historians that the Goll school belongs to what may be denoted as positivist historiography, with specific modifications. Those modifications can be found, for instance, in certain traces of the pro-Austrian Czech historiography which won a certain ascendancy after František Palacký. More convincing seems to be the description of the Goll school as a certain branch of the Rankean school. Certainly the Rankean elements cannot be neglected. But it is another question in what respect even the methodology of the Goll school was a direct product of the Rankean school, apart altogether from their obvious similarities.

This question must be answered as there existed in the past a certain danger that the influence of the Rankean school could be exploited as a demonstration not of simple but of servile dependence on German historiography on the part of the Goll school. This was the view of Pfitzner and of Marxist historians in the 1950s. Their criticism overlooked the fact that since the 1890s the influence of Rankean methodology permeated all west European historiography; there was perhaps no civilised European country where it was not felt.

Evidently—it is not possible to tackle the subject in detail here—the reception of Rankean methodology can be classified as a reaction against the widespread influence of sociologically-orientated positivism. Among Czech historians the new tendency was associated with a re-evaluation of the basic conceptions of Palacký. Ideologically it was therefore only a partial reaction against the type of historiography based on the revolutionary events of 1848. Clearly, the historical concepts of Palacký were rooted in a different situation and could not be applied in an epoch characterised by its own revolutionary trends.

But the rethinking of methodology cannot be explained solely on the basis of a change in ideological tendencies. Innovation in ideology, as the only underlying factor, applies principally in the case of Palacký. Palacký succeeded in propounding a general conception of history based on his approach to the history of the Czech people which culminated in the Hussite revolutionary movement. It is true that Palacký projected the general traits of democracy into earlier epochs and on this basis formulated an interpretation of history which corresponded to the basic ideas of west European historical thinking, associating as it did, on a broad basis, the methodology of the Enlightenment and the French historical school with post-Kantian philosophy. In certain respects a synthesis of various elements and of different modes of historiography was now applied to Czech history. In this sense Palacký's conception appears as an apology, limtied and even provincial; but it corresponded to the picture of the primitive stage of development which the German historical school postulated concerning the origins of the German people. Palacký was certainly at a great disadvantage in shaping this theory: German historians could base their conceptions on original written sources (their error lay only in their one-sided interpretation).

But shortly after Palacký's death it became clear that his view of the pre-feudal period of Czech history was false and that the validity of certain sources used by him was open to question. It was not only scientific arguments which led to this revision. Elements of ideology were also involved. Certain post-Palacký historians, for instance, tried to adapt the picture of Czech history to the claims of Austrian historiography. In the case of such historians as Tomek, Rezek and Gindely this meant re-examining the emphasis placed by Palacký on certain aspects of Czech history.

But the revision of Palacký's view of history cannot be explained by new ideological ideas alone. It would be very naive, both in the European and the Czech context, to interpret the revision exclusively in this sense. Even in those early decades a sociological view of history was making its appearance. The Czech situation was no different from any other, in that the new sociological trend in historical thinking was represented by sociologists themselves, while the attitude of historians remained rather sceptical. The new sociological influence in historical assumptions cannot be overlooked, however, in establishing a certain continuity in Czech historical development. Sociology, based as it was on the analysis of societal realities, was much more predisposed to examining these realities than history, which was orientated towards the reality of the state. Even in the sphere of the state, however, no continuity existed in the development of Czech history and so its contribution to the new sociological trends in historical thinking cannot be dismissed. Many new problems were formulated that have been of importance until today. The sociological view of history was striving to find the connecting link between the past and the present, to explain the past out of the experience of the present. It enunciated the principle that history must be explained on the basis of fundamental laws, analogous to those established by natural science. But it is well known from the history of English and French positivism that the new programme could hardly be realised; although the critical remarks directed against the traditional forms of historiography appeared to be very convincing.

Nevertheless, traditional historians were appalled by these tendencies. They sensed that they could no longer maintain their own naive views and that it would be necessary to re-examine the underlying principles of historical science.

From this point of view it would be interesting to compare any articles on historiographical methodology that appeared in Europe in the 1890s. Concurrently with French historiography, and with one exception, some years earlier than German historiography, Czech historians responded to the new programme and to the questions raised by sociology. The similarities of these reactions are quite astonishing. The application of Rankean methodology to criticism of the positivist view of history was not only apparent in Germany but even in England, France and Bohemia. This gave rise to a new form of political historiography which was to guarantee the independence of historical science against possible impacts from sociology. It was to liberate history from the necessity of exploring the general laws of historical development, which would have lead historians to admitting the impossibility of foreseeing the future or of explaining the general tendencies of contemporary events.

In his famous methodological treatise Goll left this task of prediction in history to the philosophy of history. That was the real lesson of his methodological article, which founded his school. Contrary to neo-Rankean historiography in Germany, in which the controversy with positivism was driven to extremes on the political level, Czech historiography made more concessions to liberalism and in methodology to positivism. Despite his philosophically anti-positivist attitude, Goll made more allowances for sociology and cultural history than did the contemporary neo-Rankean school in Germany.

From the specific Czech situation, as compared with German historiography, many peculiar consequences ensued. History was in one respect conceived in dependence on the state, that is to say, it was a kind of political historiography. Yet this did not preclude another approach to historical reality. Goll regarded the political moment mainly as an element which permeated the whole cultural sphere. In sharp contradiction to nationalist-orientated historiography, he did not reject the possibility of universal history in the future. He was merely sceptical of its feasibility for the time being.

But there is other evidence that the methodology of the Goll school was more akin to the positivist view of history than the contemporary neo-Rankean historiography in Germany. Josef Pekař dealt in a treatise with the problems of the so-called Lamprecht Streit in Germany. Lamprecht, contrary to the majority of German historians, sought to apply to historical science the principles of methodology prevalent in the sociology-orientated historiography of England and France. Significantly Pekař conceded the validity of many of Lamprecht's arguments, for instance, the German historian's appraisal of the collective movement in history. Contrary to many neo-Rankean opponents of Lamprecht, Pekař did not agree with the charge of Marxism levelled against Lamprecht. According to Pekař, Lamprecht remained within the usual limits of historical science. This sober appreciation differs considerably from the many criticisms levelled at Lamprecht by the German historians of the pre-war period.

All Goll's disciples were open to new ideas in European historiography. Josef Šusta, another leading historian of the first Republic, was not opposed to a political conception of historiography derived from Rankean methodology. But he was also capable of re-integrating a great number of elements of French positivism, cultural history and economic history (for instance Sombart and Weber), which neo-Rankean historiography in Germany was only seldom willing to recognise. Šusta openly called attention to the new sociological currents in French historiography. The adherents of the Goll school adopted a positive attitude to the school of Annales and favourably viewed the sociological trends in this historiography.

Another feature of Czech historiography was the relatively favourable appraisal of Soviet historical science. Many of the reviews of the writings of Soviet historians were characterised by much more objectivity and understanding than was typical of west European historiography as a whole. However, with the exception of Mendl, a leading Czech economic historian, the Goll school in general failed to integrate Marxism as a constituent element in its outlook and even Mendl never went beyond Max Weber's view. Slavík was the only Czech historian who in a certain sense came directly under the influence of Soviet Marxism. He can perhaps be described as the founder of a new branch of democratically-oriented Sovietology, and although himself a student of Goll he was opposed to many basic views of the Goll school. His was not the attitude towards Marxism characteristic of Czech historians. Generally, however, their capacity to integrate and synthesise various elements of west European historiography meant that they did not simply rule out Marxism as totally unacceptable. This was certainly in contrast to German and English historians.

In conclusion, let us re-examine the criticism of Czech historiography which Josef Pfitzner made before the second world war. Pfitzner attributed the provincialism of Czech historiography to the necessary limits of the subject itself. Anybody concentrating on the history of a small nation could hardly avoid the danger of provincialism. Only the historiography of a great nation he argued, could have a world-wide significance. But this view overlooks two basic facts. Firstly, Czech historiography developed in the heart of Europe: Prague represented at various epochs a point of interaction of European history. Secondly, it is not only the subject which determines the character of historiography: it is in many cases the method applied. What I have been striving to demonstrate is that Czech historiography consisted of various methodological elements integrated into a synthesis which allowed for the existence of democratically-orientated historians.

The Irish in Victoria, 1851–91: A Demographic Essay

Oliver MacDonagh

I

The interaction of cultures is a branch of history which receives small attention. In these islands, distinctive cultures have not merely co-existed—not to say, collided—for centuries; they have constantly worked upon and helped to shape each other. But this process of interaction is scarcely yet seen as an area for historical investigation in its own right, requiring, so to say, an historical grammar of its own. The present paper is concerned with one small portion of that grammar: the uses of demography in the study of a particular interaction.

Demographically, Australia may have a special interest for modern Irish historians. During the period of the Act of Union, the *proportions* of Irish and Catholics amongst the total population of the United Kingdom fell to approximately one-third of their original size. There may have been a corresponding, though doubtless less drastic, fall in the per capita income of the Irish and Catholic elements in the United Kingdom *vis-à-vis* the rest. But in Australia the case was different. In 1801 the ethnic and religious proportions in the population closely matched those in the new United Kingdom; but, in Australia, these proportions were preserved, like the fly in amber, down to 1914 and perhaps even longer. Moreover, political and civil parity were substantially established in the Australian colonies by the mid-nineteenth century, so that the comparative numerical and social strength of the Catholic and Irish elements could make themselves felt during the formative stages of the new societies. Historians cannot make controlled experiments, and they are constantly buffeted by idiosyncrasies in the phenomena with which they deal. But, even so, the student of Ireland under the Union may gain new insights, may find new questions forming in his mind, as he observes the interaction of the Irish and the British cultures in conditions where the relative proportions of race and religion at the time of the Act of Union remained constant, and where moreover the slow political revolution of the nineteenth century in these islands was anticipated by fifty years or more.

Conversely, modern Ireland has, or should have, a particular interest for Australian historians. Down to a generation or so ago, Australians—at least the sort of Australians who wrote scholarly books and read papers to learned gatherings—tended to assume that Irish emigration had intruded a large and alien body into an essentially British community. It was commonly implied, if not actually stated, that this intrusion presented problems of assimilation, after the fashion of the minorities in the United States. But surely such attitudes were misconceived. In Australia, the Irish were never a small proportion of the whole, nor did they come late to fit, for their term, the lower slots in a fixed social and economic hierarchy. In the the very first settlements of all, whether as soldiers or as convicts, they were a founding people, constituting almost one-third of the entire community; and for more than a century, the flow of Irish emigration maintained substantially the same proportion. En masse, the Irish may have lagged economically behind their English or Scots neighbours, but if so it was only by a step; the difference appears to have been one of degree—and small degree, at that—and not of kind. In short, for Australian historians the Irish emigration of the nineteenth century is of significance in terms of communal contributions no less than numbers; and in the culture and circumstances from which this emigration derived must lie many of the keys which explain the formation and character of their early colonial society.

II

Both the colony of Victoria and the years 1851–91 have particular advantages in a demographic enquiry into the Irish overseas. The first advantage is that the present state of Victoria was settled comparatively late. The colonisation of Port Phillip and the surrounding hinterlands did not begin until 1836, almost half a century after the first colonisation of New South Wales. For the first decade and a half, the settlement at Port Phillip was very small, so that 1851 (the year of the first 'Victorian' census with which we are concerned), may be fairly taken to mark the commencement not only of a phase of prodigious economic expansion, but also of the first significant upsurge of population. Thus, in dealing with Victoria from 1851 to

1891 we are dealing with what is essentially a new society, and with a population largely composed of direct immigrants and their immediate descendants. We are dealing with much less than a lifespan, biologically; and the fanciful—amongst whom I should perhaps include myself—might add, with the infancy and first childhood of a state. The years 1851–91 also represent, more or less, a distinctive era in the political and social orders in the colony. They begin with a decisive challenge to colonial and oligarchic rule, and the substitution therefor of parliamentary and democratic government. They end in the 1890s when the rise of labour as an organised political interest and party first reveals the configuration of modern politics in Victoria. To summarise the first advantage, 1851–91 is useful because it comprehends the first stage in the development of a society; because in almost all these years Victoria was dominated by its immigrants; and because the colonial life of this period possesses an intrinsic unity, most obviously of all in terms of politics. Each of these factors helps us to identify, and to speak with confidence of, a distinct and coherent Irish element in the community.

Secondly, for our purpose, the Victorian census material is superior to that for any of the other Australian colonies in the nineteenth century, and, it may even be, superior to that for any other region of Irish settlement overseas. The Victorian material is not of course superior at every point. It provides, for example, no direct evidence on the occupations of the foreign born, such as that furnished by certain of the New South Wales returns. But the Victorian censuses provide one vital set of data which all others lack, namely, the birth-place and the religion of all inhabitants, divided according to both the civil and electoral divisions. I call this information 'vital' because the proportion of foreign born falls very quickly in every settlement, even in one so new and young as nineteenth-century Victoria. In fact, between 1854 and 1891, the proportion of Irish-born in the total population of Victoria fell from 16·77 to 7·48 per cent. It follows that generalisations about an ethnic group based solely upon birth-place returns become progressively more circumscribed and tenuous, as time proceeds. They also become less meaningful because racial identification is a subjective rather than an objective business. To treat the Irish element in Victoria in our period as strictly synonymous with those inhabitants actually born in Ireland would be most misleading. As I have said, we are concerned, almost exclusively, with new or first generation Australians in whom identification with country of origin or extraction was extremely powerful.

In the case of Victoria, this difficulty can be largely overcome because, as we shall see, the correlation of Irish-born and Catholics was extraordinarily and persistently high. Religion appears to change but slightly and slowly by generation. Hence the data which the statistics of religion provide becomes increasingly more informative, census by census, than that furnished by the returns of foreign born. In the very short period with which we deal, moreover, we need not concern ourselves unduly with the counter-forces of religious out-marriage and of changes in national identification: even by 1891, these forces had not yet had time to weaken materially the original connections. In short, we can trace with fair confidence the behaviour and the fortunes of our ethnic group through the medium of its preponderant religion. This is the special value of the Victorian demographic data. In the continuously matched returns of birth-place and religious affiliation, the growing deficiencies of the first, as a source of relevant information, can be substantially supplied by the second.

The third advantage in the topic concerns Ireland itself, and the Irish population of the colony. The Irish question was never far below the surface of Victorian politics during our period. At the very outset, the affair of the Eureka stockade, the midwife—it might be argued—of democratic government in Victoria, was shot through with Irish implications whether we take the leader-ship, the amorphous ideology or the nationality of the victims as the criteria. Again, although Victoria was not a penal settlement, it was part of a continent where the arrival and departure of political prisoners repeatedly engaged public attention down to 1870: in particular, this process familiarised Australians with the phenomenon of Fenianism, and rendered it a major issue at several junctures. Our concluding decade 1881–91 was of course the period when colonial interest and involvement in the Irish struggle was most intense. Aptly enough, 1891 proved the exact terminal date in this connection. The fall of Parnell immediately marked the end of the era when the Irish factor was always, to some degree, a serious consideration in the colony.

On the other hand, Victoria was a colony where the Irish element was prominent and clearly discernible in the years in question. Else-where in Australia that element may have been more numerous, or constituted a higher proportion of the total population. But nowhere was its impress more deep and clear, nowhere was its part in the cultural interchanges more vivacious. To an extent, this may have been an accident of time. The rise of Victoria coincided exactly with the final spasms of the great Irish famine, with the last disintegration of Young Ireland, and with the failure of the Independent Irish Party. The coincidence appears to have been responsible for a species of chain migration amongst Irish politicians, journalists, lawyers, physicians and dons. Every Australian capital was enriched, in some degree, by this flight from the stricken professions and broken politics in Ireland; but none—or so it seems to me—to nearly the same extent as Melbourne. The deeper one penetrates the early Victorian political and legal systems, the more apparent become the links of past association and relationship amongst the many Irish immigrants involved in their operation. The Tenant League, the Munster Bar, the University of Dublin, are prime examples of the nodal points of these networks of acquaintance and common action; and at this level, of course, Church of Ireland men and non-conformists, as well as Catholics, were numerous and prominent, and the ties of friendship and former agitation often crossed the sectarian boundaries. The extent of the incursion may be gauged from the fact that each of the six speakers in the Victorian Legislative Assembly in our period was Irish-born—including Gavan Duffy and Peter Lalor. In the same 35 years, three out of every four of the attornies and solicitors-general in the colony were Irish-born. The two men of highest intellectual powers in early Victorian politics, Hearn and Higinbotham, were Irish-born: in so far as the colony possessed a de Tocqueville and a Charles James Fox, these were they.

More significant still perhaps were the political interests and expertise which arrived with the baggage of the Irish. In some respects, the Victorian situation of the 1850s was ripe for the application of contemporary Irish radicalism. The critical issues of the decade were self-government, the establishment of an ascendancy, and land. The translation of ideas and techniques was easy. It was for this reason, I believe, that the Irish supplied more than their proportionate share of the political leadership of the new colony—at any rate, of the élite and leadership of the 'left'. And quite as interesting as their collective impact in shaping the new system and alignments, was the diversity of the political strains which they introduced. To look no further than the three Irish premiers and the leading Irish radicals of our period, O'Shanassy was the very type of a Repeal lieutenant in O'Connell's most clericalist phase; Duffy, the sedulous mid-century liberal; O'Loghlen, the schooled Home Ruler, ready to march with popular discontent; Longmore and Gaunson, Ulster presbyterians of a dying species, bitter enemies not only of landlordism and the established church, but also of the British connection; Wilson Gray, the unlikely brother of Sir John, who preached Fintan Lalor's agrarian doctrines, and read Victorian politics in terms of a class struggle.

III

So much for the setting of our subject. Let us now turn to the data of five successive Victorian censuses, those of 1857, 1861, 1871, 1881 and 1891. The correlation coefficients for the Catholic and the Irish-born proportions of the populations of the 21 counties and pastoral districts into which Victoria was divided were, in these censuses, respectively, ·907, ·943, ·907, ·897 and ·879. Such correlations provide of course, a most remarkable instance of social continuity, and are statistically significant to a very high degree. Given that we are dealing with a time space of only forty years, and with first and second generation immigrants exclusively, this means that the Catholic and Irish communities can be treated as substantially synonymous, and that we can extrapolate the Catholic findings with a fair degree of confidence. This is important as I have said because the statistics according to religion enable us to follow trends in the distribution and location of the ethnic group, for which the figures for the actual foreign born are increasingly inadequate, with the passage of time.

The first striking feature of the Catholic—and by extension, the Irish—element in Victoria is its constancy. In eight censuses of 1851–1901, the Catholic element constituted, successively, 23·29, 19·05, 18·83, 20·44, 23·32, 23·60, 21·80 and 21·95 per cent of the total population of the colony. The increases in the middle of the period correspond with increases in the volume of assisted emigration, on which the Irish were particularly dependent. In most contexts, this run of percentages would be in no way remarkable: or, rather, it would be the extent of the variations which would prove arresting. But the nineteenth century Victorian context was quite extraordinary. Here we are faced with a population increase of 1,200 per cent in forty years, from less than 80,000 persons in 1851 to 1,140,000 in 1891. Moreover the bare totals conceal wild demographic fluctuations in between. The net immigration of the three years, 1851–4, was twice as great as the total population of 1851; and at several junctures, there was very considerable emigration from as well as immigration into the colony. Meanwhile the age structure and the masculinity rate of the population were changing dramatically, while the regions and intensity of settlement grew with amazing speed. It is this context of demographic ferment which renders the stability of the Catholic element so remarkable.

The general stability of the Catholic element in the colonial population as a whole was matched by stability in the Catholic elements in the various localities. Let us start with the census of 1857, the first in which the data enables us to correlate—to coin a horrid language of convenience—the 'catholicity' and the 'hibernicity' rates. The 21 counties and pastoral districts divide conveniently into three groups of 7, characterised respectively by above average, near average and below average catholicity and hibernicity. If we follow this pattern through the next four censuses, those of 1861, 1871, 1881 and 1891, we find that 5 of the 7 relatively high counties remain in this category throughout, that 5 of the near average counties remain in this category throughout, and that 5 of the relatively low counties remain in this category throughout. The significance of this constancy may become more apparent if we look at the relevant figures for particular counties. I propose to take as a sample the first three in alphabetical order: they are in fact altogether typical of the whole. The Catholic element in the population of Anglesey, a sparsely populated agricultural county, was 22·75 per cent in 1857. The Anglesey percentages of Catholics in the next four censuses were 21·96, 25·09, 24·61 and 23·15, respectively. The Catholic element in the population of the County of Bourke (in effect, greater Melbourne and its hinterland) was 20·72 per cent in 1857. The next four percentages for Bourke were 21·76, 23·51, 22·75 and 20·60. The population of Dalhousie, the county which included Kilmore and had at most times the highest catholicity and hibernicity rates in the colony, was precisely one-third Catholic in 1857. In the next four censuses, the Catholic element in Dalhousie constituted 34·19, 38·43, 37·07 and 35·83 of the whole. The pattern of gradual increase and gradual decline is identical in all three cases; and in this respect all other counties resemble Anglesey, Bourke and Dalhousie. But the measure of stability becomes fully apparent only when we note the total population changes in the 34 years under review. Between 1857 and 1891, the total population of Anglesey grew from 879 to 8,405; that of Bourke from 133,163 to 514,341; and that of Dalhousie from 10,087 to 21,426. In other words, one population grew almost tenfold, a second quadrupled and a third more than doubled, all in the span of a single generation, and yet not only were the variations in the Catholic elements extraordinary slight, they were completely regular.

The great value of the county statistics is that their boundaries were constant throughout our period. But a second type of division, that into the parliamentary constituencies, also retailed the religion and the birth-place of the inhabitants from 1857 onwards, and has other uses. Here the areas did change, four times in fact, from 37 units in 1857, to 49 units in 1861, to 55 units in 1881 and to 84 units in 1891. The changes were of course governed by the increases in, and the variations in the distributions of, the general population. On the constancy of the Catholic element, the statistics for the electoral districts both confirm and supplement those for the administrative counties. Similarly, the figures for the municipal districts proper reinforce our conclusion. The percentage of Catholics in the cities of Melbourne and Geelong in 1857 were, respectively, 19·86 and 19·46. In the next four censuses, the Melbourne percentages read 20·19, 22·77, 22·30 and 20·79, and the Geelong percentages, 21·19, 24·49, 23·79 and 21·80.

The next striking feature of the catholicity and hibernicity rates is their *evenness* of distribution throughout the colony. In *each* of the six censuses taken between 1857 and 1901, almost one-half of the counties and pastoral districts show catholicity and hibernicity rates within 3 per cent of the colonial average. The highest percentage of Catholics shown in any of the 126 relevant returns was the 39·02 per cent for the county of Villiers in 1881, and the lowest, the 11·30 per cent for the county of Hampden in 1857. In 1871, the highest percentage was 38·43 for Dalhousie, and the lowest 17·51 for Evelyn; and only 5 of the 21 areas deviated by more than 5 per cent from the colonial average. In 1891, the highest percentage was 36·16 for Villiers and the lowest 16·47 for Evelyn; and again only 5 of the 21 areas deviated by more than 5 per cent from the colonial average.

The nicer measurement, according to electoral divisions, generally confirms this pattern. Of the 37 parliamentary constituencies of 1857, 22 had catholicity rates within 5 per cent of the average and 34 had rates within 10 per cent of average. Of the 49 constituencies of 1871, 29 had rates within 5 per cent, and 44 rates within 10 per cent of average. Of the 84 constituencies of 1891, 45 had rates within 5 per cent, and 75 rates within 10 per cent of average. Next, the electoral division returns establish that the range of variation for municipal areas, taken as whole units, was significantly less than the range of variation in the rural districts, throughout the second half of the nineteenth century. Finally, the Catholic proportions in the several constituencies have, of course, an intrinsic political significance. At any particular stage, there was but one constituency with an absolute majority of Catholics. This was Kilmore in the early decades, than (ironically) Belfast and finally Warrenheip—all of them safe seats for the O'Shanassys and Duffys of the day. On the other hand, in only one constituency did the Catholic proportion of the population ever fall below 10 per cent of the whole. Almost everywhere, the Catholics constituted at all times a more or less considerable minority. To particularise by taking the censuses of 1857 and 1881 as examples, in 1857, the Catholic proportion was 10–15 per cent of the whole in 3 constituencies; 15–20 per cent in 12 constituencies; 20–25 per cent in 8 constituencies; 25–30 per cent in 6 and 30–35 per cent in 2; while in 1881 it constituted 10–15 per cent in 2 constituencies; 15–20 per cent in 17 constituencies; 20–25 per cent in 20 constituencies; 25–30 per cent in 7 and 30–35 per cent in 10; in addition, of course, in either case, to the single constituency where Catholics predominated. The absolute extremities in these censuses were Catholic proportions of 12·70 and 53·52 per cent in 1857; and of 12·52 and 52·95 per cent in 1881. These findings are of course of prime interest in the political geography of nineteenth century Victoria.

Certain general characteristics of the Catholic population—and, by extension, of the great mass of the Irish immigrants—in the colony are by now apparent. But some of the minor deviations are as interesting, in their way, as the major pattern. If, for example, we distinguish the main types of administrative county, even in a rough and ready way, the following conclusions may be drawn. First, the areas with the highest ratios of Catholics and Irish-born were rural and agricultural. This is not to say that every predominantly agrarian county had high ratios; but that the ratios of these counties in toto were high, and markedly high in particular instances. Conversely, the Catholic and Irish-born population of the towns and cities were generally below the average for the colony. In Melbourne, Bendigo and Castlemaine, for instance, they fell below the colonial average in every census after 1860. In fact, only in the case of Geelong were they consistently close to—and even there not always above—the medial line. Third, and not least surprising, the mining districts tended to have relatively low catholicity and hibernicity rates. The Ballarat rates, for instance, were usually the lowest for any town or city in the colony.

If we examine the more detailed constituency statistics towards the end of our period, other features become apparent. The areas with the very highest proportions of Catholics and Irish-born were, on the one hand, small and mixed farming districts around Kilmore in the North-Central, and Warnambool and Port Fairy in Western province; and on the other hand, certain wards in central Melbourne, such as Melbourne itself, Melbourne East and West and Carlton South. Conversely, the areas with the lowest proportions of Catholics and Irish-born were other mixed farming districts in the Central and Western provinces, and certain other parts of Melbourne, in particular the prosperous suburbs of South Yarra, Hawthorn and Toorak. If we use a stronger microscope, further minutiae come into view. To continue with our last example, the prosperous suburbs of Melbourne are one of the few areas where the relative proportion of Irish-born exceeds significantly the relative proportion of Catholics; and the masculinity rate for the Catholics in these same suburbs is, in turn, abnormally low.

IV

Now all these findings reinforce, clarify and illuminate our other knowledge. At the outset, I suggested that the all-important factor for the nineteenth century Irish emigration to Victoria was that here the Irish did not come to a ready made society, but were a founding people. They entered the social, economic and political race on more equal terms than in the older colonies, Tasmania and New South Wales, and of course on very much more equal terms than in any region in Great Britain or North America. Partly because of the lateness of the settlement, and partly from a variety of accidents, even the predominant Catholic element amongst the Irish contained a considerable number of middle class immigrants; as to the rest, Victorian society was unusually fluid and unfixed in the first quarter century of the colony's existence. Herein, I think, lies the ultimate explanation of the stability and evenness of ethnic distribution which the demographic data has revealed; and conversely this data furnishes a firm foundation—and indeed inspirations—for general argument.

Even the minor demographic deviations only serve to show, on the one hand, that the Irish places on the Victorian social ladder were rather lower, *pari passu*, than the places of the remainder of the population; and on the other hand, that the chances of first settlement tended to determine subsequent expansion for half a century or more. To illustrate these points, the relatively high proportion of Irish-born as against Catholics in the prosperous suburbs of Melbourne is readily explicable by the greater affluence of the anglican and presbyterian elements in Irish immigration, while the abnormally low masculinity rates for the Catholic populations of these districts is readily explicable by the large number of female domestic labourers ministering to Melbourne's haute bourgeoisie. Correspondingly, the abnormally high and abnormally low catholicity and hibernicity rates found in similar—sometimes even adjoining—agricultural districts is explicable in terms of the original choice of tenants to populate a selection. For example, William Rutledge chose Irish tenants to settle the land granted to him in 1841 in the Warnambool-Port Fairy district; and doubtless other proprietors in other places may have chosen exclusively English or Scottish tenants at the beginning. Again, central Melbourne contained the most 'working class' wards in the city; it is no surprise that these should also have been the wards where Catholics constituted roughly one-third of the local population, as against roughly one-sixth in the 'good' eastern suburbs.

The low catholicity and hibernicity rates in the mining districts can be partly explained by two factors. First, the relatively high proportion of females amongst Irish immigrants: the Catholic and Irish-born masculinity rates were always significantly lower than that for the colony at large: 127 and 121 as against 181 in 1857, and 95 and 88 as against 101 half a century later. Secondly, Irish emigration to Victoria was largely a state-aided business, whereas the influx of would-be diggers in the 1850s was very much a manifestation of private enterprise—or occasionally perhaps of a relative-assisted movement of black and greyish sheep.

The Irish emigration to Australia was but a fragment of a great nineteenth century diaspora, less than 5 per cent of the whole; and that to Victoria, at less than 2 per cent, was even more minute. Nonetheless, it suggests several lines of general new inquiry. The accepted syndrome of the overseas Irish is more or less as follows: concentration in large urban areas; selection of particular cities for heavy settlement; confinement to the lowest social strata for two generations; employment in manual and unskilled labour; and the eschewing of agriculture and rural life. Overall, the geographical, and probable occupational, distribution of the Irish in Victoria does not fit this syndrome. This alone—and quite apart from the different constitutional and economic climate of the colony—ensured that the Irish in Victoria would not follow the same courses as in other places. For example, a social conflict in which the Irish rural element was not only considerable, but even disproportionately large, was inevitably different from one in which that element was negligible. Support campaigns for Irish agitations were very different. The provision of an autonomous educational system where Catholics were dispersed and socially disparate presented very different problems to its provision in poor, massed communities. In short, as even these few instances may indicate, the demographic data opens up questions of very general, no less than particular, relevance.

V

Let me, finally, attempt to illustrate the uses of this data more specifically by considering, briefly, one special aspect of the matter, the Victorian political system from the formal constitution of the colony to 1891. 1856 marks the final failure of both oligarchic government and the efforts to reproduce in the new colony the current British politics of deference. At the other end of our time scale, in the 1890s, coherent political parties in the modern sense were forming, and the conventional European polarisation of right and left was gradually making way. At first sight, Victorian politics in the intervening years defy categorisation. A Victorian conservative of the 1850s, it was said, was one who accepted only four points of the People's Charter; and Victorian ministries came together and divided, re-grouped and moved apart again, with the apparent randomness of logs drifting in a river. But politics are never really incoherent. It was not that Victoria lacked political groupings, bodies of legislative demands and cultural affinities. It was rather that the social and economic pressures had not yet been sufficiently simplified and stabilised, and that the process of Australianisation was not yet sufficiently advanced, for these to issue in two or three universal parties. The new interests and the order of political priorities were still unfixed; and the confusion was compounded by the active politicians, who were almost without exception foreign born, and brought to their business exogenous, and often irrelevant, European sympathies and antipathies. The coherent Catholic and Irish groupings in part help to explain, and are in part explained by this situation.

Broadly speaking, Catholics and Irish cohered politically in three causes. The first we might term the 'democratic-radical' and here it was the land issue which predominated in the early years, and the assault upon the powers of the upper house which predominated later. The second cause was the sectarian, and here if civil equality was the chief theme at first, secular education was the storm centre of the late 1860s, the 1870s and the early 1880s. The third was Ireland itself; and although, incidentally, this led the Irish into the camp of colonial autonomy and separation, its primary role in Victorian politics was to bind men politically in support of, or in hostility to, the Irish agitations of the day. In none of these causes did the Irish and the Catholics constitute an entirely undivided, or an isolated, force; but for each they were a main coherent corps. In other words, catholicity and hibernicity produced powerful political forces and counter-forces, which could be and were often used in the struggle for place, power and control of policy.

These forces and counter-forces can be seen clearly at work in both the formation and defeat of O'Shanassy's first and second ministries in 1857–9, which included Duffy and Richard Ireland, an old associate of Duffy's on the *Nation*. But it was in the closing decades of our period that they operated most effectively. Duffy's ministry of 1871–2 was assailed—in the end, successfully—for the use of patronage in favour of his Catholic and seditious fellow-countrymen, amongst them Hoey, his successor as editor of the *Nation*.

The defeat was avenged with the formation of Berry's administration in 1877. This rested to a considerable extent upon the Catholic and Irish support which had been mobilised at the preceding general election by a programme of land radicalism and the prospect of concessions to denominational education. Half the members of Berry's cabinet, which included Lalor, Longmore and O'Loghlen, were Irish-born; and O'Loghlen carried a normally conservative seat by organising the Irish minority, as a political enemy declared, to vote en bloc 'for the old country and the old faith'. When Berry in turn failed the denominationalists, a Roman Catholic Education Defence League was formed in 1879 to throw the Catholic vote into the scales in favour of candidates, of whatever faction, who would pledge themselves to oppose every government which maintained the full secular system. The object was a demonstration of Catholic political power, to make and unmake ministries *ad nauseam* until the Catholic demands were met. Although it was, for obvious reasons, repudiated even by many of the Irish Catholic career politicians, the League had some negative success. A small group of eight members did bind themselves completely to League policy, and in 1880–1 succeeded in bringing down three ministries within a year. By 1881 however, the Parnell issue was already beginning to supersede the Catholic cause; and over the next decade the Home Rule question operated as an important force both centrifugally and centripetally, within the political system. It was a neat illustration of the change that denominationalism should have helped O'Loghlen to power in 1881, but that the Phoenix Park murders should have helped to bring him down eighteen months later.

Enough has been said to indicate, on the one hand, the significance of catholicism and Irishness in the group politics of the day, and, on the other, the close correlation of these forces with our demographic data. In only half-a-dozen constituencies did Irish Catholics represent more than one-third of the population; and these were generally Irish Catholic preserves. But in the considerable majority of the constituencies in the 1870s and 1880s, Irish Catholics probably constituted one-fifth, or thereabouts, of the electorate. Clearly, such minorities, if coherent, were very powerful; but equally they could be overcome with ease, should the countervailing forces in the community be aroused and compacted. The Irish minority was most effective in a general front, such as movements for land or constitutional reform, and least effective when it exhibited what was more or less idiosyncratic to the group, as was substantially the case with denominational education after 1870, or with Home Rule down to the publicisation of Gladstone's conversion in 1886. It was by forces and counter-forces of this kind that the early Victorian political system operated. Part of the 'code' which explains its functioning may be found, perhaps, in our columns upon columns of statistics.

VI

It will long have been obvious that I am not a demographic historian by trade. A true demographer would doubtless have expressed my findings in a dozen graphs and algebraic formulae, and not entangled himself in the difficulties of clothing quantitative relationships in literary forms. The true demographer is probably inured to the disproportion between his vast statistical labours and the modest scale of his results. He is probably inured to the common absence of surprise at his most painful discoveries. But he may console himself—certainly he should—with Namier's observation, 'True history almost always seems obvious after it has been told'.

But the interaction of cultures interests all of us; and if demography can assemble materials for its study which no other discipline can provide, the general practitioner may perhaps be forgiven for venturing into another's field.

NOTE ON SOURCES

Most of the matter in this article is based on statistical material contained in the census returns for the colony of New South Wales for 1836, 1841, 1846 and 1851, and for the colony of Victoria for 1854, 1857, 1861, 1871, 1881, 1891 and 1901. For reasons of space only those series of statistics which are of first importance for the argument are published below. The figures for total, Irish-born and Roman Catholic populations set out in the tables are taken from the relevant printed census returns; but the percentages which also appear in the tables, as well as the other percentages etc. used in the text, have been calculated by me. The returns accompanying the printed annual reports of the colonial land and emigration commissioners down to 1873 have furnished some additional information on immigration.

The contemporary *Victorian Year Books* contain further statistical matter, of some interest but uncertain value. One item, for example, suggests that the adult Catholic illiteracy rate may have been 50+ per cent above the colonial mean: 12·79 per cent as against 6·62 per cent in the 1870s, 3·88 per cent as against 2·28 per cent in the 1880s and 1·59 per cent as against 1·08 per cent in 1892 (*V.Y.B. 1893*, 261–2). Another series suggests that the crime rate (especially for crimes of violence and drunkenness) of the Irish-born, and still more of the Catholics, was higher than average. In 1882, for instance, ·099 per cent of the Irish-born, and ·106 per cent of the Catholic, population were committed for trial as against a colonial mean of ·069 per cent

(*V.Y.B. 1882–3*, 403–6). These 'findings'—in conjunction with the facts that the Victorian illiteracy and crime rates were, by contemporary standards, low, and that lesser groups (those born in continental Europe or in Australian colonies other than Victoria, for example) often stood higher in these inglorious scales than ours—tend to support the view that, on average, the Irish-born and Catholics were poorer than the other major elements in the population, but that the social differences between groups in the colonial community were comparatively small. But this evidence has not been used in the text because it is of very doubtful strength. The literacy figures were based, solely, on signings in marriage registers, and the crime figures were most often for arrests or committals or both, rather than convictions.

For general background, the paper owes much, of course, to such basic secondary material as, amongst contemporary writings, Charles Gavan Duffy's *My life in two hemispheres*, 2 vols., col. edit. London, 1898; amongst pioneering work, H. G. Turner's *A history of the colony of Victoria*, 2 vols., London, 1904; and amongst the fruits of modern scholarship, G. Serle's *The golden age*, Melbourne, 1966. On particular topics, it is especially indebted for information on the Berry administration to Miss J. Parnaby's unpublished dissertation, 'The economic and political development of Victoria, 1877–81' (University of Melbourne); for information on the Home Rule issue in Victorian politics to Miss P. Breen's unpublished B.A. essay, 'The reaction to the Irish question in Victoria' (University of Melbourne); for information on William Rutledge and the Farnham Survey to Miss Martha Rutledge; and for information on the Roman Catholic Education Defence League to the minutes and correspondence of the Catholic Education Committee preserved in the diocesan archives in Melbourne.

Not least, I acknowledge warmly the patient and generous help given to a semi-numerate by Professor W. M. Borrie and other members of the Department of Demography at the Institute of Advanced Studies in the Australian National University, Canberra. So far as my statistical procedures are sound, the credit is theirs; and the converse is most certainly true.

Table I

CENSUS OF VICTORIA 1857

County or pastoral district	*Population*	*Population born in Ireland*	*Local Irish-born population percentage of local population*	*Roman Catholics*	*R.C. percentage of local population*
Anglesey	879	172	19·57	200	22·75
Bourke	133,163	25,072	18·83	26,996	20·72
Dalhousie	10,087	2,451	24·30	3,362	33·33
Dundas	2,215	346	15·62	441	19·91
Evelyn	2,589	443	17·11	436	16·84
Follett	510	65	12·75	86	16·86
Grant	59,460	9,316	15·67	11,397	19·17
Grenville	16,142	2,071	12·83	2,463	15·26
Hampden	1,850	182	9·84	209	11·30
Heytesbury	574	137	23·87	138	24·04
Mornington	2,657	463	17·43	624	23·49
Normanby	5,913	858	14·51	884	14·95
Polwarth	1,638	260	15·87	346	21·12
Ripon	5,377	757	14·08	840	15·62
Talbot	42,356	5,411	12·78	7,397	17·46
Villiers	10,731	2,575	24·00	3,078	28·68
Gippsland	3,600	519	14·42	832	23·11
The Lodden	50,065	8,150	16·28	10,084	20·14
Rodney	1,764	273	15·48	315	17·85
The Murray	19,346	3,969	20·52	4,908	25·35
The Wimmera	4,627	715	15·45	813	17·57
Ships etc.	3,723	387	—	651	—
Migratory	4,348	672	—	839	—
Chinese, Aboriginals	27,152	—	—	12	—
Total	410,766	65,264	15·89	77,351	18·83

Table II

CENSUS OF VICTORIA 1861

County or pastoral district	*Population*	*Population born in Ireland*	*Local Irish-born population percentage of local population*	*Roman Catholics*	*R.C. percentage of local population*
Anglesey	1,749	324	18·52	384	21·96
Bourke	166,746	30,889	18·52	36,283	21·76
Dalhousie	20,502	5,385	26·27	7,010	34·19
Dundas	3,588	511	14·24	694	19·34
Evelyn	3,617	524	14·49	529	14·63
Follett	696	86	12·36	111	15·95
Grant	65,519	10,348	15·79	14,177	21·64
Grenville	30,154	3,401	11·28	4,054	13·44

Table II (*continued*)

CENSUS OF VICTORIA 1861

County or pastoral district	*Population*	*Population born in Ireland*	*Local Irish-born population percentage of local population*	*Roman Catholics*	*R.C. percentage of local population*
Hampden	3,265	411	12·59	492	15·07
Heytesbury	969	233	23·01	304	31·37
Mornington	4,368	691	15·82	933	21·35
Normanby	8,026	1,078	13·43	1,282	15·95
Polwarth	2,171	333	15·34	450	20·73
Ripon	10,000	1,447	14·47	1,554	15·54
Talbot	65,528	7,360	11·23	9,989	15·24
Villiers	13,892	3,348	24·10	4,478	32·23
Gippsland	6,398	905	14·15	1,395	21·80
The Lodden	64,969	9,651	14·85	12,744	19·62
Rodney	3,280	448	13·66	604	18·41
The Murray	31,931	5,360	16·79	6,689	20·95
The Wimmera	27,675	4,242	15·33	5,402	19·52
Ships etc.	1,918	195	—	271	—
Migratory	3,361	509	—	638	—
Total	540,322	87,669	16·23	110,467	20·44

Table III

CENSUS OF VICTORIA 1871

County or pastoral district	*Population*	*Population born in Ireland*	*Local Irish-born population percentage of local population*	*Roman Catholics*	*R.C. percentage of local population*
Anglesey	5,492	863	15·71	1,378	25·09
Bourke	236,778	36,392	15·37	55,669	23·51
Dalhousie	26,471	5,314	20·07	10,173	38·43
Dundas	6,888	874	12·69	1,362	19·77
Evelyn	5,997	698	11·64	1,050	17·51
Follett	1,240	128	10·32	236	19·03
Grant	73,828	9,787	13·26	18,713	23·35
Grenville	60,917	7,229	11·87	11,967	19·64
Hampden	7,172	1,028	14·33	1,660	23·15
Heytesbury	3,059	492	16·08	876	28·64
Mornington	7,397	898	12·14	1,499	20·26
Normanby	10,750	1,075	10·00	1,884	17·53
Polwarth	3,837	463	12·07	892	23·25
Ripon	14,010	1,994	14·23	2,753	19·65
Talbot	84,762	8,471	9·99	15,525	18·32
Villiers	21,031	4,138	19·68	7,552	35·91
Gippsland	18,197	2,475	13·60	4,336	23·83

Table III (*continued*)

CENSUS OF VICTORIA 1871

County or pastoral district	*Population*	*Population born in Ireland*	*Local Irish-born population percentage of local population*	*Roman Catholics*	*R.C. percentage of local population*
The Lodden	63,411	7,422	11·70	13,769	21·71
Rodney	7,390	1,103	14·93	1,783	24·13
The Murray	46,252	7,022	15·18	12,652	27·35
The Wimmera	23,655	2,457	10·39	4,260	18·01
Ships etc.	2,252	145	—	396	—
Migratory	742	—	—	—	—
Total	731,528	100,468	13·73	170,620	23·32

Table IV

CENSUS OF VICTORIA 1881

County or pastoral district	*Population*	*Population born in Ireland*	*Local Irish-born population percentage of local population*	*Roman Catholics*	*R.C. percentage of local population*
Anglesey	6,156	642	10·43	1,515	24·61
Bourke	307,582	33,379	10·85	70,018	22·75
Dalhousie	21,375	2,969	13·89	7,924	37·07
Dundas	7,790	804	10·32	2,085	26·77
Evelyn	7,227	604	8·36	1,264	17·49
Follett	2,336	155	6·64	452	19·35
Grant	66,173	6,905	10·43	17,320	26·17
Grenville	44,159	3,772	8·54	8,743	19·80
Hampden	7,253	725	10·00	1,676	23·11
Heytesbury	4,676	512	10·95	1,246	26·65
Mornington	11,467	1,026	8·95	2,232	19·46
Normanby	11,624	923	7·94	2,154	18·53
Polwarth	5,530	458	8·28	1,199	21·68
Ripon	12,341	1,232	9·98	2,595	21·03
Talbot	67,963	5,016	7·38	12,834	18·88
Villiers	20,751	3,040	14·65	8,099	39·02
Gippsland	30,920	2,912	9·42	7,197	23·28
The Lodden	84,268	7,465	8·86	18,919	22·45
Rodney	18,159	2,196	12·09	5,276	29·05
The Murray	66,832	7,659	11·46	19,686	29·46
The Wimmera	53,967	4,216	7·81	10,522	19·05
Ships etc.	1,846	123	—	524	—
Migratory	1,951	—	—	—	—
Total	862,346	86,733	10·06	203,480	23·60

Table V

CENSUS OF VICTORIA 1891

County or pastoral district	*Population*	*Population born in Ireland*	*Local Irish-born population percentage of local population*	*Roman Catholics*	*R.C. percentage of local population*
Anglesey	8,405	659	7·84	1,946	23·15
Bourke	514,341	39,911	7·76	105,958	20·60
Dalhousie	21,426	2,426	11·32	7,678	35·83
Dundas	8,181	618	7·55	2,172	26·55
Evelyn	9,814	636	6·48	1,616	16·47
Follett	2,736	140	5·12	508	18·57
Grant	68,943	5,390	7·82	16,611	24·09
Grenville	41,553	2,664	6·41	8,006	19·27
Hampden	8,140	629	7·73	1,951	23·97
Heytesbury	6,014	447	7·43	1,379	22·93
Mornington	19,586	1,366	6·97	3,522	17·98
Normanby	11,496	724	6·30	2,209	19·22
Polwarth	8,335	541	6·49	1,822	21·86
Ripon	11,663	1,025	8·79	2,426	20·80
Talbot	57,976	3,485	6·01	11,022	19·01
Villiers	21,747	2,332	10·72	7,864	36·16
Gippsland	53,705	3,901	7·26	11,558	21·52
The Lodden	79,195	5,657	7·14	17,182	21·70
Rodney	19,021	1,717	9·03	5,703	29·98
The Murray	83,039	7,200	8·67	24,284	29·24
The Wimmera	71,537	3,715	5·19	12,623	17·65
Ships etc.	2,401	124	—	314	—
Migratory	1,209	—	—	—	—
Chinese etc.	9,942	—	—	237	—
Total	1,140,405	85,307	7·48	248,591	21·80

Table VI

CENSUS OF VICTORIA 1857

Electoral district	*Population*	*Population born in Ireland*	*Local Irish-born population percentage of local population*	*Roman Catholics*	*R.C. percentage of local population*
Alberton	1,543	256	16·59	396	25·66
Anglesey	2,680	645	24·07	820	30·60
Belfast	1,869	362	19·37	404	21·62
East Bourke	14,314	3,004	20·99	3,173	22·17
South Bourke	7,722	1,411	18·27	1,478	19·14
West Bourke	12,053	2,543	21·10	2,896	24·03
Brighton	3,699	503	13·60	515	13·92

Table VI (*continued*)

CENSUS OF VICTORIA 1857

Electoral district	*Population*	*Population born in Ireland*	*Local Irish-born population percentage of local population*	*Roman Catholics*	*R.C. percentage of local population*
Castlemaine Boroughs	4,037	558	13·82	616	15·26
Colac	791	146	18·46	196	24·78
Collingwood	21,430	2,753	12·85	2,722	12·70
Dundas and Follett	2,725	411	15·08	527	19·34
Evelyn and Mornington	5,246	906	17·27	1,060	20·21
Geelong	23,307	3,879	16·64	4,536	19·46
Gippsland	2,057	263	12·79	436	21·20
North Grant	20,860	3,578	12·36	2,142	15·06
South Grant	15,293	2,859	18·69	3,719	24·32
North Grenville	15,455	1,957	12·66	2,336	15·11
Kilmore	2,330	739	31·72	1,247	53·52
Kyneton Boroughs	3,900	936	24·00	1,088	27·90
The Lodden	37,155	5,326	14·33	6,626	17·83
Melbourne	37,646	9,264	24·61	10,692	28·40
South Melbourne	8,496	1,277	15·03	1,382	16·27
Murray	3,967	811	20·44	1,074	27·07
The Murray Boroughs	1,831	368	20·10	493	26·93
Normanby	3,208	511	15·93	487	15·18
The Ovens	13,817	2,850	20·63	3,418	24·74
Polwarth, Ripon, Hampden and South Grenville	8,761	1,167	13·32	1,326	15·14
Portland	2,705	347	12·83	397	14·68
Richmond	10,078	1,609	15·97	1,591	15·79
Rodney	3,551	516	14·53	645	18·16
The Sandhurst Boroughs	12,150	2,667	21·95	3,300	27·16
St Kilda	14,189	2,059	14·51	1,805	12·72
Talbot	39,079	5,010	12·82	6,939	17·76
Villiers and Heytesbury	7,854	2,030	25·85	2,449	31·18
Warrnambool	1,582	320	20·23	363	22·95
Williamstown	3,536	649	18·35	742	20·98
The Wimmera	4,627	715	15·45	813	17·57
Remainder of Population (*a*)	35,223	1,059	—	1,502	—
Total	410,766	65,264	15·89	77,351	18·83

(*a*) Persons in ships and hulks, travellers, unnumerated population, Chinese and roving aborigines.

Table VII

CENSUS OF VICTORIA 1861

Electoral district	*Population*	*Population born in Ireland*	*Local Irish-born population percentage of local population*	*Roman Catholics*	*R.C. percentage of local population*
Ararat	4,032	502	12·45	607	15·05
Avoca	18,999	2,323	12·23	3,024	15·92
Ballarat East	16,800	2,551	15·18	3,539	21·07
Ballarat West	17,678	2,058	11·64	2,374	13·43
Belfast	2,342	428	18·27	587	25·06
East Bourke	10,164	2,205	21·69	2,706	26·62
East Bourke Boroughs	6,781	1,218	17·96	1,392	20·53
South Bourke	11,380	2,004	17·61	2,086	18·33
West Bourke	20,635	5,074	24·59	6,116	29·64
Brighton	4,349	602	13·84	590	13·57
Castlemaine	26,764	3,088	11·54	3,766	14·07
Collingwood	24,475	3,140	12·83	3,424	13·99
Creswick	32,877	3,739	11·37	5,395	16·41
Crowlands	23,107	3,707	16·04	4,701	20·34
Dalhousie	8,367	2,207	26·38	2,762	33·01
Dundas	4,284	597	13·94	805	18·79
Emerald Hill	8,924	1,422	15·93	1,683	18·86
Evelyn	3,617	524	14·49	529	14·63
Geelong East	11,752	2,175	18·51	2,944	25·05
Geelong West	11,234	1,473	13·11	1,926	17·14
North Gippsland	4,022	526	13·08	761	18·92
South Gippsland	2,376	379	15·95	634	26·68
South Grant	20,386	3,412	16·74	4,714	23·12
Grenville	16,573	1,894	11·43	2,485	14·99
Kilmore	2,897	940	32·45	1,517	52·36
Kyneton Boroughs	7,391	1,926	26·06	2,286	30·93
Maldon	8,059	629	7·80	922	11·44
Mandurang	19,574	3,209	16·39	4,271	21·82
Maryborough	7,013	722	10·30	1,039	14·82
East Melbourne	12,981	3,079	23·72	3,914	30·15
North Melbourne	16,798	3,597	21·41	4,510	26·85
West Melbourne	11,023	2,874	26·07	3,543	32·14
Mornington	4,368	691	15·82	933	21·36
Murray	14,074	2,513	17·86	3,061	21·75
Murray Boroughs	2,652	514	19·38	677	25·53
Normanby	5,222	691	13·23	837	16·03
Ovens	15,644	2,435	15·57	3,074	19·65
Polwarth and Sth. Grenville	3,421	519	15·17	699	20·43
Portland	2,804	387	13·80	445	15·87
Richmond	13,140	2,047	15·58	2,446	18·61
Ripon and Hampden	10,345	1,456	14·07	1,549	14·97
Rodney	6,437	982	15·26	1,310	20·35
Sandhurst	17,211	3,301	19·18	4,316	25·08
Sandridge	3,496	486	13·90	615	17·59
St Kilda	18,108	2,519	13·91	2,399	13·25
Villiers and Heytesbury	10,308	2,718	26·37	3,658	35·49
Warrnambool	2,211	425	19·22	537	24·29
Williamstown	4,492	622	13·85	859	19·12

Table VII (*continued*)

CENSUS OF VICTORIA 1861

Electoral district	*Population*	*Population born in Ireland*	*Local Irish-born population percentage of local population*	*Roman Catholics*	*R.C. percentage of local population*
Wimmera	3,456	435	12·59	591	17·10
Ships, hulks, etc.	1,918	195	10·17	271	—
Migratory popn. (estimated)	3,361	509	15·14	638	—
Total	540,322	87,669	16·23	110,467	20·44

Table VIII

CENSUS OF VICTORIA 1871

Electoral district	*Population*	*Population born in Ireland*	*Local Irish-born population percentage of local population*	*Roman Catholics*	*R.C. percentage of local population*
Ararat	6,203	855	13·78	1,398	22·54
Avoca	17,111	1,483	8·67	2,601	15·20
Ballarat East	21,130	3,016	14·27	5,484	25·95
Ballarat West	42,702	5,215	12·21	8,340	19·53
Belfast	2,485	360	14·49	667	26·84
East Bourke	9,951	1,619	16·27	2,605	26·18
East Bourke Boroughs	8,704	1,450	16·66	1,894	21·76
South Bourke	15,440	2,063	13·36	2,864	18·55
West Bourke	23,851	3,977	16·67	7,170	30·06
Brighton	4,912	636	12·95	778	15·84
Castlemaine	19,825	1,836	9·26	3,453	17·42
Collingwood	34,145	4,195	12·29	6,436	18·85
Creswick	46,588	5,104	10·96	9,226	19·80
Crowlands	18,243	1,863	10·21	3,171	17·38
Dalhousie	16,237	3,456	21·28	6,458	39·77
Dundas	8,128	1,002	12·33	1,933	23·78
Emerald Hill	17,488	2,276	13·01	3,647	20·85
Evelyn	5,997	698	11·64	1,050	17·51
Geelong East	12,165	1,689	13·88	3,148	25·88
Geelong West	10,498	1,189	11·33	2,385	22·72
North Gippsland	15,530	2,138	13·77	3,553	22·88
South Gippsland	2,774	351	12·65	727	26·21
South Grant	21,626	2,814	13·01	5,526	25·55
Grenville	23,670	2,661	11·24	5,023	21·22
Kilmore	2,838	736	25·93	1,497	52·75
Kyneton Boroughs	7,133	1,219	17·09	2,178	30·53
Maldon	8,424	626	7·43	1,054	12·51
Mandurang	24,633	3,142	12·76	6,010	24·40
Maryborough	9,898	899	9·08	1,782	18·00

Table VIII (*continued*)

CENSUS OF VICTORIA 1871

Electoral district	*Population*	*Population born in Ireland*	*Local Irish-born population percentage of local population*	*Roman Catholics*	*R.C. percentage of local population*
East Melbourne	13,461	2,901	21·55	4,477	33·26
North Melbourne	33,983	6,091	17·92	9,777	28·77
West Melbourne	15,331	3,384	22·07	5,142	33·54
Mornington	7,397	898	12·14	1,499	20·26
Murray	22,813	3,947	17·30	6,903	30·26
Murray Boroughs	3,864	640	16·56	1,149	29·74
Normanby	8,378	849	10·13	1,499	17·89
Ovens	20,245	2,558	12·64	4,741	23·42
Polwarth and Sth. Grenville	6,791	895	13·18	1,666	24·53
Portland	2,372	226	9·53	385	16·23
Richmond	20,435	2,817	13·79	4,132	20·22
Ripon and Hampden	16,906	2,355	13·93	3,421	20·24
Rodney	12,368	1,732	14·00	3,016	24·39
Sandhurst	21,777	2,809	12·90	5,199	23·87
Sandridge	6,098	721	11·82	1,353	22·19
St Kilda	25,853	3,505	13·56	3,963	15·33
Villiers and Heytesbury	17,806	3,690	20·72	6,812	38·26
Warrnambool	3,799	580	15·27	949	24·98
Williamstown	7,126	757	10·62	1,431	20·08
Wimmera	3,402	400	11·76	652	19·17
Persons in ships	2,252	145	—	396	—
Migratory popn. (computed)	742	Undifferentiated			—
Total	731,528	100,468	13·73	170,620	23·32

Table IX

CENSUS OF VICTORIA 1881

Electoral district	*Population*	*Population born in Ireland*	*Local Irish-born population percentage of local population*	*Roman Catholics*	*R.C. percentage of local population*
Ararat	6,393	651	10·18	1,398	21·87
Avoca	21,732	1,617	7·44	3,902	17·96
Ballarat East	18,558	2,137	11·52	5,158	27·79
Ballarat West	32,140	2,768	8·61	6,078	18·91
Barwon	10,197	829	8·13	1,887	18·51
Belfast	4,812	878	18·25	2,548	52·95
Benambra	7,595	774	10·19	2,180	28·70
Boroondara	11,832	1,154	9·75	1,824	15·42
Bourke East	8,020	852	10·62	1,843	23·60
Bourke Boroughs East	11,548	1,304	11·29	2,611	22·61
Bourke South	9,583	947	9·88	1,708	17·82

Table IX (*continued*)

CENSUS OF VICTORIA 1881

Electoral district	*Population*	*Population born in Ireland*	*Local Irish-born population percentage of local population*	*Roman Catholics*	*R.C. percentage of local population*
Bourke West	20,762	2,740	13·20	6,233	30·02
Brighton	7,627	709	9·30	1,117	14·65
Carlton	13,589	1,484	10·92	3,515	25·87
Castlemaine	15,665	1,168	7·46	2,718	17·35
Collingwood	22,389	2,133	9·53	4,919	21·97
Creswick	29,300	2,345	8·00	6,324	21·58
Dalhousie	7,976	1,251	15·68	3,540	44·33
Delatite	9,889	1,278	12·92	3,111	31·46
Dundas	6,477	625	9·65	1,567	24·19
Emerald Hill	25,374	2,447	9·64	5,542	21·84
Evelyn	7,227	604	8·36	1,264	17·49
Fitzroy	24,180	2,114	8·74	4,581	18·95
Footscray	6,785	524	7·72	1,146	16·89
Geelong	19,255	1,900	9·87	4,671	24·26
Gippsland North	21,049	1,958	9·30	4,949	23·51
Gippsland South	9,969	968	9·71	2,291	22·98
Grant	14,930	1,765	11·82	4,890	32·75
Grenville	13,380	1,146	8·57	3,055	22·83
Kara Kara	12,592	946	7·51	2,192	17·41
Kilmore and Anglesey	9,346	1,196	12·80	3,054	32·68
Kyneton Boroughs	6,092	742	12·18	1,812	29·75
Maldon	6,205	361	5·82	777	12·52
Mandurang	34,226	3,329	9·73	8,947	26·14
Maryborough and Talbot	16,793	1,142	6·80	3,015	17·95
Melbourne East	16,204	2,492	15·38	5,163	31·86
Melbourne North	29,156	3,913	13·42	8,719	29·90
Melbourne West	17,451	2,738	15·69	5,509	31·57
Moira	32,523	3,955	12·16	10,208	31·39
Mornington	11,467	1,026	8·95	2,232	19·46
Normanby	8,044	670	8·33	1,830	22·75
Ovens	16,790	1,651	9·83	4,159	24·77
Polwarth and Sth. Grenville	8,038	668	8·31	1,739	21·63
Portland	7,074	560	7·92	1,204	17·02
Richmond	28,135	2,858	10·16	6,168	21·92
Ripon and Hampden	10,024	949	9·47	1,907	19·02
Rodney	22,213	2,605	11·73	6,294	28·33
Sandhurst	29,829	2,654	8·90	6,391	21·43
Sandridge	8,771	837	9·54	2,042	23·28
Stawell	9,145	650	7·11	1,709	18·69
St Kilda	36,550	3,415	9·34	5,518	15·10
Villiers and Heytesbury	18,536	2,304	12·43	5,814	31·37
Warrnambool	7,457	922	12·36	2,408	32·29
Williamstown	9,034	647	7·16	1,617	17·90
Wimmera	28,621	2,310	8·07	5,908	20·64
Shipping	1,846	123	6·66	524	—
Migratory	1,951	Undifferentiated			—
Total	862,346	86,733	10·06	203,480	23·60

Table X

CENSUS OF VICTORIA 1891

Electoral district	*Population*	*Population born in Ireland*	*Local Irish-born population percentage of local population*	*Roman Catholics*	*R.C. percentage of local population*
Albert Park	12,693	877	6·91	2,046	16·12
Anglesey	12,802	1,100	8·59	3,342	26·11
Ararat	8,136	734	9·02	1,814	22·30
Ballarat East	13,877	752	5·42	2,089	15·05
Ballarat West	27,195	1,520	5·59	4,585	16·86
Barwon	10,440	655	6·27	1,702	16·30
Benalla and Yarrawonga	11,739	1,069	9·11	3,893	33·16
Benambra	7,789	626	8·04	2,035	26·13
Bogong	8,346	787	9·43	2,395	28·70
Borung	11,553	648	5·61	2,307	19·97
Bourke East	11,810	1,054	8·92	2,716	23·00
Bourke West	10,149	1,232	12·14	3,385	33·35
East Bourke Boroughs	42,768	3,157	7·38	8,249	19·29
Brighton	15,581	996	6·39	2,120	13·61
Carlton	15,689	1,301	8·29	3,957	25·22
Carlton South	12,187	1,203	9·87	3,740	30·69
Castlemaine	13,107	898	6·85	2,366	18·05
Clunes and Allandale	8,365	580	6·93	1,688	20·18
Collingwood	29,333	2,005	6·84	5,960	20·32
Creswick	7,918	533	6·73	1,733	21·89
Dandenong and Berwick	15,706	1,029	6·55	2,466	15·70
Daylesford	9,028	530	5·87	2,101	23·27
Delatite	10,339	973	9·41	3,043	29·43
Donald and Swan Hill	11,524	773	6·71	2,736	23·74
Dundas	9,489	643	6·78	2,307	24·31
Dunolly	8,091	485	5·99	1,523	18·82
Eaglehawk	8,509	339	3·98	1,113	13·08
Eastern Suburbs	21,015	1,521	7·24	3,101	14·76
Emerald Hill	14,881	1,290	8·67	3,726	25·04
Essendon and Flemington	24,352	1,314	5·40	3,863	15·86
Evelyn	12,386	815	6·58	2,106	17·00
Fitzroy	28,800	1,927	6·69	5,609	19·48
Footscray	20,151	1,101	5·46	3,438	17·06
Geelong	23,167	1,649	7·12	5,127	22·13
Gippsland Central	10,963	826	7·53	2,432	22·18
Gippsland East	10,353	548	5·29	2,395	23·13
Gippsland North	9,714	664	6·84	2,065	21·26
Gippsland South	10,015	806	8·05	2,332	23·29
Gippsland West	15,059	1,211	8·04	3,165	21·02
Grant	8,685	714	8·22	2,343	26·98
Grenville	13,980	1,136	8·13	3,229	23·10
Gunbower	10,522	856	8·14	2,846	27·05
Hawthorn	19,551	1,118	5·72	2,569	13·14
Horsham	10,778	477	4·43	1,599	14·84
Jolimont and West Richmond	12,780	1,033	8·08	2,496	19·37
Kara Kara	8,863	471	5·31	1,552	17·51
Kilmore, Dalhousie and Lancefield	9,671	1,209	12·50	3,771	38·99

Table X (*continued*)

CENSUS OF VICTORIA 1891

Electoral district	*Population*	*Population born in Ireland*	*Local Irish-born population percentage of local population*	*Roman Catholics*	*R.C. percentage of local population*
Korong	8,630	774	8·97	1,665	19·29
Kyneton	9,574	1,143	11·94	3,355	35·04
Lowan	13,120	409	3·12	1,628	12·41
Maldon	7,302	435	5·96	1,230	16·84
Mandurang	8,580	746	8·69	2,240	26·11
Maryborough	9,714	434	4·47	1,563	16·09
Melbourne	9,436	1,740	18·44	3,720	39·42
Melbourne East	19,318	2,367	12·25	6,088	31·51
Melbourne North	17,235	1,737	10·08	4,981	28·90
Melbourne South	14,103	1,102	7·81	3,318	23·53
Melbourne West	13,927	1,736	12·46	4,640	33·32
Mornington	14,687	994	6·77	2,583	17·59
Normanby	8,793	589	6·70	2,144	24·38
Numurkah and Nathalia	11,310	938	8·29	2,936	25·96
Ovens	7,460	592	7·94	1,945	26·07
Polwarth	10,954	713	6·51	2,472	22·57
Port Fairy	7,179	1,001	13·94	3,459	48·18
Port Melbourne	13,065	879	6·73	2,999	22·95
Portland	8,479	510	6·01	1,422	16·77
Prahran	16,340	886	5·42	2,435	14·90
Richmond	31,090	2,483	7·99	7,557	24·31
Ripon and Hampden	11,457	808	7·05	2,198	19·18
Rodney	21,655	1,924	8·88	6,377	29·45
Sandhurst	22,491	1,580	7·03	5,133	22·82
Sandhurst South	8,957	654	7·30	2,127	23·75
Shepparton and Euroa	11,046	968	8·76	3,471	31·42
South Yarra	15,400	1,071	6·95	2,163	14·05
St Kilda	19,112	1,600	8·37	3,458	18·09
Stawell	9,422	515	5·47	1,548	16·43
Talbot and Avoca	7,555	426	5·64	1,229	16·27
Toorak	19,722	1,066	5·41	1,920	9·74
Villiers and Heytesbury	10,320	885	8·58	3,030	29·36
Wangaratta and Rutherglen	10,377	845	8·14	2,985	28·77
Warrenheip	7,397	1,198	16·20	4,054	54·81
Warrnambool	9,256	866	9·36	2,691	29·07
Williamstown	15,950	785	4·92	2,518	15·79
Windermere	6,591	599	9·09	1,593	24·17
Shipping	2,401	124	—	314	—
Migratory	1,209	Undifferentiated		—	—
Chinese	9,377	—	—	231	—
Aborigines	565	—	—	6	—
Total	1,140,405	85,307	7·48	248,581	21·80

PART II: IRISH HISTORY

The Aggrandisement of Armagh

Liam de Paor

The controversy about St Patrick, his mission, his chronology, his singularity or duality, has been in progress in its present phase since 1942.[1] It has concentrated on the figure of the fifth-century missionary himself, making use of documents, some of which are much later than his time, for the light they might shed on him. These documents in turn, in this capacity, have been severely criticised. They do, however, supply evidence for other matters besides the career of Patrick, and they deserve to be looked at from other points of view.

It has more than once been pointed out that many of these later documents were designed to serve a purpose, that of furthering the interests of Armagh, and that because of this they are untrustworthy sources of information about St Patrick. 'Nothing whatsoever of Tírechán, the *Book of the Angel*, the *Tripartite Life* and similar documents may be admitted as evidence for Patrick's work in Ireland', writes J. Morris in a recent paper, '. . . though persons named may be real . . . these works can carry no weight, for their purpose was to invent connection with Patrick'.[2] And James Carney goes so far as to suggest that the very foundation of Armagh itself by Patrick was an invention.[3]

Dr Morris is, of course, quite right, up to a point. Tírechán's *Breviarium* and the similar documents are not good evidence for St Patrick's work in Ireland, with which they purport to deal, but the reasons for their inadequacy in this respect may not have to do wholly with the ulterior motives of their authors, who experienced

[1] This is to date the present phase of the controversy from T. F. O'Rahilly's lecture on 'Palladius and Patrick', delivered in Dublin on 20 March 1942, published as *The Two Patricks*, Dublin 1942, re-issued 1957.

[2] J. Morris, 'The Dates of the Celtic Saints', *Journal of Theological Studies*, New Series, xvii (Oct. 1966), 342.

[3] J. Carney, *The Problem of St Patrick*, Dublin 1961, 38.

difficulties of their own in the seventh and eighth centuries in dealing with events of the fifth. D. A. Binchy, who has expressed himself as forcefully as any other on the distortions produced by the writers 'who were primarily propagandists for the claims of Armagh',[4] has also pointed out most cogently that the method of recording events in a chronological framework 'had to be evolved slowly and painfully' in Ireland, and has said that he does not believe 'there is a single "genuine entry" throughout the whole of the fifth century'.[5] Writers like Tírechán were themselves faced with a Patrician problem.

This paper is not concerned with St Patrick, but with the begin ning of the rise of Armagh to its position of pre-eminence in the Irish Church—an end which the documents were explicitly con cerned to serve. If we look at them in this light we find that as propaganda they fall far short of the modern techniques of the big lie. The *Book of Armagh* itself, for example, does not attempt to claim Armagh as the oldest bishopric in the country, but expressly states that Trim was founded by Lommán many years earlier,[6] and relatively little effort is directed to establishing Patrick's connection with Armagh, which is largely taken for granted. The chief concern is to establish Patrick himself in his position as apostle of the Irish: the claims of Armagh follow from this.

Although many points of detail are obscure, the broad outlines of Armagh's later rise to primacy are relatively clear and have been well expounded by Dr Kathleen Hughes in her book on *The Church in Early Irish Society*.[7] This rise, or revival perhaps, appears to have begun in the seventh century and to have been well advanced by the beginning of the ninth. Sparse as the evidence is for the early period, it leaves little doubt that Armagh, however much its fortunes may have declined with the rise of great monasteries and monastic federations in the sixth and seventh centuries, had always enjoyed, with Patrick its founder, some recognition of priority. The letter of Cummian to Segéne, abbot of Iona, written in the early 630s after consultation with the heads of the churches of Emly, Clonmacnoise, Clonfert-Molua and, probably, Birr and Mungret, refers to Patrick in connection with the system of calculating Easter dates he is said to have brought to Ireland, and gives him the title *papa noster*.[8] The name of the bishop of Armagh, Tomméne, heads the list of ecclesiastics of the northern half of Ireland to whom John, pope-elect,

[4] D. A. Binchy, 'Patrick and his biographers; ancient and modern', *Studia Hibernica*, ii (1962), 76.
[5] D. A. Binchy, *op. cit.*, 71.
[6] *The Book of Armagh*, ed. John Gwynn, 32a.
[7] K. Hughes, *The Church in Early Irish Society*, London 1966, 111, 275.
[8] Ed. Migne, *P.L.*, 87, cols. 969–78.

wrote in 640, urging conformity in Easter observances and extirpation of the Pelagian heresy.[9] This position of priority in the list of names is very interesting, even if it gives us no more than a hint that in 640, in Rome (which had been visited by a delegation from the southern Irish churches a few years previously) Armagh was regarded as being at least *primus inter pares* in a group which probably included the great churches of Clonard, Clonmacnoise and Bangor.

It has been suggested that a cult of Patrick, or at least some Patrician documents, were brought to continental Europe at about this time by St Fursa[10]—for such a cult later flourished at Peronne, which was the ultimate source of some of our texts of Patrick's writings. This seems unlikely, since Bede, who informs us about Fursa and who plainly had access to documentary material connected with him (probably at Burgh Castle), appears to know nothing of Patrick, and did not even include him in his martyrology (although the name was added later, in France). Indeed, it is possible, if we take up a suggestion made by Fr Grosjean,[11] that the text of Patrick's *Confession* may have come *into* Ireland at this time, from Britain or the Continent. Grosjean's suggestion was that the short version of the *Confession* (a document which is in fact a letter addressed probably to British bishops) was the preliminary draft, kept in Ireland and copied ultimately into the *Book of Armagh*, while the long version, which we have from continental manuscripts, was the full text of the letter as sent out of Ireland. Grosjean's full hypothesis fails by a simple test: the long version of the *Confession* is quoted in the *Book of Armagh*, and the short version is in fact, as Dr Binchy has shown,[12] a shortened, indeed a censored, version. But it is not impossible that the transmission of the text down to the seventh century may have occurred outside Ireland. At any rate, whatever their source, copies of this important document must have existed, probably at more than one place, in Ireland by about the middle of the seventh century.

We are not without indications therefore that Patrick had a reputation and a name, in some Irish churches at least, in the early seventh century, and that Armagh had some measure of precedence. But there are also indications, admittedly of a negative character, that in some of the monastic traditions the name of Patrick had been all but forgotten, or was irrelevant. There are more positive indications that in the second half of the century Armagh, at least in the eyes of its own supporters, was given far less than its due recognition in Ireland. Columbanus, alumnus of the school of Bangor, makes no

[9] Bede, *Historia ecclesiastica gentis Anglorum*, ed. Plummer, 2, 114.
[10] Carney, *St Patrick*, 115.
[11] P. Grosjean, 'The Confession of St Patrick', in J. Ryan, ed., *St Patrick*, Dublin 1958, 88.
[12] D. A. Binchy, 'Patrick and his biographers', 40.

reference to Patrick, and although Columbanus in general mentions few names, there is at least one context in which we might expect him to refer to Patrick, had Patrick been regarded as 'papa noster' by the community of sixth-century Bangor. This is the letter of 612 or 613 to Pope Boniface IV in which Columbanus actually makes reference to the conversion of the Irish. In Ireland, he says, 'the Catholic faith, just as it was first transmitted from you, that is the successors of the holy apostles, is maintained unchanged', and he describes the Irish as 'disciples of Saints Peter and Paul'.[13] This is inconclusive. Bede's silence, however, we must surely take as an indication that Patrick had little or no place in the Columban tradition of the seventh century. Adomnán, writing towards the end of the century, has just one passing reference to Patrick when he mentions a Columban monastery which was founded next door to a monastery founded by a disciple of 'the holy bishop Patrick'.[14]

Putting together these isolated pieces of evidence, as well as further evidence which will shortly be considered, I think that we may reasonably infer that in the seventh century Patrick was not forgotten or unknown in Ireland; that his name was honoured in a special way in some churches, probably in some of the older churches especially; that in some other churches, probably especially the larger monastic federations whose traditions essentially went back only about a hundred years, he was little more than a name; that in general he was a remote figure of the distant past, whose situation and circumstances were so different from those of the seventh-century monastic Church as to be beyond comprehension; and that this remoteness reflected on the status, in real and practical terms, of Armagh. There appears to be no indication of even the slightest plausibility that there was at any stage in Armagh's history any questioning of its title to Patrick. On the contrary, the general recognition of this claim is implicit in every move the supporters of Armagh made in their assertion or reassertion of their church's primacy: this is the premiss from which they argued.

The older churches referred to above were in the main those of the primary missionary period, and it is clear from a range of consistent evidence that a great many, although not all, of them had fallen into obscurity by the seventh century. We may take as a fairly clear demarcation between this primary period in Irish church history and the ensuing phase of rapid monastic development the great plague which appears to have reached Ireland in the 540s.[15] Monasticism was probably already established when the plague arrived, although

[13] G. S. M. Walker, *Sancti Columbani Opera*, Dublin 1957, 38, 39.
[14] A. O. and M. O. Anderson, *Adomnan's Life of Columba*, Edinburgh 1961, 182.
[15] The Justinian Plague. See Hughes, *Ch. in early Ir. soc.*, 67.

it is as well to be cautious in accepting the testimony of later documents on this point. Places such as Kildare were not necessarily founded as monasteries, at least in the sense of later times. There are some aspects of the beginnings of the monastic movement in Ireland which might be better explained if we were to envisage efforts, round about the beginning of the sixth century, to found not monasteries but episcopal cities—*civitates*.[16] The plague at any rate occurred at a crucial period in the development of the Irish Church: mortality was severe, as all our evidence testifies. The worst source of infection was Gaul, which had been badly affected, and therefore the churches which were still in contact with Gaul (and we know from archaeological evidence that there was at this time a flourishing connection) would have been, as it were, singled out by the pestilence. This visitation must thus explain in part the decline or disappearance of many of the earliest churches.

We may imagine a period of recovery after the great plague, which is known to the annalists as the Buidhe Conaill, and we know that the monastic movement flourished. Foundations dated to the sixth and early seventh centuries are numerous. By the early seventh century too, Irish native culture had gone far on the way to assimilating the alien Roman import of Christianity: this process may have been regarded at first with no great favour by churches which still preserved a tradition stemming from the missionary period. At any rate there does emerge from the seventh-century texts some consciousness among the older foundations of their difference as a group from the newer. We may, if we wish, picture these older churches, respectable in their antiquity and genteel in their latinity, looking down their noses at the parvenu monasteries with their wealth and influential royal connections. Tírechán, for example, in mentioning a place-name, will say, *Loig-les in scotica, nobiscum Uitulus Ciuitatum.*[17] Or, when he speaks of 'monks' of Patrick who from their names appear to be Irish, he calls them *barbaros, Conleng et Ercleng, barbaros monachos sibi.*[18] When Adomnán, who belonged to the other (the monastic) group, translates an Irish word, he does not do it in that tone of voice: . . . *matrem Aethneam nomine, cujus pater latine filius navis dici potest, scotica vero lingua mac naue.*[19]

At the beginning of the seventh century the old foundations were almost certainly separate and isolated. We can obtain some idea of the nature of the work of one fifth-century missionary—Patrick himself—from his own writings, and the impression received is of a

[16] See the '*Liber Angeli*', *Bk Arm.*, 40–43; and Binchy, 'Patrick and his biographers', 64.
[17] *Bk Arm.*, 20a.
[18] *Bk Arm.*, 22a.
[19] Anderson, *Adomnan's Life of Columba*, 186.

man travelling and working largely in isolation. There is no suggestion of the organiser, of the man concerned with founding an ecclesiastical system or administration. It seems from later evidence that the episcopal church was the church of the *tuath* (and Tírechán, for example, to quote him again, refers to *Ultanum episcopum Chonchuburnensium*):[20] so that even the different churches founded by the same missionary, whether Patrick or another, would not have, or be intended to have, any continuing connection with one another.

A crisis was brought about in the affairs of the Irish Church by the paschal controversy of the seventh century, and it was a crisis which called for the adoption of a common policy and therefore demanded meetings and negotiations between the heads of various churches. The beginnings of Armagh's move towards the primacy are, it seems, closely connected with this controversy. This crisis was probably what first stimulated the older churches to work out a common policy to defend their common interest in maintaining the precedence due to their antiquity and seniority. It appears from the *Book of Armagh* that Bishop Aed of Slébte negotiated an agreement with Segéne, bishop of Armagh (whose death is recorded in the Annals of Ulster in 688), bringing a 'bequest' and acknowledging Armagh as head of a *paruchia*. In this, these churches of the missionary age were following the pattern, well established by the 680s, of monastic federation. Dr Hughes, following and commenting on Zimmer, has a full discussion in her book of the episode, and of the extent to which it is connected with the Easter question.[21] She surmises very reasonably that by or about this time Armagh conformed to the Roman Easter. I suspect, incidentally, that the term *romani*, which is used of the paschally orthodox of this period, has a deeper implication than the merely paschal; that it may well involve a reference to the policy of papal control and rationalisation of the organisation of western Churches which had been forwarded by Gregory the Great and his successors. It may even imply a recognition of the special position of churches whose foundation derived from the Roman mission.

The mid-century developments are of special interest for the historian because documents began to issue, to revive the memory of the primitive Irish church and thus bring the grievances and claims of the older foundations before an interested ecclesiastical public. In this matter Armagh was not to the fore. The oldest of such texts extant (and in fact the first to be issued, if a reference by Muirchú in the *Book of Armagh* is so to be interpreted) is the *Life of Brigid* by Cogitosus. This important manuscript, which exists in a large

[20] *Bk Arm.*, 17b.
[21] Hughes, *Ch. in early Ir. soc.*, 116.

number of late manuscripts outside Ireland, has not been edited since the seventeenth century.[22] The *Life* is non-historical. It contains a collection of miracles of Brigid, but it has an introduction stating the claims of Kildare to supremacy over the churches of 'almost all of Ireland', an epilogue of very great interest giving a description of the seventh-century city of Kildare, and a good deal of incidental detail of informative value for social history. The name 'Kildare' (*Cell dara*), incidentally, appears to be later than the time of Cogitosus, to whom the place is still *civitas Brigidae*. The dating of the text of Cogitosus to the middle of the seventh century depends largely upon an emendation, generally accepted, to Muirchú's work on St Patrick in the *Book of Armagh*.[23] It was probably soon after the middle of the seventh century that Armagh and Kildare negotiated the arrangement for mutual support and advantage which is enshrined in the later *Book of the Angel* (in the *Book of Armagh*),[24] where the paruchia of each is defined, the precedence of Armagh being recognised, but the autonomy of Kildare protected.

The south midlands were a main centre of ecclesiastical controversy and turmoil in the seventh century, because not only did the paschal dispute produce a division between north and south, but there was growing pressure from the southern Uí Neill and their monastic protégés on the traditional border between the two halves of Ireland. The legend of the expulsion of Carrthach from Rahan (a place lying just a mile or so south of the border) crystallises this conflict in the favourite Irish form of a good story.[25] There were in this area fairly numerous churches which traced their history back to the missionary period—notably the churches of Slébte, Trim, Ardbraccan, Kilcullen, Dunshaughlin and Killashee. Some of these appear to have taken the initiative in organising a form of alliance of the old churches against interlopers—under the aegis of Patrick and Armagh. Thus it is not from Armagh itself but from Ardbraccan and Slébte that the first Armagh documents emanate. Incidentally, the output of hagiographical documents on the other side, in Iona, appears to have begun in the same period with, to quote Adomnán, *Cummeneus albus in libro quem de virtutibus sancti Columbae scripsit*.[26]

In the meantime another severe plague, or series of plagues, appears to have afflicted Ireland, and we have the testimony of Tírechán that, at least in the west, this had disastrous effects on some

[22] By Colgan, in *Trias Thaumaturga*, Louvain 1647.
[23] See *Bk Arm.*, xix.
[24] *Bk Arm.*, 40–43.
[25] C. Plummer, *Bethada Náem nÉrenn*, Oxford 1922, I, 300 ('*Indarba Mochuda a rRaithin*') and Plummer, *Vitae Sanctorum Hiberniae*, Oxford 1910, 170 ('*Vita sancti Carthagi siue Mochutu episcopi de Less Mor*').
[26] Anderson, *Adomnan's Life of Columba*, 474.

of the primitive churches, some of them being subsequently taken over by monastic interlopers.[27]

The first documents in support of Armagh were hagiographical. The claims of the Armagh supporters were, briefly, as follows: Armagh had been founded by St Patrick and was the seat of his successors; Patrick was the chief apostle of the Irish; therefore Armagh was the chief church of the Irish. What this supremacy involved in the minds of its seventh-century advocates must remain for the moment an open question. The documents in which jurisdictional claims are spelled out are mostly of a later date, but the situation had probably changed by then—indeed it appears to have been changing rapidly in the late seventh century as the growing Armagh federation accommodated itself to the monastic pattern.

As an abundance of documents testifies, the basis of Armagh's claim was the standard argument put forward by any church which wished to claim local or regional pre-eminence or jurisdiction, an argument based on the pre-eminence and claims to status of its founder. A great deal of our hagiography in fact ratifies, as it were, agreements made between churches by arranging retrospectively a meeting between their saintly founders.[28] A church putting forward a claim to rents, tribute, or other recognition based on its founder's status showed its 'title-deeds', and these in early medieval times consisted usually not of charters or other written documents, but of the physical possession of the tomb and major relics of the founder, backed by a carefully fostered hagiographical tradition. 'Rome is head of the churches of the world', Columbanus wrote to Pope Boniface, '—saving only the singular prerogative of the place of resurrection of the Lord'.[29] Armagh in this respect was in a peculiarly difficult position. It did not possess, nor could it claim to possess, the body of Patrick: it was not his 'place of resurrection'. Yet there is no evidence of any challenge to Armagh on these grounds. The church had been founded near the ancient and famous Emhain Macha, royal site of the prehistoric Ulaid, and it is a plausible supposition that Emhain Macha was still capital of the Ulaid when Armagh was founded. It may well be that Emhain Macha was overrun in the time of Patrick himself; it may be that Patrick moved east into the diminished area which was to be held by the Ulaid in the historic period. At any rate, Armagh, from some date very early in its

[27] *Bk Arm.*, 23a.

[28] Thus, in the *Life* of Ailbhe (Plummer, *Vitae SS. Hib.*, I, 46), he is brought together with Ibor and Patrick at Cashel (par. xxiv) and with Brigid at Kildare (par. xxvi), while in the *Life* of Declan (Plummer, *Vitae SS. Hib.*, II, 32), he works out, again at Cashel, spheres of influence with Patrick, Ailbhe, Ciaran of Saighir, and Ibor (par. xviii).

[29] Walker, *S. Columbani Opera.*

history, instead of being at the centre of a great and powerful kingdom, was situated in a territory of political obscurity and unimportance.[30]

Yet its connection with Patrick appears not to have been challenged, and the historical kings of the Ulaid maintained a connection with ecclesiastical Armagh. The church did possess relics, and important ones. According to the *Book of the Angel* it had relics of Peter, Paul, Laurence and Stephen. These have been discussed at some length by Professor Carney in his book on *The Problem of St Patrick*.[31] A secondary entry in Irish (quoting the *Book of Cuanu*) in the Annals of Ulster records how relics of Patrick were revealed by an angel to Columba, who distributed them to Down, Armagh and Iona.[32] The existence of some such story by the beginning of the ninth century is confirmed by a reference in the *Book of Armagh*.[33] Tírechán too, in the seventh century, mentions a distributed group of relics which he himself had seen in the church of Patrick in Armagh, in the church of Elphin and in the church of Bishop Sacellus, at Basilick.[34]

The relics were backed by a mass of hagiographical material compiled from the seventh century onwards. The great dossier of this material is of course the early ninth-century *Book of Armagh*—we are not here concerned with the later elaboration of the Patrick legend or the later history of Armagh. The *Book of Armagh* collection, as is well known, includes a shortened version of the *Confession*, a collection of notes on Patrick's journeys made in the late seventh century by Bishop Tírechán (a man from the west of Ireland) at the instance of Bishop Ultan of Ardbraccan, an account of Patrick by Muirchú written at the end of the seventh century under the sponsorship of Aed of Slébte, and a miscellany of notes and jottings, including the *Book of the Angel*. This material is well known, especially since it has been much discussed in the literature on St Patrick.

One of the interesting features of the work of both Muirchú and Tírechán is that although they make use of the *Confession* as a source, they have in fact no interest in the real St Patrick or understanding of him. They are concerned to tell a dramatic and interesting story in the heroic vein and to display Patrick as an invincible wonder-worker whose malediction is as powerful as his blessing: a dangerous enemy and a mighty friend. Loegaire has been chosen as the king who figures in the most dramatic part of both works, the confron-

[30] This was probably a disability in its early years, but it was probably in later times an advantage not to be too closely connected with any one branch of a powerful dynastic grouping.
[31] Carney, *St Patrick*, 46.
[32] *A.U.*, *s.a.* 553.
[33] *Bk Arm.*, 15a.
[34] *Bk Arm.*, 22b.

tation of the new faith with the old heathendom at Tara, but in these saga-like parts of the narrative details from secular tales, biblical history and early Christian story-telling have been freely drawn upon, and the *dramatis personae*—indeed the whole Tara setting—are just as likely to have been borrowed for the occasion. There are perhaps some distorted reflections of the seventh-century political scene in the accounts of Patrick's dealings with the ancestors of kings who were contemporary with the writers, but essentially what we have here is simply a marvellous story. There are in both accounts passages which show a somewhat more serious effort to retail traditions collected about Patrick's work, and evidence of an attempt to reconstruct his early life. But for the purpose of the present essay the main interest of the material is the light it sheds on the seventh-century situation.

Of the two, the work usually referred to as the *Breviarium* of Tírechán is generally regarded as the earlier. A scribal or editorial introductory note ascribes this work to Tírechán, pupil or fosterling of Bishop Ultán of Ardbraccan,[35] and this appears to be confirmed by the text, although the name of the writer does not occur in it. The text may be accepted therefore as being in the main a work of the late seventh century, but some caution is necessary. Some interpolation can be demonstrated, and the work has no clear ending but tails off in a series of short notes and cryptic passages whose date is uncertain. In the main text there are a few explicit citations from earlier works and one or two passages, differing in style from their context, which appear to have been quoted, but without acknowledgment, from earlier works.

Tírechán's narrative is divided into two parts, the first of which begins without preamble. At its close we are told: 'here ends the first book, completed in the territory of the Uí Néill'.[36] The second book has an introduction, or rather several introductions, the first of which tells us that it was completed *in regionibus Connact*. Then we are told that the first book concerned what was done in 'your territory'— that is in the territory of the Uí Néill—and it is indicated that the material in it was well known, in contrast to the material in the second book.

There follows a passage which is of special interest here:

Cor autem meum cogitat in me de Patricii dilectione, quia uideo dissertores et archiclocos et milites Hiberniae quod odio habent paruchiam Patricii, quia substraxerunt ab eo quod ipsius erat. Timentque quoniam si quaereret heres Patricii paruchiam illius, potest pene totam insolam sibi reddere in paruchiam, quia Deus dedit illi totam insolam per anguelum domini. Et legem domini

[35] *Bk Arm.*, 17b.
[36] *Bk Arm.*, 21b.

docuit illis, et baptismo Dei babtitzauit illos, et crucem Christi indicauit et resurrectionem eius nuntiuit. Sed familiam eius non dilegunt, quia non licet iurare contra eum et super eum et de eo, et non lignum contra mitti; quia ipsius sunt omnia primitiuae aeclessiae Hiberniae. Sed iuratur a se omne quod iuratur.

The passage is difficult and probably corrupt. The following is a tentative translation.

My heart is heavy within me from love of Patrick, since I see that bards and satirists and nobles of Ireland hate his paruchia, because they have taken from him what is his. And they are afraid, since if the heir of Patrick were to demand his paruchia, almost the whole island might be surrendered to him as his, for God, through the angel of the Lord, gave him the whole island. And he taught them the law of the Lord, and he baptised them with the baptism of God, and he showed Christ's cross and announced his resurrection. But they do not love his community, for it is not lawful to swear against him or to overswear him or to swear from him, or to cast lots against him, since all the primitive churches of Ireland are his. But his oath overswears all oaths.

Here the precedence of Armagh is expressed in terms of the legal status of Patrick, or his successor.[37] Two points of interest to note are, firstly, that it is secular powers who are condemned for the state into which Armagh has fallen, and, secondly, that *all* the primitive churches are claimed for Patrick.

In the book which follows, Tírechán describes Patrick's journeys west of the Shannon. In fact, as is clear from internal evidence in the text, he is describing his own journeys in search of early churches, writing up his notes in the evenings. Intermingled with legends about Patrick he gives us vivid glimpses of the state of the primitive churches in his time, some of them virtually reduced to the care of a part-time priest or, as one passage would suggest, to the care of a lay family. He occasionally protests where churches have been taken over by monastic federations (Iona and Clonmacnoise being the chief offenders), makes reference now and then to the 'recent plagues' and their effects, and once or twice tells a story which implies that there were missionaries working in some areas *before* St Patrick. On the whole it appears to be a reasonably honest, if somewhat gossipy and gullible, account, clearly of little value as evidence for St Patrick's work. In a story of the resurrection of a giant, we are told that he had been killed exactly one hundred years earlier. For Tírechán or his informant a century was a sufficient measure of antiquity to bring the story into the realm of the fabulous.

Tírechán has forewarned us of his prejudice: wherever he can find an ancient church he will claim it for Patrick. His narrative is fairly

[37] The meaning of the legal terms is briefly discussed by Binchy, 'Patrick and his biographers', 62.

detailed and circumstantial as it rambles to and fro in the west from the Shannon to the Erne. At times it convinces us that Tírechán has collected a genuine tradition or folktale about Patrick; more often that he himself has introduced Patrick into a tradition which concerns some other missionary. Then there is a fairly hasty summary of the eastward journey across Ulster to Armagh, then an even more hasty summary, reading very like an afterthought or addition, bringing Patrick south to Cashel. By this stage the work is so scrappy that it is impossible to be certain where the work of Tírechán ends. There is one item of considerable interest towards the end, where it is mentioned, quite casually, that Patrick ordained one Victoricus bishop of Armagh and founded a great church for him.[38] This may possibly be a garbled version of the story, found elsewhere,[39] that Patrick's 'angel' Victor (a legendary conflation of the unnamed angel who indicated to Patrick in a vision that he should flee from his captivity and the named man whom he saw in a dream bringing letters from Ireland) pointed out the site of Armagh to him.

Muirchú's account, a collection of legends and saga-like stories about Patrick, tells us less about the seventh-century situation. He gives an account of the founding of Armagh which suggests that Patrick himself spent some time there, but the account of Patrick's death clearly implies that Patrick had by then moved on from Armagh. The death-story, in fact, is a legend to account for the absence of Patrick's grave from Armagh.

But the *Book of Armagh* collection does not exhaust the Armagh documentation of this period. The supporters of Armagh went on from hagiography to attempt something more nearly resembling history: for the early section of our annals is in large part an 'Armagh document' in this sense.

There is now general agreement that our early annals, as we have them, are the result of an initial compilation early in the eighth century, *circa* 730–40.[40] In other words, up to about A.D. 735, the annals are not annals, but a synthetic reconstruction which may or may not be based in part on true annalistic material. Our manuscripts, of course, are all much later than this, and show the work of many redactors. There were not simply scribes who transcribed, but scholars (often good scholars) who edited, corrected, revised, and added footnotes (which of course they did not put in as footnotes but embodied in the text). But a good deal of the material before 735 is

[38] *Bk Arm.*, 30a.

[39] E.g., in Muirchú's account. See the discussion in Carney, *St Patrick*, 164.

[40] See T. F. O'Rahilly, *Early Irish History and Mythology*, Dublin 1946, 235; S. Mac Airt (ed. and trans.) *The Annals of Inisfallen*, Dublin 1951, xvi–xxii; J. Carney, *Studies in Irish Literature and History*, Dublin 1951, 363; Chadwick, *Studies in the Early British Church*, 57, 117.

common to the main collections of annals and shows a common source. By this date there were copies of foreign chronicles and histories in Ireland, and these were used in part as model, in part as framework, for the Irish compilation. Furthermore there are many indications that the place of compilation was Bangor.

It needs only a glance at the annals for the fifth century to see how large the Patrician entries bulk in them, and throughout the pre-compilation period the Armagh record is, in annalistic terms, full. In this sense, the earliest section of our annals is an Armagh document, and it serves the same purpose as the other Armagh documents. What kinds of sources did the compilers use?

They produced in fact two compilations, the first a world chronicle borrowed from external sources with Irish pseudo-historical material fitted in at convenient intervals, so that we get the dates of an interesting collection of events, such as the death of Cormac mac Airt or the birth of Cú Chulainn assigned their due place in world history; the second a chronicle from the early fifth century onward, in which the external chronicles continue to be used as a framework and careful attention has been given to the reconstruction of the chronology of Irish events of three centuries. The secular Irish events fitted into this framework, drawn from the Irish secular learning, must have been, like the prehistory from which that tradition does not distinguish them, essentially dateless: they can only have been provided with dates by synchronism with ecclesiastical events—and such synchronisms must often have been quite speculative and artificial. It has been shown that Paschal cycles figure in the ecclesiastical records[41] and it has been suggested that important names and events would have been noted on the paschal tables kept in the churches for practical purposes, and that it is from these that the early annals ultimately derive.

The Annals of Ulster may preserve in the form of the obits a reflection of the various native ecclesiastical sources from which the compilation was made. There is a standard convention, which has previously been noted, by which secular obits are recorded with the formula *mors* followed by the genitive of the name, while an ecclesiastical obit is generally recorded with a different formula. In the Annals of Ulster there is a variety of these. The following forms occur: *quies, quievit*; *mors, moritur, mortuus est*; *pausa, pausatio, etc.*; *dormitatio, etc.*; *obiit, obitus*. When these are analysed it is found that they fall into groups broadly corresponding to particular regions or federations of churches. The compiler, in other words, has fairly regularly copied the particular formula favoured by his exemplar. The formulae with *quies* and *quievit* relate to the missionary churches

[41] O'Rahilly, *loc. cit.*

and Armagh; *obiit, obitus* to Iona and Britain; *mors* to Bangor; the *pausa* and *dormitatio* variants to the south—probably Clonmacnoise. While there is no absolute consistency we can, by this test, group in a broad way the sources which the compiler used. The variation ceases at *circa* 735, and the Bangor formula prevails thereafter for some years. This serves us as a crude indicator to isolate the group of source materials which is likely to be associated with Armagh. It includes references to a number of churches in the north, especially in the north-east, and in Louth and north Leinster (the modern province). It tends to dominate the earliest part of the historical record.

The real starting date for this period is A.D. 431, the date of the mission of Palladius, derived from Prosper's *Chronicle*. This was the first date in Irish history available to the compiler, as it is to us. But he had no information to add to it. He could say nothing further about Palladius, and the next event he knew to have happened was the arrival of Patrick, for which no date was available. To supply one he devised a schematised chronology and synchronism, as follows:

431 Palladius;
432 Patrick arrives; 4th year of Loegaire;
433 Patrick converts the Irish; 5th year of Loegaire.

It is an open question whether the 'compiler' of this scheme was the annalistic compiler of *circa* 735 or an earlier chronologist, for we have parallel texts in the Annals of Inisfallen[42] and at the beginning of Tírechán's *Breviarium.*[43] The computation in Tírechán may well be, not the work of that writer, but an editorial 'footnote' (it interrupts the narrative) added in the eighth century in the course of transmission of the text before it assumed the form in which we have it in the ninth-century *Book of Armagh*. On the whole it seems more likely that the compilation belongs to the second, eighth-century, phase of Armagh documentation. At any rate the highly schematic nature of the chronology is clearly shown by the plain statement in both the Annals of Inisfallen and Tírechán that Patrick achieved the conversion of Ireland in 433.

This neat scheme, however, led the compiler into difficulties. The awkward Palladian date of 431, coming from a source outside Ireland, must have brought him back much farther than any of his genuine written sources in Ireland might reasonably be expected to go, and after he had fitted Patrick in at 432 and 433 we may surmise that he was at a loss. The mid-fifth century is padded with vague Patrician entries, and of course with the confusion of Patrician dates which has caused so much discussion in recent years. But the vacuum

[42] *Ann. Inisf.* (ed. Mac Airt), 45, 57. The scheme in *Ann. Inisf.* is concealed in the edition by the break made by the editor between the pre-Patrician and post-Patrician entries.

[43] *Bk Arm.*, 17b.

had to be filled somehow, and events or pseudo-events were spaced out through the fifth and sixth centuries to fill it. Some of them have the ring of the chronicler's desperation about them—*Patricius in Christi doctrina floruit*—while some seem to have a muffled contact with reality.

The obits of the heads of the church of Armagh are found in orderly and unbroken sequence from St Patrick on. What kinds of records had Armagh to provide this? Here we must refer to another text, existing in four manuscripts, the earliest of which is the late twelfth-century *Book of Leinster*. This is a list of the successors of Patrick, and it has been studied by Lawlor and Best.[44] They showed that the list as we have it dates from the eleventh century. Carney, who made use of the list in his study of St Patrick,[45] has been criticised for using so late and obviously fictitious a source, and indeed the list is unlikely to throw much light on the fifth century. But it gives the lengths of tenure of office of the coarbs of Patrick, which can also, of course, be calculated from the dates given in the Annals of Ulster. It emerges that the two sources are not independent, diverging only for a period in the late sixth century. There is internal evidence in the list of coarbs that it was compiled from the diptychs on which were recorded the names of those for whom prayers were offered at Mass. These, not paschal tables, were the sources for the Armagh obits in the Annals of Ulster, and this helps to explain some puzzling features in the list.

For, especially when the other missionary churches agreed to give full acknowledgment to the priority and precedence of Armagh, Patrick was believed to have founded many churches, and so he would have had successors elsewhere than in Armagh. There is indeed a strong suspicion that some of the early part of the list (as incorporated in the annals) derives from the names of heirs of Patrick gathered in the seventh-century period of Patrician collecting which has been examined above, and perhaps thereafter preserved on the altar of Armagh. Of the first four or five names, suspicion certainly attaches to those of Secundinus (of Dunshaughlin), Benignus (of Kilbennan?), Iarlath (of Tuam?), and Cormac (of Trim?). Dubtach and Ailill are doubled. David (in the Annals of Ulster only) is almost certainly an error (for Fiachra, recorded in the other sources here) arising perhaps from confusion with some reference to David of Wales.

Two tentative conclusions emerge: first, that we may have a number of intruders filling up the intolerable vacuum created by an expanded chronology at the beginning of our annals; second, that Armagh had virtually no authentic records of its own early history.

[44] H. J. Lawlor and R. I. Best, 'The ancient list of the coarbs of Patrick', *Proceedings of the Royal Irish Academy*, xxxv, section C, 316.
[45] Carney, *St Patrick*, 173.

No conscious falsification by Armagh or Bangor is necessarily implied, although this may have taken place.

A comparison of the Annals of Ulster with the Annals of Tigernach leads to further doubts about the chronological system at the beginning of the annals. The Annals of Ulster has A.D. dates in the main hand, which left the ferials blank. These were filled in by a later hand. The whole chronicle is the culmination of a long period of careful medieval chronological work and revision. It is not to be tested by the dates of external events, for the chronology is based on these. The Annals of Tigernach, a badly botched transcript, has ferials for the period to A.D. 735 which so consistently disagree with the Annals of Ulster (this disagreement being masked in the published edition by the editor's provision of A.D. dates derived from the Annals of Ulster) that they cannot wholly be the result of mistranscription. There are long runs of ferials, however, in the earlier sixth century which would be correct for dates generally about ten to fifteen years later than the Annals of Ulster, and these are perhaps a relic of an earlier stage of the struggle by the annalistic redactors to make sense of a recalcitrant chronology. At any rate, there appears to be enough evidence to suggest that the emergence at an early date of a historiography serving Armagh and the cult of Patrick raised problems which have distorted the whole chronology of the early annals.

To sum up briefly the somewhat speculative conclusions which have been reached, it seems that Armagh from shortly after its foundation suffered vicissitudes which left it in a sorry state throughout most of the sixth century—declining perhaps from the fall of Emhain into an obscurity saved from being total only by the reputation of its founder, and perhaps by the irredentist sentiment of the Ulaid. Even though the memory of Patrick grew fainter with the passage of time, his name and reputation were not forgotten, but were sufficient in themselves to serve as a base on which his chief church (if it was that) might be rebuilt. The traditions of the fifth century, of the Church of Romans ministering to barbarians, were preserved not at Armagh itself, which was possibly monastic at the beginning of the seventh century, but in other churches in the midlands. Yet when these churches found it necessary to seek a bulwark against the encroachments of monastic establishments, it was only through Patrick, and hence Armagh, that they could achieve this. Their efforts to provide documentation for their new counter-monastic federation (soon itself to be monastic in character) led to the production of a learned pseudo-history which provides us with more than a century of ecclesiastical pseudo-annals. They should be read in this light.

English Monks and Irish Reform in the Eleventh and Twelfth Centuries[1]

Denis Bethell

Of all the many unexplored problems which constitute the challenge, excitement and difficulty of Irish medieval history, particularly of native Irish medieval history, Irish Church reform in the eleventh and twelfth centuries is perhaps the easiest for the amateur to approach and study. In a period when most writing came from, and was preserved in, churches and monasteries, the subject had a peculiar interest for those who were writing and preserving records. It was a period when Irishmen themselves wrote much: though what interested them then seems not to have been the present, but the past. This was the age of the great compilations of early literature, of laws and genealogies, of the writing of the history of Ireland's struggle with the Vikings, or the lives of long dead saints. It is true that some native writings on the reform survive to us, but these are slight and few, and for the most important period there is a great lacuna in the annals. For this reason, and because of the great destruction of so many native Irish records, Church reform is easier to deal with in the long, comparatively neglected, period of Irish history which lies between the battle of Clontarf in 1014 and the Norman invasion of 1169 because, of all the important events in that important period, it alone attracted foreign commentators. Finally, Fr Gwynn has built a whole series of distinguished articles,[2] shortly to be published as a

[1] This paper was originally read at a seminar held by Professor F. J. Byrne in University College, Dublin. I am most grateful to him for comments, and for lending me the text of his unpublished *Thomas Davis* lecture on twelfth century Ireland; to Rev. Professor A. Gwynn S.J. for allowing me to see the revised text of his collected articles (shortly to appear with the Oxford University Press); to Rev. Professor F. X. Martin O.S.A. for comments and the loan of offprints, and to Dr K. Hughes for reading this paper in manuscript form and commenting on it.

[2] For a list see *Medieval Studies presented to Aubrey Gwynn S.J.*, ed. J. Watt, J. Morrall and F. X. Martin, Dublin 1961, 502–7.

collection, upon the foundations laid by Archbishop Ussher[3] and Professor Kenney,[4] and has made brilliant summaries of all that he has written in his *History of the diocese of Killaloe*[5] and in the section on *The twelfth century reform* in the *History of Irish catholicism*.[6]

A general view of the work which has been done would result, I think, in the conclusion that two great tasks remain. First, that the concentration has so far been on the reformers rather than on what was reformed, and that the native, conservative, tradition still awaits its historian; and that the major task in this field lies in a fuller exploration of Irish hagiography. Second, that despite a great deal of light which has been thrown on the politics of this period by Fr Ryan,[7] the political implications of the reform have been missed and greatly require clarification. This paper will do neither: it is the work of an amateur in Irish history, and pursues the easier task of following where Fr Gwynn has led.

Both Fr Gwynn and Fr Ryan (in a most useful series of notes which he used to issue to his students at University College, Dublin),[8] in their general surveys of the reform can be said to divide the history of the reform under four main headings: *first*, the Irish contacts with the continent in the pre-reform era, the presence of Irish monks in Flanders, Lorraine and Germany, and Irish contacts with Rome; *second*, the foundation of the see of Dublin in the 1020s or 1030s, and the relationship of the bishops of Dublin, Waterford and Limerick with the archbishop of Canterbury; *third*, the holding of the great national reform synods—the synods of Killaloe in 1050, of Cashel in 1101, of Rath Breasail in 1111, of Kells in 1152 and of Cashel in 1172—as the result of which a diocesan system was proposed for Ireland for the first time in 1111, and an independent hierarchy was set up by the legate Cardinal John Paparo in 1152; *fourth* the arrival in Ireland of the new regular orders, the Cistercians and the Canons Regular. The concern of this paper is with the first two of these, with Irish contacts overseas before the reform and Irish contacts with the

[3] Especially in his collection of texts, *Veterum Epistolarum Hibernicarum Sylloge*, Dublin 1632, reprinted in *The Whole Works of the Most Rev. James Ussher*, ed. C. R. Elrington and J. H. Todd, Dublin 1847–1864, IV, 383–573.

[4] J. F. Kenney, *The Sources for the Early History of Ireland, Ecclesiastical*, Columbia 1929, reprinted Dublin 1966.

[5] The first two chapters of D. F. Gleeson, *A History of the Diocese of Killaloe*, Dublin 1962.

[6] Ed. P. J. Corish, II, chap. 1, Dublin 1968.

[7] 'The O'Briens in Munster after Clontarf', *North Munster Antiquarian Journal*, 2 (1941), 141–52, 3 (1942), 1–52, 3 (1943), 189–202, and *Toirdhealchach O'Conchubhair* (O'Donnell lecture, Dublin 1966). For further references, and a survey of recent work in the field see F. J. Byrne, 'Thirty Years Work in Irish History: II, Ireland before the Norman Invasion', *Irish Historical Studies*, 16 (1968), 1–14.

[8] For another brief survey of the reform and a valuable history of the earlier Irish Church see K. Hughes, *The Church in Early Irish Society*, London 1966.

English Church. Further clarification of the work of the synods, of the papal legates who held them and of the new orders of the twelfth century may now indeed be said to wait upon the reconsideration and exploration of native Irish Church history and politics mentioned above as the next major step in this whole subject.

First of all then, the question of Irish contacts with Rome and the continent. Dr Hughes has shown how the tradition of Irish pilgrimage abroad changed during the ninth century: 'Now they came either on a Roman style pilgrimage *ad limina*, or they settled for long periods under patronage in some fixed hospices which Carolingian legislation attempted to maintain in efficient working order so that pilgrims need not be a drain on diocesan funds'.[9] The *Scotti vagantes* still wandered, but in a more controlled sort of way. These scholars had their period of greatest influence in the Carolingian and episcopal courts of the ninth century, but in the tenth century they were still to be found all over the Frankish empire, and particularly in that empire's cultural centres: Lotharingia—that is, Ghent, Liège, Metz, Toul, Verdun; the great bishoprics and abbeys of the Main valley, in particular Würzburg, but also at Mainz and Fulda; in the great Bavarian episcopal cities and abbeys, especially Regensburg, Passau, and Salzburg; in the great Alpine abbeys, St Gall, Reichenau, Einsiedeln. The tenth and eleventh centuries saw indeed the foundation of wholly new communities on the continent, at Waulsort in the Ardennes by St Cadroe of Armagh in 946, which was followed by his making an Irish foundation at Metz in the 970s.[10] At the same period we have a description of a crowd of Irish priests who were kept by St Gerard of Toul, who died in 994. Gero, archbishop of Cologne, brought Irish monks to St Pantaleon's 'Cologne' a little later. This movement seems to have had its main links with northern Ireland.

In the late eleventh and early twelfth centuries there was another burst of foundations. In 1052 the young Marianus Scotus became a monk at Moville, Co. Down. In 1056 he went overseas to Germany, to Cologne. In 1058 he left Cologne for Fulda, and in 1059 he was ordained priest at Würzburg. Two months later he was solemnly walled up as an *inclusus*[11] at Fulda. In 1069 he moved to Mainz, and

[9] Kathleen Hughes, 'The Changing Theory and Practice of Irish Pilgrimage', *Journal of Ecclesiastical History* 2 (1960), 146; cf. her article 'On an Irish Litany of Pilgrim Saints compiled c. 800', *Analecta Bollandiana*, 77 (1959), 305–331.

[10] Add to previous references in Kenney and Gwynn, B. de Gaiffier, 'Notes sur le culte des St Clement de Metz et St Caddroe', *Analecta Bollandiana*, 85 (1967), 21–44.

[11] On the duties of an *inclusus*, which included writing and teaching, see B. MacCarthy, *The Codex Palatino—Vaticanus No. 830* (Royal Irish Academy Todd Lecture Series, III, 1892), 5–6.

there, in 1082[12] he died, after compiling a valuable world chronicle which was much used by the influential twelfth century chroniclers Sigebert of Gembloux and 'Florence' of Worcester. In the old tradition of northern Ireland he was a skilful computist, and his work on computistics and chronology (which he prefixed to his chronicle) was much used and excerpted by contemporary chronologists, in particular by Robert, the Lotharingian bishop of Hereford and close friend of St Wulfstan of Worcester.

In 1067 another Marianus, from Donegal, set out on pilgrimage to Rome. His route, significantly enough, lay through Germany and he ended up at Bamberg, where he and his companions spent a whole year in the priory of the Michelsberg. He then moved to Regensburg, where he founded a priory, St Peter's, and where he died in 1088. In Regensburg in 1111 another abbey of Irish monks was founded at St James. From St James, under its third abbot, Christian MacCarthy, further foundations were made—at Würzburg (1134), Nuremburg (1140), Constance (1142), Erfurt (1150), Vienna (1155) and Eichstadt (1183). By the early twelfth century the connections of these houses were probably closer with Munster.

Two reflections occur after reading Fr Gwynn's work on this subject which I have thus just rapidly summarised. First, that the contact of Irish monks was with what had been the centres of Carolingian Europe, and what were by the mid twelfth century the rather conservative intellectual centres of the German empire. We have the most positive evidence that these monks did not get on well with the Cluniac reformers. Fr Gwynn's paper 'Irish monks and the Cluniac reform'[13] is in some ways a misnomer—it ought to be 'Irish monks *versus* the Cluniac reform'.[14] At Verdun the young Richard of St Vannes tried out his vocation under Abbot Fingen. He found the experience thoroughly unsatisfactory and migrated to Cluny. Abbot Odilo of Cluny sent him back to Verdun; there once again he was going to run away when a certain holy woman interfered and told Abbot Fingen. But on Fingen's death he was elected abbot, and proceeded to remodel his abbey on Cluniac lines. We have the same picture in the fight between Archbishop Pilgrim of Cologne (1021–26), who was an ardent pro-Cluniac, and the Irish monks at Cologne.

Not only were these Irish monks disapproved of by the Cluniacs, but they seem to have been pro-imperialist. Fr Gwynn says: 'Those

[12] Wilhelm Wattenbach and Robert Holtzmann, *Deutschlands Geschichtsquellen im Mittelalter, Die Zeit der Sachsen und Salier*, II, ed. F. J. Schmale, Darmstadt 1967, 447, note 13, 'Waitz: 1082 oder 1083. Da die Chronik mit dem 17 April 1082 endet, dürfte dieses jahr wahrscheinlich sein'.

[13] *Studies*, 29 (1940), 409–30.

[14] *Ibid.*, 428: 'It is obvious that men like Fingen and Elias were fighting a losing battle against the triumphant forces of Cluniac Benedictinism'.

who have read the last section of the world chronicle of Marianus Scotus will remember that this Irish *inclusus* was a steadfast supporter of Gregory VII'.[15] With all respect, a reading of Marianus will not lead to so strong a conclusion. Marianus died three years before Gregory VII and passed no judgement on his pontificate. Under 1077 we have the words: 'At a council of twenty four bishops, and of many abbots and clergy held at Worms in March in the presence of King Henry it was decreed that no one should pay attention to the ban of Pope Hildebrand and that he was no pope. The pope excommunicated the king with his followers in Lent for three causes, the infamy of his sins, his alliance with simoniacs and the division of the Church. Hence in this apparently just cause—*causa quasi justa*—the princes of the kingdom opposed the king as if he were excommunicate—*quasi excommunicato*, trying to drive him from his kingship'.[16] This is as near as Marianus got to a judgement; otherwise he is pure chronicler. It may be observed that the continuation of his chronicle which came to Worcester (via St Alban's, Mainz)[17] and which was copied there by 'Florence' was violently anti-Gregorian: 'The apostolic pope Hildebrand in his death agonies called to himself one of the cardinals whom he greatly loved, and confessed that he had greatly sinned in his pastoral duty and had incited anger and hatred againt the human race at the direct suggestion of the devil. He sent his confessor to the emperor and the whole Church to beg forgiveness and he put on his vestments and denounced and dissolved all his bans against the emperor'.[18] It would be hard to find a better piece of anti-Gregorian wish fulfilment. As is well known, David the Scot of Würzburg accompanied Henry V to Rome in 1110, and wrote a history of his expedition against Paschal II which William of Malmesbury describes as 'more written to please the emperor than

[15] 'Ireland and Würzburg in the Middle Ages', *Irish Ecclesiastical Record*, 78 (1952), 405; cf. 'Ireland and Rome in the Eleventh Century', *ibid.*, 57 (1941), 213–232; 232: 'This Irish exile was a devoted supporter of Gregory VII'.

[16] 1077 (1099) 'In concilio 24 episcoporum, abbatum multorumque clericorum Vurmatia mense Martii facto, presente Heinrico rege, decretum est, ut bannum Illibrandi papae nullus curaret, nec papa esset. Papa vero regem cum suis in quadragesima tribus excommunicavit causis, ob infamiam peccatorum suorum, et unitatem suam cum simoniacis, et hanc scisuram ecclesiae inter papam et alios. Inde causa quasi justa primates regni quasi excommunicato contradicunt regi, temptantes eum projecire regno.' *Mariani Scotti Chronicon*, ed. D. G. Waitz in *Monumenta Germaniae Historica, Scriptores* V, Hanover 1844, 561.

[17] Wattenbach and Holtzmann, ed. Schmale, 449.

[18] 'Apostolicus papa Hildebrandus in extremis suis ad se vocavit unum de 12 cardinalibus, quem diligebat multum, et confessus est . . . valde se peccasse in pastorali cura . . . suadenteque diabolo contra genus humanum odium et iram incitasse . . . Tunc misit . . . confessorem suum ad imperatorem et ad totam ecclesiam ut optarent illi indulgentiam . . . et tam cito induebat se angelicam vestem et dimisit ac dissolvit vincula bannorum omnium suorum imperatori . . . Teste Moguntino archiepiscopo.' *Maria nus, Continuatio*, ed. Waitz, *ed. cit.*, 563.

accords with the impartiality of history'.[19] In 1112 Henry V gave Regensburg the privilege of *Reichsunmittelbarkeit*.[20] Indeed it would be most surprising if the Irish monks were not imperialist. Mainz, Bamberg, Regensburg '*im kaisertreuen Bayern*'[21] were imperialist centres; Bishop Gunther of Bamberg with his love of heroic tales and the vernacular, his pomp and his pilgrimages[22] seems, like Archbishop Siegfried of Mainz, to have been precisely the type of bishop among whom the Irish would find patrons.

Now in this area of continental contact and sympathies the world of these Irish monks was emphatically the world of the English monks of the tenth century reform, and therefore of the post-conquest communities of Evesham, Worcester, Glastonbury, Winchester and Canterbury, which also had to face strong French monastic disapproval after the conquest[23] and a definite attack by the Cluniacs in the 1120s and 1130s.[24] This indeed is what we might expect. St Dunstan was brought up by Irish scholars,[25] and his surviving classbook from Glastonbury contains Irish material.[26] Professor Finberg has recently reminded us of this, and plausibly suggested reasons for the establishment of the Irish there, and their responsibility for the Patrick and Brigid legends of Glastonbury.[27] Dunstan must certainly have met Irish scholars at the court of Athelstan.[28] St Cadroe went to see Archbishop Oda of Canterbury at Winchester on his way to the continent between 940 and 946.[29]

I have only examined the surviving manuscripts of one community of this period for Irish contacts: Worcester, where the Irish names of monks in the Durham *Liber Vitae*,[30] the Worcester origin of Bishop Patrick of Dublin,[31] the letters written to St Wulfstan by the Irish kings,[32] the survival of Gregory VII's letter to King

[19] Gwynn, 'Ireland and Würzburg', 404.
[20] *Ibid.*
[21] Wattenbach and Holtzmann, ed. Schmale, 548.
[22] *Ibid.*, 479–80: 'ein prachtliebendes Weltkind . . . ein Liebhaber der deutschen Heldensage': he accompanied Siegfried of Mainz to Jerusalem.
[23] M. D. Knowles, *The Monastic Order in England*, Cambridge, second edition, 1963, 111–119.
[24] See Denis Bethell 'Black Monks and Episcopal Elections in the 1120s' in the *English Historical Review*, 84 (1969), 673–98.
[25] *Memorials of St Dunstan*, ed. W. Stubbs, London 1874, 257.
[26] *St Dunstan's Classbook from Glastonbury*, ed. R. W. Hunt, *Umbrae Codicum Occidentalium* no. 4, Amsterdam 1961.
[27] H. P. R. Finberg, 'St Patrick at Glastonbury', *West Country Historical Studies*, Newton Abbot 1969, 70–89.
[28] J. Armitage Robinson, *The Times of St Dunstan*, Oxford 1923, 70 and elsewhere.
[29] Gwynn, 'Irish monks and the Cluniac Reform', 414–5.
[30] *Liber Vitae Dunelmensis*, ed. J. Stevenson, Surtees Society Vol. 13 (1841), 14.
[31] *The Writings of Bishop Patrick 1074–1084*, ed. A. Gwynn S.J., *Scriptores Latini Hiberniae* I, Dublin 1955, 1–7.
[32] *Vita Wulfstani*, ed. R. R. Darlington, *Camden Society*, 40 (1928), 59.

Toirdhealbhach Ua Briain in a Worcester manuscript,[33] all suggested that earlier contact might be strong. (So did the relics of St Wulfstan at Christchurch,[34] the discovery of a reliquary of Wulfstan in the High Street excavations,[35] and the miracles worked, admittedly on Anglo-Norman invaders, by St Wulfstan's body in King John's reign.)[36]

So indeed it turned out. At Worcester in the tenth and eleventh centuries copies were made of Bishop Duncaht's commentary on Martianus Capella,[37] Bishop Israel's work on metre,[38] of the Irish canon collection,[39] of the writings of St Patrick.[40] One might add the works of Pseudo-Augustine,[41] of Smaragdus,[42] Aethicus Ister,[43] and the Rithmimachia of a clerk of Würzburg[44]—one of those games of numbers which made Irish scholars popular at the court of Athelstan. If only our sources were fuller we should know more of the clerks who carried these texts, and the messengers who came to Worcester from Ireland via Bristol, Chester and Wales. Only one stray eleventh century reference tells us of the many Irish pilgrims at nearby Evesham,[45] while another tells of the poor wandering Irishman who murdered his benefactor, the abbot of Ramsey,[46] and another of the Irish traders who came to Cambridge to sell cloaks.[47] But everything leads us to think that there were many such callers, traders, pilgrims, teachers and intellectual pedlars. The works of

[33] MS. Cotton Claudius A I.

[34] *The Book of Obits and Martyrology of . . . Christ Church Dublin*, ed. J. C. Crosthwaite, Dublin, for the Irish Archaeological Society, 1844, 3.

[35] An ampulla lettered + IN b(=h) ONORE . SAN(c)TI WLSTANI, + INb(=h) ONORE . SAN(c)TE . MARIE . VIRGIN(i)S was found in the National Museum excavations at the High Street excavation in 1968 (Reg. No. NMI. 171: 3661). I owe this information to Mr Brendán Ó Ríordáin.

[36] *Vita Wulfstani*, 141–5, 154.

[37] Leland noted the 'Comment. Duncaht pontificis Hibern. super Martianum Capellam' at Worcester, of which a leaf is now to be found in B.M. MS Royal 15 A 33, a Worcester MS; see Kenney, 573 for further references.

[38] Worcester Cathedral MS Q 5, a handsome CX MS. On Israel see Gwynn 'Irish monks and the Cluniac Reform', 411–13. Also add to Kenney's references (610) for manuscripts of Bishop Israel's work on metre Bibliothèque Sainte Genevieve at Paris, MS 2049, f.118v–119.

[39] Bodleian MS Hatton 42, Corpus Christi College Cambridge MSS 265 and 279.

[40] B.M. MS Cotton Nero E I—the Worcester Passional.

[41] Bodleian MS Hatton 30.

[42] Bodleian MS Hatton 40, Worcester Cathedral MS F 91 (Expositio Libri Comitis, *Patrologia Latina*, 102).

[43] B.M. MS Cotton Vespasian B X.

[44] Bodleian MS Auct. F.1.9.

[45] *Chronicon Monasterii de Evesham*, ed. W. D. Macray, London 1863, 91.

[46] *Chronicon Abbatiae Rameseiensis*, ed. W. D. Macray, London 1886, 155.

[47] 'Quidam institores de Hybernia cum variis mercibus et sagis apud civitaculum que Grantebrygge nuncupatur, appulerunt et, expositis mercibus, contigit quod prefatus presbyter Leofstanus subduxisset saga eorum. Quod cum patefieret, petiit patrocinium civium'—in the time of King Edgar—*Liber Eliensis*, ed. E. O. Blake, *Camden Society* 92 (1962), 107.

Bede made pre-conquest monks always conscious of Ireland: the feasts of Patrick and Brigid were universal in their houses,[48] and the world of their learning was still that of Aldhelm and Boniface, the world of history, hagiography, games, grammatical puzzles, metres, ornamental cosmography, computistics and the monastic classics, high among them Smaragdus, with his devotional grammar.[49] Older scholars used to pronounce the end of Irish influence on English learning and devotion at the Synod of Whitby. Edmund Bishop throught he saw it waning in the early ninth century, but Dr Hughes has recently shown in her O'Donnell lectures how strong it then remained, by a study of Irish prayers and devotions in ninth and tenth century English prayerbooks. Its true epitaph was probably pronounced by William of Malmesbury in the twelfth century: 'The Irish today promise great things of their knowledge of language and grammar, but the truth is that they are less than safe guides to the formation of Latin words and the proper speaking of Latin'.[50]

On both sides of a pre-conquest England however there is every reason to feel that there was much contact between the two countries: on the West Saxon, Old English side in its great traditionalism and continued re-reading of the works of Bede, Aldhelm and the Irish scholars: on the Scandinavian-Danish side with the Norse court at Dublin, and the cities of the Ostmen in which Iceland and Ireland formed part of a single world. Both sides of course intermingled with each other, as they did in Ireland. Godwine's wife belonged to the house of Canute, and it will be remembered how often members of his house took refuge in Dublin, but his daughter was married to Edward the Confessor.

It is in the light of this that we should look at Irish contacts with the continent and with Rome. Both the areas of contact and the high period of pilgrimage were the same. English contacts with the continent in the pre-conquest period were above all with the great abbeys of the Rhine and Flanders.[51] It was that way that English trade went—English wool for German silver;[52] English princesses were married into the Saxon and Flemish royal houses. We find an

[48] F. Wormald, *English Benedictine Kalendars Before A.D. 1100. Vol. 1*, Henry Bradshaw Society 1932.

[49] On Smaragdus see Kenney, 543–4: J. Leclercq, *The Love of Learning and the Desire for God*, New York 1961, 52–4, and references there given. See also B. Bischoff, 'Muiredach Doctissimus Plebis — ein irische grammatiker des neunten jhrdts', *Mitteralterliche Studien*, Stuttgart 1967, II, 51–6.

[50] *Memorials of St Dunstan*, 257.

[51] P. Grierson, 'The Relations between England and Flanders before the Norman Conquest', *Transactions of the Royal Historical Society*, fourth series, 23 (1941), 71–113.

[52] P. H. Sawyer, 'The Wealth of England in the Eleventh Century', *ibid.*, fifth series, 15 (1965), especially 160–162.

English embassy at St Gall,[53] Anglo-Saxon glosses in St Gall manuscripts;[54] this shared contact may be exemplified by the English scribe Eadberct who in the ninth century copied a collection of the Irish canons for the St Gall library.[55] In the eleventh century England was obtaining her bishops and hagiographers from Lotharingia. Edward the Confessor's Normans are famous, but the Lotharingians were more important and numerous. The influence goes back at least to the time of Grimbald of St Bertin's in Alfred's reign, it was strengthened by St Dunstan's stay at Ghent, but became of major importance in Canute's reign with the appointment of Duduc to the bishopric of Wells. Other important Lorraine bishops were Leofric of Exeter, Giso of Wells and Hermann of Sherborne. Among lesser clergy may be mentioned the Lorraine canons of St Paul's, and Adelard of Liège whom Earl Harold placed in charge of his foundation of Holy Cross Waltham; among writers, the Encomiast of Queen Emma, Goscelin of St Bertin's, and Hermann of Lorraine, the author of the *Miracles of St Edmund*.[56]

Fr Gwynn has shown how the way to Rome for both Ostman and Irish kings was opened by the agreement which the Emperor Conrad brought about between Canute and Rudolf of Burgundy in 1028.[57] It opened too the high point of English pilgrimage there, including the pilgrimages of Harold and Tostig; this was the first time since the eighth century when we know of papal legates in the Severn valley. The common nature of Irish, Scottish and English pilgrimage at this period may be symbolised for us not by kings, but by an ordinary Irishman, the cripple Gillemichel, who, so Aelred of Rievaulx tells us, had made the pilgrimage to Rome six times, and then came to be cured of his ills by Edward the Confessor.[58] This high period of pilgrimage was precisely the era of the Lorraine popes. Now it was possible to be a supporter of Pope St Leo IX and not of Pope St Gregory VII. The contacts of Harold and of Archbishop Aldred of York with the imperial court are to be noted. So are those of Edward

[53] J. M. Clark, *The Abbey of St Gall as a Centre of Literature and Art*, Cambridge 1926, 64.

[54] N. R. Ker, *A Catalogue of Manuscripts containing Anglo-Saxon*, Oxford 1957, 477–81.

[55] Henry Bradshaw, *The Early Collection of Canons Known as the Hibernensis*, Cambridge 1893, 9.

[56] On the Lorrainers see F. Barlow, *The English Church 1000–1066. A Constitutional History*, London 1963, 82–4 and elsewhere; C. H. Talbot, 'The Liber Confortatorius of Goscelin of St Bertin', *Studia Anselmiana*, 37 (Rome 1955), *Analecta Monastica*, third series, 1–22; C. N. L. Brooke, 'The Composition of the Chapter of St Paul's, 1086–1163', *Cambridge Historical Journal*, 10 (1951), 122; *Encomium Emmae Reginae*, ed. A. Campbell, *Camden Society*, third series, 72, xix-xxiii.

[57] Gwynn, 'The Origins of the See of Dublin', *Irish Ecclesiastical Record*, 57 (1941), 97–112.

[58] *Patrologia Latina* 195, col. 744–5.

the Confessor: an imperial embassy came to congratulate him on his accession in 1043[59] and in 1049 Edward allied with the Emperor Henry III against the Count of Flanders.[60]

The note of these pilgrimages seems to be struck when we find Abbot Aelfstan of St Augustine's Canterbury magnificently received at Rome by the Emperor Henry III who asked him for a relic of St Augustine of Canterbury for the greater glory of the Empire.[61] The ties of the house of Godwin with Flanders are well known; and the presence of refugees in Lorraine after the conquest may explain the rumour reported by Lampert of Hersfeld that William the Conqueror was planning to attack Lorraine in 1074.[62]

Similarly it may be noted that the marriage of Matilda of Scotland to Henry I and the restoration of the Old English line to the throne brought about the *rapprochement* of the imperial and English courts and the marriage of the Emperor Henry V with the princess Matilda in 1109. Henry V specifically wrote to Queen Matilda to thank her effusively for promoting the alliance, and it may be noted that the letter survives at Bamberg.[63] Similarly the letter of the excited Burchard of Aachen reporting Henry V's success over Paschal II at the Ponte Mammolo survives at Worcester,[64] and 'Florence' of Worcester is a strongly imperialist writer.

Indications are slight but it can be suggested that Old English monks after the conquest were, like the continental Irish, pro-imperialist. Certainly Honorius of Autun says so, writing at Canterbury and Worcester in the early twelfth century: 'I have fixed my tent in Ethiopia, I live among scorpions, I am a confrater of dragons, and an acquaintance of ostriches',[65] a picturesque way of saying that no one shared his high Gregorian views. It is certain that the strongly Godwinist nunnery of Wilton made an appeal to the antipope Clement III[66] and with the thesis of this paper in view the presence

[59] K. J. Leyser, 'England and the Empire in the Early Twelfth Century', *Transactions of the Royal Historical Society*, fifth series, 10 (1960), 62.
[60] *Ibid.*
[61] 'Praestantissimus autem abbas Aelstanus Romam proficiscens, a praecellentissimo imperatore Henrico . . . magnifice suscipitur . . . piisimus princeps insistebat magnopere venerando abbati, quatenus illud tam preciosum decus Romani imperii, ac generis humani jam transferret, sibique aliquid tam sacrorum pignorum conferret.' Goscelin of St Bertin's, *Historia Translationis Sancti Augustini*, *Patrologia Latina* vol. 155, col. 31. The whole text deserves reading.
[62] Leyser, *art. cit.*, 61.
[63] *Ibid.*, 64.
[64] *Ibid.*, 78.
[65] 'En fratres sancti, cogitis me in Aethiopia figere tentorium (*Hab.* 3, 7) ut habitem in medio scorpionum (*Ezek.* 2, 6) et frater fiam draconum et socius strucionum (*Job* 30, 29)', *Offendiculum*, ed. I. Dieterich *Libelli de Lite*, III, ed. E. Duemmler, *Monumenta Germaniae Historica*, Hanover 1897, 38.
[66] F. Liebermann, 'Lanfranc and the Antipope', *English Historical Review*, 16 (1961), 329, 331.

of 'clerks of the Picts' at Wilton deserves mention.[67] Someone encouraged the antipope to write to Lanfranc and to speak of Gregory VII in terms of which Lanfranc strongly disapproved,[68] but which were no different from those used by the Worcester chronicler. Someone urged the imperial case to St Anselm.[69] The Canterbury community tended to be hostile to St Anselm and were inclined to see his struggle as a fuss about nothing.[70] Archbishop Ralph, his successor was much more as wax in their hands; he was accused of having made common cause with the Emperor in 1114 and stayed with him on his Roman journey in 1116.[71]

Fr Gwynn sees the stoppage of Irish pilgrimage to Rome after 1066 as the result either of the conquest of England or of the troubles of Gregory VII's pontificate.[72] Irish annalists do not mention the conquest but the Ostman kings gave shelter and aid to Godwin's sons. That there was some coolness is suggested by the Anglo-Saxon chronicle's remark that if William had lived a year longer he would have conquered Ireland. This may have been a blind; there is slightly more evidence that, if anything, William intended an expedition against Galicia in Spain.[73] There can be no doubt however that the Irish continued to come to England. For one thing, there was a good deal of trade. Muirchertach Ua Briain 'from some unknown cause', says William of Malmesbury, 'acted for a short time rather superciliously towards the English, but soon after on the

[67] *Patrologia Latina*, 155, col. 114–5.
[68] Liebermann, *art. cit.*
[69] Leyser, *art. cit.*, 73.
[70] R. W. Southern, *Saint Anselm and his Biographer*, Cambridge 1963, 236, 306; cf. the poem by Gilbert Crispin, Abbot of Westminster, begging him to return from a pointless exile (J. Armitage Robinson, *Gilbert Crispin, Abbot of Westminster*, Cambridge 1911, 22), which among other things accuses him of neglecting the Irish:

'Anglia tota,
gens populosa:
Scotia tota:
insula longe
longior illis,
gens numerosa,
sunt et Hiberni:
quando revisa
regna perampla
ista fuere?
nemo revisit:
annus et anni
praeteriere:
ergo timendum'

[71] 'William of Corbeil and the Canterbury-York Dispute', *Journal of Ecclesiastical History*, 19 (1968), 153 and 153 note 9.
[72] Gwynn, 'The Twelfth Century Reform', 2.
[73] *Historia Compostellana* in *Patrologia Latina* vol. 170, col. 1033. cf. M. Desfourneaux, *Les Francais en Espagne aux XIe et XIIe siècles*, Paris 1949, 194ff.

suspension of navigation and foreign trade, his insolence subsided'.[74] Irish ships certainly came to Chester and Bristol and, so William of Malmesbury says, to York.[75]

There were also intellectual contacts. Although the reputation of the Irish as teachers sank in the twelfth century, they were most important purveyors of romance and hagiography. It is in these two sorts of literature that we may hope to find most evidence of contact. Thus, to take a stray example, the prologue to the unprinted *Life of St Modwenna* of Burton-on-Trent by Geoffrey of Burton (abbot c.1114–1150) tells how he sent to Ireland for a manuscript Life of the saint: 'I sent many messengers to Ireland, and letters to a certain Irish bishop'.[76] The Life he received shows us that earlier an Irish writer of saints' lives, Conchubranus, had come to England with the opposite intention, to obtain English information on St Modwenna of Killeavy.[77] The result is a fantastic mixture

[74] *De Gestis Regum*, ed. W. Stubbs, London 1889, I, 484–5.

[75] *Gesta Pontificum*, ed. N. E. S. A. Hamilton, London 1870, 208, 'Naves a Germania et Hibernia venientes'.

[76] B.H.L. 2097. Geoffrey of Burton's Life survives in two MSS, B.M. MS Royal 15 B IV and Mostyn 260, now in the possession of Professor Wormald. An Anglo-Norman version in verse has been printed in an edition begun by the late Professor A. T. Baker, and completed by Dr Alexander Bell (*Anglo-Norman Texts* No. 7, Oxford 1947). The prologue was most kindly transcribed for me by Mr Christopher Hohler from the British Museum MS, f. 76: '*Incipit prefatio Gaufridi Abbatis Burtonie in vitam Sancte Modvenne virginis*. Diu desideravi estuans animo reperire aliquid certum de patria, de genere, de vita et virtutibus sanctissime virginis Modvenne; et multis vicibus ad ipsam quoque super hac re corde intento deprecatus sum, multoque studio vigilavi ut quererem. Nec cecidit in cassum labor meus, quia tandem contigit, eadem iuvante, ut quod quesieram, habundantius quam speravi, per Dei gratiam invenirem. Misi enim nec una vice legatos ubi forte indicatum est michi : misi literas ad quemdam episcopum in Hiberniam : sed et ipse, ut potui, curavi plurimos interrogare per Angliam, et tandem (MS, *tanta*), Deo administrante, inveni de illa per eius suffragium, partim hic, partim illic, quanta nec valui universa conscribere, neque ut tot essent illius (MS, *illa*) miracula potuerim antea vel aliquando cogitare. Codex siquidem de Hibernia michi allatus est, in quo fodi thesaurum absconditum, continentem divitias inestimabiles, et habentem in se preciosores cunctis opibus absque ulla comparatione virtutes. Set quoniam displicebat stilus et in locis aliquibus eiusdem libelli mixta erat quasi quidem inordinata confusio, materie autem ac veritate (MS, *veritatis*) auctoritas certissima et fundatissima est; sicut de mina per vigilantium multi studii laboriose metallum egeritur, ita etiam ex hoc codice et sermone (MS, *sermons*) Hyberniorum, non sine laboris sudore quam plurimo, de lingua barbara velud de abstrusis et abditis, patria, ergo, vita, habitus et conversatio, signa quoque beate virginis, docente nos divina gratia, in sequenti opusculo proferentur. Cetera vero, que, preter hunc codicem, non immerito superadicienda (MS, *aditientia*) putaveris, veracium valde virorum qui vel didicerunt a maioribus, vel ipsi viderunt atque affuerunt presentes, fidelissima atque probatissima narratione cognovi. Partem vero nos ipsi vidimus, unde et illa que videre nequivimus maiore securitate narramus. Accipite itaque me quicunque legeritis vitam huius sacratissime virginis sicut translatorem fundatissimum (MS *fundatissime*), nec tanquam mendaci ore commentatorem; alioquin tacere michi multo melius, quam falsitatum commenticia fabricare. Explicit Prefatio.'

[77] Conchubranus' Life was edited by M. Esposito, *Proceedings of the Royal Irish Academy*, 28, section C (1910), 202–51. See Kenney, 366–70.

of marvels and anachronisms, but it tells us of literary contact.

When the vast, largely unsifted, corpus of English twelfth century hagiography has been sorted and edited we may hope for more such instances. But it is significant that in so far as these can now be recovered that they point to contact in surroundings where Old English sympathies were strong.

First of all, the Scottish court. We know that there were Irish clergy at that court: we know that King Alexander of Scotland commissioned verses on the Life of St Columba.[78] We know that it was through the medium of that court that Irish hagiography reached the monks of Durham. 'We have heard some of the greatest men, and not a few Irish bishops perorate on the Irish birth of St Cuthbert . . . St Malachy told King David of Scotland many things on this matter, and Maurilius his successor afterwards confidently asserted it and Eugenius bishop of Ardmore discussed it more exactly, and so did two other bishops whose names have been forgotten, and so did their companions, priests and clerks at various times'.[79] It is particularly interesting that Irish hagiography reached Durham as well through the medium of the family of Aelred of Rievaulx,[80] King David's steward, the boy who spent too much of his youth listening to the tales of King Arthur. For Aelred was the writer of the work on Henry II's descent from the Confessor,[81] the man in whom Irish contacts, the Scottish court, Angevin politics, the Cistercian order and the Old English past all formed an amalgam which is important for understanding what happened in the 1140s. It also explains the run of Irish material and interests through the northern houses which were influenced by Rievaulx and Durham, so that we find a letter of Gilbert of Limerick's in a Sawley manuscript which

[78] Kenney, 434.

[79] The 'Irish' Life of St Cuthbert by Laurence of Durham, ed. J. Raine, in *Miscellanea Biographica*, Surtees Society series 8 (1838), II, 86–7: 'Haec de Scottorum paginis et scriptis exscripsimus, sed quia seriatim exponente interprete verba singula liquidius transferre nequivimus, sensibus explicandis operam dedimus et in linguam istam transtulimus. Quia maximis viris et nonullis Hybernensium episcopis perorantibus de Beati Cuthberti natalibus praeclara quaedam audivimus . . . sanctus e quidem Malachias regi David Scottorum quam plurima de hiis retulit, et Maurilius successor eius (? Malachy II of Down, 1148–1175) archiepiscopus (or ? Maurice, archbishop of Cashel) eadem postmodum confidenter astruxit, quibus Eugenius Hardmoniae (?Ardmore) episcopus quaedam distinctius annexuit : sed et duo alii episcopi quorum jam nomina exciderunt, una cum sociis ipsorum presbyteris et clericis sub diverso tempore nostris uberius in auribus infuderunt'.

[80] A. Hoste, 'A Survey of the Unedited Work of Laurence of Durham, with an Edition of his Letter to Aelred of Rievaulx', *Sacris Erudiri*, 2 (1960), 249–65. The letter printed is Laurence's preface to his Life of Brigid, which came to him in a manuscript given to him by Eilaf, Aelred's father, the hereditary priest of Hexham. On him and Aelred see *The Life of Aelred of Rievaulx*, ed. F. M. Powicke, London 1950, xxviii–xxxiii.

[81] *Patrologia Latina 195*; cols. 711–738.

contains a magnificent drawing of Woden among his descendants,[82] and the writings of Bishop Patrick of Dublin at Rievaulx and Rufford.[83] This is to run ahead however. The lady whom Aelred and all Old English saw as restoring the rightful blood to the usurping Norman kings was Matilda of Scotland, and it was with her that Irish hagiography came to London. Her court was the place for Irish story telling with its love of the marvellous and exotic, for the saints' lives which read like space fiction. The verses written at her court attacking the *Life of St Brendan* as heretical fiction illustrate very well the sensible manner in which many Norman clerics attacked what may be called Hiberno-English piety with its cultus of innumerable improbable saints, its highly emotional and extravagant devotions and its strong element of the unlikely and the fictitious.[84] Later, as is well known, the Normans came to use these stories as the vehicles for their own fiction: partly, of course, as the result of the work of Geoffrey of Monmouth, but also as the result of contact with the court of King David of Scotland, especially during its residence at Carlisle in the 1140s.[85]

The second area of contact was with the Old English monastic communities. Our chief knowledge of that contact comes of course from the correspondence of Lanfranc and Anselm, and from the monastically trained bishops in Ireland.[86] Here we may note the predominance of the highly conservative cathedral communities of Worcester, Winchester and Canterbury. That contact survived to a surprisingly late date, as is exemplified by the Irish miracles of Thomas Becket. Many of these are connected with Henry II's Irish campaign, like that concerning Tancard Carew, wounded by an Irish arrow in Cork, and advised by an Irish doctor, *medicus Hibernicus*, to take his wounds to St Thomas.[87] But there were also native Irish pilgrims. The most striking was Connor, *cognatus* to the High King Rory O'Connor, who suffered from elephantiasis and on the advice of a certain Abbot Marianus, made two pilgrimages to

[82] Corpus Christi College Cambridge MS 66.

[83] Gwynn, *Writings of Bishop Patrick*, 24–5.

[84] Kenney, 417. For evidence that these verses were originally written not for Queen Alice of Louvain, but Queen Matilda see R. L. G. Ritchie, 'The Date of the Voyage of St Brendan', *Medium Aevum*, 19 (1950), 64–66.

[85] R. L. G. Ritchie, *Chrétien de Troyes and Scotland*, Oxford 1952.

[86] Gwynn, 'Lanfranc and the Irish Church', *Irish Ecclesiastical Record*, 57 (1941), 481–500, *ibid.*, 58 (1941), 1–15; 'The Origins of the Diocese of Waterford', *ibid.*, 59 (1942), 289–96; 'St Anselm and the Irish Church', *ibid.*, 59 (1942), 97–109; 'Bishop Samuel of Dublin', *ibid.*, 60 (1943), 81–88; 'The First Bishops of Dublin', *Repertorium Novum*, 1 (1955), 1–26; 'The Diocese of Limerick in the Twelfth Century', *North Munster Antiquarian Journal*, 5 (1946), 35–48.

[87] *Materials for the History of Thomas Becket, Archbishop of Canterbury*, ed. J. C. Robinson, London 1875, II, 279–80.

Canterbury to cure it.[88] There were humbler pilgrims as well—a poor Irish boy called Colum who begged silver from the monks of Canterbury, and then stole a bottle to hold the holy water poured over the saint's bones; he confessed the sin to an Irish deacon (after he had got an appalling tumour on the neck) and did penance at the shrine.[89] There was Sihtric from the central region of Ireland, who suffered from dropsy and redness of the nose, to whom St Thomas personally appeared in Canterbury cathedral and spoke with in the Irish language.[90] William of Canterbury, who is the source of these miracles, has one remark which is worth quoting. Speaking of one Theobald, who was wounded in the Irish war, he says: 'It served him right, or so those thought who saw no reason for the disquieting of a neighbouring nation, who, however uncivilised and barbarous, were remarkable and noteworthy practisers of the Christian religion'[91]—a remark worth noting by those who would blame the Canterbury community for attempting to stir up an invasion of Ireland in the 1150s.

But though William of Canterbury praised the Christianity of the Irish, he reprehended their barbarism. The praise represents the long tradition which goes back to Bede in which the Irish were admired for their sanctity and learning. It has been the purpose of this paper so far to show how strong that tradition still was in the eleventh century; up to 1066 we can still say that English and Irish monks shared a common cultural world in which the Irish could still be teachers. This community of interest was strengthened by the fact that abroad both Irish and English looked to the German empire, that they went to Rome under the patronage of the German emperor, and that both disliked and disapproved of, if not the ideas of Leo IX, certainly of those of Gregory VII. In 1066 Ireland could still be regarded as *insula sanctorum*. After 1066 Irish learning gradually became outdated, but the Irish still came to the Scottish court, where the Old English royal family had taken refuge, and to the conservative Old English monasteries, particularly as pilgrims to their shrines. As late as the 1170s they will be found there in numbers, and their piety served to keep a certain sympathy and admiration for the Irish alive among English monks.

But long before this date much more hostile judgments were being given. 'Barbarity' had become, and was to remain, a cliché in describing the Irish—with about as much truth as the previous

[88] *Ibid.*, I, 431.
[89] *Ibid.*, I, 308.
[90] *Ibid.*, I, 221. St Thomas said: 'Heri aere nech flantu'—'Eirigh, Eirionach, slánta'. For other Irish miracles see *ibid.*, I, 181, 219, 278, 301, 379, 457, 477, 507, 527, 545; II, 213.
[91] *Ibid.*, II, 364–5.

'sanctity'. By 1156 Ireland was *insula barbarorum* to the Winchester annalist. In the ninety years between the Norman conquest of England and the accession of Henry II even the Old English monastic communities, where the memories of the shared piety and learning of the past were strongest, had come to feel superior, hostile and alien. The chief reason for this change of view lies in the fact that, after the conquest, English Benedictines came to Ireland and failed in what they wished to achieve there. But given the previous long common tradition and sympathy, why did they fail? Perhaps the reasons are obvious enough, but they may bear further discussion. Since the Irish continued to be welcomed, and in their way influential in England, why did the English monks fail in Ireland?

I say 'English' advisedly. The monks who came to Ireland in the late eleventh century came partly in pursuance of a pre-conquest tradition (since Dublin's connection with Canterbury dates from the reign of Canute),[92] but even more as part of that diaspora of Old English monasticism which followed the Norman conquest of England: some fled to Denmark, some to Flanders and some to Scotland. The atmosphere was well expressed when in 1107 Gilbert of Limerick wrote to St Anselm to congratulate him on having tamed 'the untamed minds of the Normans'—the *indomitas Normannorum mentes*.[93] In the Severn valley where Old English superiors lasted so long—St Wulfstan at Worcester and Aethelwig at Evesham—this movement of Old English monastic dispersal had quite remarkable ramifications. It led to the foundation by monks from Worcester and Evesham and Winchcombe of the northern English monasteries. We see that influence at St Mary's York, Durham and Whitby. Not only did these monks from the Severn and Cotswolds go to northern England and attempt to revive there quite consciously the age of Bede[94] (and hence for them the attraction of Ireland), but they went also to Scotland and Denmark.[95] At a time when new Norman liturgies were being introduced into southern England, not without some bloodshed, these monks carried with them into northern England a markedly conservative Old English liturgy. Thus, till the Dissolution, St Mary's York continued to have the most conservative liturgy of any English monastery.[96] Their learning

[92] Gwynn, 'The First Bishops of Dublin', *ref. cit.*

[93] *Sancti Anselmi Cantuariensis archiepiscopi Opera Omnia*, ed. F. S. Schmitt, V, London 1960, 374, ep. 428.

[94] This included excavation of the Bedan sites and the reshrining of the Bedan saints, see e.g. for Whitby, *Gesta Pontificum*, 24–5; for Jarrow, *Symeonis monachi opera omnia*, ed. T. Arnold, London 1882, I, 88; II, 261; for Hexham *ibid.*, II, 48–9.

[95] For the Danish settlement see Peter King, 'The Cathedral Priory of Odense in the Middle Ages', *Saga Book of the Viking Society*, vol. 16, 1962/5, 192–215.

[96] *The Ordinal and Custumal of St Mary's Abbey York*, ed. by the Abbess of Stanbrook and J. B. L. Tolhurst, Henry Bradshaw Society 1936, III, appendix 1, i–iv.

also was of a highly conservative character. Fr Gwynn has demonstrated how the monks of Dublin came from Worcester and the Cotswolds, and the connection of the annals in the Black Book of Christchurch, Dublin, with Winchcombe.[97] In this connection it may be hazarded that the Aldwin to whom Bishop Patrick dedicated so many of his poems was not the Aldwin monk of Worcester with whom Fr Gwynn identifies him, but a greater Aldwin, Aldwin, monk of Winchcombe, the reformer of northern monasticism.

In many ways when these English monks came to Scotland and Ireland they found an intellectual world which suited them admirably, as can be seen from Fr Gwynn's edition of the verses of Bishop Patrick on the *Wonders of Ireland*, or the verses that Simeon, an English monk at the Scottish court, wrote, under the direction of William, bishop of Man, on St Columba, for King Alexander.[98] But though intellectually these monks were highly conservative, they could scarcely be so ecclesiastically; like Anglican converts of the nineteenth century they fled to what they thought were good old-fashioned Catholic countries, and found them less Catholic and more old-fashioned then they wished. They were used to a world of great celibate monastic communities, ruled over by monk bishops who owed their appointment and duty to a king of a strong centralised monarchy. Men of the tenth century living in the eleventh, they came to Ireland and Scotland and found men living in the ninth and to married, highly hereditary bodies of clergy using liturgies that pre-dated the Carolingian liturgical reform. Owing to the biographer of St Margaret of Scotland (Turgot, prior of Durham, and later bishop of St Andrew's) and owing to two recently discovered letters of Pope Paschal II to Turgot and the Scottish people, written in 1114,[99] we know of the debates between the English monks in Scotland and the local Hiberno-Scottish clergy. These enable us to reconstruct debates between English monks in Dublin—and perhaps in Limerick and Waterford—with the Irish clergy, of which we catch echoes in the letters of Lanfranc, St Anselm and Gregory VII to Ireland.

Thus Paschal II's letter to Bishop Turgot tells us that the question of the giving of communion to infants at baptism was a controversial issue in Scotland; this must reflect the Stowe Missal's practice, which we may thus suppose to have been a general Irish practice—that children were given the Eucharist when baptised, as in the modern

[97] Gwynn, 'Origins of the See of Dublin', *Irish Ecclesiastical Record*, 57 (1941), 51.
[98] Kenney, 434.
[99] In Peterhouse Cambridge MS 74. See Denis Bethell, 'Two letters of Pope Paschal II to Scotland', *Scottish Historical Review*, 49 (1970), 33–45.

Greek Orthodox Church.[100] This renders necessary a reinterpretation of Fr Gwynn's view of Lanfranc's letter to Bishop Domhnall Ua h'Enna, the Dalcassian 'chief bishop of Ireland'—that Domhnall had written to Lanfranc about this practice because he had heard that 'certain overseas churches' believed that infants who were not given communion when they were baptised, and who subsequently died before they received it were thus liable to damnation.[101] Lanfranc's words are: 'Know clearly and without any possible ambiguity that neither the churches overseas nor we English believe what you think about children', *hanc de infantibus tenere sententiam quam putatis*. The rest of the letter is a hot polemic against this appalling view, pointing out that St Augustine had shown that it was necessary to take communion when one reached the age of reason. Lanfranc then somewhat chillingly declines to solve a series of puzzles and riddles: 'When we were children that amused us: but the administration of a diocese has led us to renounce such games'.[102] That renunciation marks the passing of an intellectual tradition.

What the English monks found in Scotland and Ireland was a Church without organisation, a Church which differed in many ways from their own, and, of course, a social context entirely outside their experience. To solve what seemed to them terrible abuses of the sacraments—marriage, confession and ordination in particular—they found themselves forced like any other person in eleventh century Europe to turn to authority, to the archbishop of Canterbury and the see of Peter. Yet they had not themselves the authority to determine the answers: those answers could only come through the hierarchy of the secular clergy. By demanding it they doomed themselves, for a strong secular clergy, strong bishops and metropolitans essentially meant the passing of that monk-ruled world in which they had grown up. They did their best to find Carolingian precedents, but when Bishop Gilbert of Limerick used a Frankish treatise[103] to write that authoritative description of the hierarchy of the Church which it was felt that the Irish situation required he says quite unequivocally: 'It is not for monks to baptise, give communion or in any way to minister to the laity'.[104] For that reason the influence of English monks upon the Irish Church could only be temporary.

[100] *The Stowe Missal*, ed. Sir George F. Warner, Henry Bradshaw Society 1915, II, 32; F. J. Byrne, 'The Stowe Missal', *The Great Books of Ireland*, unpublished Thomas Davis Lectures (Dublin 1967), 45.

[101] Gwynn, 'Pope Gregory VII and the Irish Church', *Irish Ecclesiastical Record*, 58 (1941), 107: 'The Irish bishops were in doubt as to the doctrine held in England and France on the question of baptism'.

[102] *Sylloge*, 495: *Patrologia Latina*, vol. 150, col. 532, ep. 33.

[103] Gwynn, *The Twelfth Century Reform*, 36.

[104] *Sylloge*, 502: 'Non est monachorum baptizare, communicare, aut aliquod ecclesiasticum laicis ministrare'.

To their conservatism, and to the difficulties which a secular reform was bound to bring to old-fashioned English Benedictines, though not to regular canons or Cistercians, there was added their loyalty to an archbishop of Canterbury who governed an ecclesiastical *imperium* which had only ever existed in their imaginations. To understand the claim we must first of all go back to Bede. Bede, say the Canterbury community writing to Pope Calixtus II,[105] quite clearly distinguishes between the *Scotti* who inhabit Ireland and those who inhabit Scotland, and although the charge of the Irish was not given to St Augustine, Bede also says quite distinctly that it was given to his successor Laurentius: 'Henceforward he had not only the charge (*curam gerebat*) of the new church collected among the Angles, but also of the ancient inhabitants of Britain and of the Irish who inhabit the isle of Ireland next door to Britain: and of them too he took pastoral care'—*necnon et Scottorum qui Hyberniam insulam Britanniae proximam incolunt, populis pastoralem impendere sollicitudinem curabat.*[106] Henceforward, say the Canterbury community, the church of Canterbury has never ceased in its pastoral care and primacy of all Britain and Ireland until *haec Normannorum tempora*—and the sad phrase is again and again repeated—until the unheard of novelties introduced by the archbishop of York.

Such an interpretation might arise from reading Bede and treating his works as a sort of scripture to be read uncritically and literally and to be excerpted for definitive texts. But what lent strength to the conviction of Canterbury's primacy over Ireland which could be drawn from Bede's words was the belief that the tenth century kings had exercised dominion over it and had confirmed Canterbury's rights. Ussher saw this when he printed Edgar's famous *Altitionantis* charter to Worcester in the *Veterum epistolarum Hibernicarum Sylloge*: 'To me God has conceded together with the empire of the English all the islands of the ocean with their most fierce kings as far as Norway, and subjugated the greater part of Ireland with its most noble city of Dublin to the kingdom of the English'.[107]

Scholars are generally agreed that *Altitionantis* has a genuine text underlying it. They are equally inclined to agree that it has received interpolation. Our earliest authority for its text is an early twelfth

[105] *The Historians of the Church of York*, ed. J. Raine, II, London 1886, 236, and generally 228–251.

[106] *Venerabilis Bedae Historia Ecclesiastica*, ed. C. Plummer, Oxford 1896, I, 87.

[107] *Sylloge*, 569: 'Mihi autem concessit propitia divinitas, cum Anglorum imperio, omnia regna insularum Oceani cum suis ferocissimis regibus, usque Norwegiam, maximamque partem Hiberniae cum sua nobilissima civitate Dublinia, Anglorum regno subjugare; quos enim omnes meis imperiis colla subdere, Dei favente gratia, coegi.'

century MS from Worcester.[108] If the phrase quoted is interpolated, then this throws interesting light on beliefs and propaganda in early twelfth century Worcester: it was worth pretending that Edgar had subjugated Ireland and Dublin in some way to his dominion. Quite what advantage any forger in the period before the Norman invasion would have derived from putting such a phrase in the harangue to a charter which has nothing whatsoever to do with Ireland it is very hard to see. It would be better to say that this phrase was interpolated because the fact was generally believed.

A reading of other tenth century charters will show that as far as their phraseology goes there was some reason for the belief. No one will deny that the tenth century kings claimed an *imperium* over Britain; and the Earldorman Aethelweard at least thought that Ireland *was* Britain: 'Ireland, which Julius Caesar called Britain'.[109] Quite apart from that, innumerable tenth century charters assert that this *imperium* was exercised over all peoples living in Britain and the regions about it: the phrase is a common place in the charters of Athelstan, Edwig and Edgar. Without entering difficult matters of charter criticism, this *imperium* is asserted quite unmistakably in an indubitably genuine tenth century document, the *Regularis Concordia*, the rule under which all preconquest monks lived: 'Glorious Edgar, egregious king by Christ's grace of the English and all other peoples living in the ambit of the British island'.[110] Looking at such language, and many other examples of it, we shall understand better how it was that the Canterbury monks of the twelfth century, who thought of the reign of Edgar as *the* golden age, could believe so strongly in Canterbury's primacy over Scotland and Ireland.

Moreover, in the twelfth century, there existed in two tenth century manuscripts at Canterbury a charter which contains the claim that it was written by St Dunstan himself: 'I, Dunstan, unworthy abbot, at the order of King Eadred, my lord himself dictating this perpetual charter, composed and with my own fingers wrote this document'. Whether he did or not is another question. Professor Whitelock is of the opinion that the claim of itself denotes forgery; if so, it is a tenth century forgery, for sound palaeographical opinion is in no doubt as to the date of the two of the surviving

[108] W. de G. Birch, *Cartularium Saxonicum*, III, London 1893, 377–8, no. 1135; P. H. Sawyer, *Anglo-Saxon Charters, An Annotated List and Bibliography*, London 1968, 237, no. 731; see E. John, *Orbis Britanniae*, Leicester 1966, 59, 237; E. John, *Land Tenure in Early England*, Leicester 1960, 90–112.

[109] *The Chronicle of Aethelweard*, ed. A. Campbell, London 1962, 53, s.a. 914–15, 'Denique pars exercitus illius maior nec non Hiberniam petunt, Britannidem olim a Iulio magno Caesare vocatam'. Professor Campbell gives no footnote to explain this mysterious remark, which at least shows that a contemporary member of the royal house of Wessex would include Ireland in the term 'Britain'.

[110] *Regularis Concordia*, ed. T. Symons, London 1953, 1.

manuscripts. Now this charter contains the explicit statement that the archbishop of Canterbury has the power of St Peter over the whole region of Britain—not just Britain, but the *arva Brittanica*. 'I, Eadred, king by divine grace of all Albion . . . give to Christ's temple dedicated to his incomprehensible name (i.e. to Christchurch, Canterbury) . . . and to Archbishop Oda, who holds the metropolitan chair and who holds the keys of the heavenly kingdom throughout the region of Britain . . .' a series of donations.[111] In the tenth century then either King Eadred and St Dunstan, or a forger, believed in a primacy which we are sometimes invited to think of as an invention of King William and Archbishop Lanfranc.

That primacy could be seen as arising from two causes, first, the empire of the English kings over the whole region of Britain; second, that that region included all of these islands which in themselves formed an *alter orbis* of their own. That the rights of empire gave the the English king the rights of a Constantine or a Holy Roman emperor is made plain by Athelstan in a charter where he speaks of himself as 'I, Athelstan, by indulgence of divine clemency king of the English, and supervisor of the Christian household of the whole region well-nigh in the whirlpools of cataclysms'.[112] Mr John has discussed the concept of the *orbis Britanniae* in an important paper.[113] A belief in its existence in the tenth century can once again be demonstrated from the phraseology of charters: 'I, Edgar, by sceptre

[111] *Birch*, III, 33–4, no. 880; Sawyer no. 546: 'Ego Eadred rex divina gratia totius Albionis monarchus et primicerius Christo regi meo in throno regni perennis perpetualiter subthronizato et concessis mihi ab eodem labilium gazis rerum accepti tirocinii quarto mei terrestris regni anno ad templum sue inconprehensibili dedicatum nomini in urbe Dorobernia Odone archiepiscopo metropolitanam cathedram presidente et regni caelestis super arva Brittanica claves preportante ... (the minster at Reculver) . . . Ego Dunstanus indignus abbas rege Edredo imperante hanc domino meo hereditariam kartulam dictitando conposui et propriis digitorum articulis perscripsi'. Professor Whitelock's judgment is only a passing remark, which she does not extend: 'the forger's motive is obvious when a document claims the sanctity of being drawn up by St Dunstan himself'. (*English Historical Documents*, I, London 1955, 341). It is to be hoped that Mr Nicholas Brook's forthcoming study of the Christ Church charters will throw light on this and many other matters; cf. the phrase used to describe Archbishop Sigeric (990–994): 'consentaneo typici nominis praesagio Sigerico, apostolico summi praesulatus ciriceo largiflua dei gratia decorato' (*Memorials of St Dunstan*, 3).

[112] J. Armitage Robinson, *The Times of St Dunstan*, 43; F. M. Stenton, *Latin Charters of the Anglo-Saxon Period*, Oxford 1955, 53 (genuine); *Sawyer*, no. 395.

[113] Eric John, *Orbis Brittaniae*, 1–63—p. 11–12: 'Carl Erdmann . . . pointed out that for classical authors the term *orbis Romanus* was common and that this world was supposed to be bounded by the sea . . . the classical authors found a place for *Britannia* in their scheme of things by calling it an *alius orbis* . . . In the disorders of the late Empire a number of usurpers raised their standards *in Britannia* and Erdmann suggested that it was amongst these men and their supporters that the idea of an emperor for a new world arose'. John goes on convincingly to suggest that this idea of an Empire over the whole *orbis Britanniae* continued as a force throughout the Anglo-Saxon period.

bearing right Basileus of the whole *orbis Britanniae*'.[114] It is difficult to interpret this Aldhelmian rhetoric in tenth century terms: inflated terminology was loved for its own sake, but it is clear how it struck the eleventh and twelfth century monks of Canterbury.[115]

Two other pieces of evidence must have made the monks of Canterbury sure of their rights. The first was the long series of episcopal professions at consecration, which in 1066 included professions of obedience from an eleventh century bishop of Dublin and a ninth century bishop of Lindsey, Berthred, who, by styling himself *episcopus Lindisfarorum* led twelfth century monks to believe in Canterbury's rights over Lindisfarne.[116] The second was the inscriptions in their tenth century gospel books. Athelstan's dedication to Christchurch of the gospel book which he received from the Emperor Otto I reads: 'Athelstan, Basileus of the English and curagulus [ruler or guardian] of all Britain gives this book to the primatial see of Canterbury'.[117] Much more striking with Ireland in mind is the inscription in MacDurnan's Gospel which the coarb of Armagh gave to Athelstan, and he to Christchurch:

Maielbrithus MacDurnani
Istum Textum per triquadrum
Deo Digne Dogmatizat:
Ast Aethelstanus AngloSaexna
Rex et Rector Dorvernensi
Metropoli Dat per Aevum

i.e. 'Maielbridge, son of Tornan (coarb of Armagh 888–927) taught this gospel worthily for God's sake through the *triquadrum*, the Anglo-Saxon king and ruler Athelstan gives it for ever to the metropolitan church of Canterbury'.[118]

It is true that the expression *triquadrum* denies by implication that there is an *orbis Britanniae*—Orosius explains the word as meaning the earth which is divided into three portions, Asia, Europe and Africa;[119] but on the other hand here is the heir of Patrick, who was also abbot of Iona, giving a gospel to Athelstan, lord of all the peoples of Britain, who had defeated the men of Dublin in the glori-

[114] *Birch*, III, 625–6, 6, no. 1304; *Sawyer* no. 799 (Whitelock, forgery).
[115] See the clear statement of Goscelin of St Bertin's dedication of the *History of the Translation of St Augustine* (*Patrologia Latina* vol. 155, col. 14):

Dux Anselme, Patrum Pater, et vigor ecclesiarum
Quem celebrat titulis Romanus et Anglicus orbis,
Ne spernas imi pronum munus Gocelini.

cf. the words of the Canterbury community to Calixtus II (*Historians of the Church of York*, II, 229): 'Porro quod Roma Cantuariae, id Cantuaria toti Britanniae'.
[116] H. Wharton, *Anglia Sacra*, London 1691, I, 79.
[117] Robinson, *The Times of St Dunstan*, 60.
[118] *Ibid.*, 57–8.
[119] Robinson, *op. cit.*, 58.

ous battle of Brunanburh, to whom the princes of the Scots had made their submission, giving it to him as its proper keeper: and here is Athelstan presenting it to the metropolitan church of Canterbury, Athelstan 'emperor of the kings and nations *infra fines Britanniae*',[120] Athelstan 'by God's grace Basileus of the English and curagulus equally of the whole *orbis Britanniae*',[121] 'Athelstan, guardian and lover of all worshippers of the true God in the *orbis Britanniae*'.[122]

There is still something slightly heady about these tenth century formulae; it would be possible to continue quoting them at some length. Twelfth century monks did not always find them satisfactory, as is shown by the famous Canterbury forgeries, or that clause which the monks of Canterbury tacked on to a charter of Edgar's: 'and we decree that the church of Christ at Canterbury shall be the *mater et domina* of all other churches of our kingdom'.[123] But they were not wrong in the message they found there: on any literal reading, tenth century English kings do quite positively say that they have rule over all the peoples of these islands, and that the metropolitan church of these islands is the church of Canterbury. A genuine charter of Eadred uses the frequent formula 'Basileus of the English, ruler and governor of the remaining peoples living in the circuit'—*in circuitu persistentium*, that is, in the circuit, the other world, of these islands.[124] It was precisely the Old English monks of Canterbury who, in their long nostalgic studies of the life of St Dunstan,[125] met these claims again and again. For Eadmer, the precentor Osbern or Prior Nicholas of Worcester to deny them would have seemed quite unthinkable. Like everything else that came Lanfranc's way he ordered and regularised it, but the metropolitan patriarchate of Canterbury was not his invention, nor was it to him part of a passionately held heritage to be defended like the shrine and reputation of St Alphege or St Dunstan.

What prevented it from becoming a reality in Britain was first of all, of course, the resistance of the archbishops of York. In Ireland it could never have hoped for more than nominal assent; it might have its place in some sort of ideal tenth century world hierarchy, but none at all as soon as it acquired even a shadow of administrative

[120] *Birch*, II, 399, no. 700; *Sawyer* no. 406 (to Worcester, spurious).
[121] *Birch*, II, 411–12, no. 707; *Sawyer* no. 430 (authentic).
[122] *Birch*, II, 414, no. 708; *Sawyer* no. 429 (authentic).
[123] *Birch*, III, 241, no. 1039; *Sawyer* no. 1632.
[124] *Birch*, III, 5, no. 864; *Sawyer* no. 536.
[125] It is scarcely necessary to emphasise how much the English monks of this period dwelt on the golden reign of Edgar: Southern, *St Anselm* makes the point again and again (e.g. 266–7); for a good example see Dominic of Evesham (*Chron. Evesham*, 40); for a summary of the whole tradition see Aelred of Rievaulx (*Patrologia Latina* vol. 195, col. 726): 'Iste Anglis non minus memorabilis quam Cyrus Persis, Carolus Francis, Romulusve Romanis'.

reality. This is shown quite clearly by the metropolitan pretensions of Bishop Samuel of Dublin,[126] and the way in which Canterbury's rights were totally ignored at the Synod of Rath Breasail, though it should be noted that Canterbury was then vacant, and that Gilbert of Limerick's hierarchy allows for the existence of primates who govern a number of archbishops and act as intermediaries between them and the pope. Nor is it to say that like Canterbury's jurisdiction over Wales, or York's over Scotland, that Canterbury's jurisdiction over Ireland might not have been successfully vindicated at Rome. Here we must allow a major part to the changed attitude and hostility of the Scottish court. Here the expulsion of Eadmer, St Anselm's friend and biographer, from the see of St Andrew's in 1121 because he wished to pay obedience to the see of Canterbury is notable; and when Bishop Gregory was chased out of Dublin in the same year, and joined him in exile in the well beloved cloisters of Christchurch Canterbury, that too marked the end of an era.

It also marked a beginning, for from then on it became more and more plain that the Scottish kings were determined to have a Church of their own. King David was demanding an independent archbishopric for St Andrew's in 1126.[127] There can be little doubt that it was he who concerted the great attack on the Canterbury primacy from Scotland, Wales and Ireland in the 1140s. Canterbury's reaction was hastily to consecrate a new bishop of Limerick (who seems never to have gone there) and to obtain in 1145 a bull repeating Paschal's primacy privilege to St Anselm,[128] with the significant addition of a clause that it should be just as Lanfranc and Anselm enjoyed it. With Wales a tremendous mobilisation of the English hierarchy was just enough to have the case left pending: the fortunate death of Bernard of St David's in 1148, and the imposition of a new and stricter form of profession on his successor in effect defeated Bernard's ambitions[129] (and those of King David, who was backing him).[130] But Ireland was more lucky. Its chief good fortune was St Malachy's friendship with St Bernard and with the Cistercian pope, Eugenius III. But Malachy was certainly aided by the fact that the

[126] Gwynn, 'Bishop Samuel of Dublin'.

[127] Hugh the Chantor, *History of the Church of York*, ed. C. Johnson, London 1961, 126.

[128] Walther Holtzmann, *Papsturkunden in England*, III, Abhandlungen der Akademie der Wissenschaften in Göttingen, Phil Hist. Klasse, Dritte Folge no. 33 (Göttingen 1952), 34.

[129] Michael Richter, 'Professions of Obedience and the Metropolitan Claims of St David's', *National Library of Wales Journal*, 15 (1967/8), 197–213.

[130] The connection (which is clear in the documents) was as far as I know first pointed out by Professor G. W. S. Barrow, 'King David I and the Honour of Lancaster', *English Historical Review*, 70 (1955), 85–89, esp. 89: he shows that Bernard was in close touch with David; cf. the close friendship of David with St Malachy.

papacy during these years was on the worst of terms with King Stephen[131] and therefore inclined to favour the party of Matilda, and her uncle King David. Cardinal John Paparo, who took the pallia to the new Irish archbishops in 1152 had promised to obtain the pallium for St Andrew's.[132] Perhaps St Andrew's would have obtained it but for the joint accession of King Henry II and Pope Adrian IV in 1154. The short-lived Anastasius IV took the preliminary step of withdrawing the Orkneys, Sodor and Man from the jurisdiction of York;[133] but by 1155 Adrian wrote to the Scottish bishops ordering them to obey their proper metropolitan, the archbishop of York.[134] The Angevin alliance with the ambitions of the Celtic churches however explains why it was that when a revengeful Canterbury had obtained the bull *Laudabiliter*[135] to incite Henry II to invade Ireland his mother Matilda dissuaded him. The Affligem continuator of Sigebert of Gembloux tells us that 'bishops and certain religious men' wished him to go.[136] These were probably the monks of Canterbury. We know that Robert of Torigny considered that Canterbury had been grievously wronged.[137] Contemporary monastic feeling in England however received its sulphurous expression in the Winchester Annal for 1156: 'This year died the Cardinal John. When he was dead, sailors heard a voice under Mount Etna saying "Stoke up the fire"'.[138] Exactly sixty years previously the monastic community at Winchester had provided its first bishop to Waterford.

[131] R. H. C. Davis, *King Stephen*, London 1967, 98–111.
[132] John of Salisbury, *Historia Pontificalis*, ed. M. Chibnall, London 1956, 72.
[133] Philippus Jaffé, *Regesta Pontificum Romanorum*, second edition, revised G. Wattenbach, S. Loewenfeld, F. Kaltenbrunner, P. Ewald, Leipzig 1885, no. 9941.
[134] Jaffé, no. 10,000.
[135] See M. P. Sheehy, 'The Bull *Laudabiliter*: A Problem in Medieval *Diplomatique* and History', *Journal of the Galway Archaeological and Historical Society*, 29 (1961), 45–70, which contains a select bibliography of previous literature.
[136] *Sigeberti Gemblacensis, Auctarium Affligemense*, ed. D. L. C. Bethmann in *Monumenta Germaniae Historica, Scriptores* VI, ed. G. H. Pertz, Hanover 1844, 403: 'Henricus iunior rex Anglorum, exercitum copiosum et magni bellum apparatum, quem proposuerat ducere in Hiberniam, ut eam suo dominio subiugaret fratrem que suo consilio episcoporum et religiosorum virorum illi insule regem constitueret, convertit contra regem Francorum.'
[137] *Ibid.*, 500, *Roberti de Monte Cronica*: 'Eugenius papa Iohannem Romane ecclesie cardinalem presbiterum cognomento Paparo, destinavit legatum in Hiberniam cum quatuor pallis . . . Et hoc factum est contra consuetudinem antiquorum et dignitatem Cantuariensis ecclesie a quo solebant episcopi Hibernie expetere et accipere consecrationem'; and 505: 'Circa festum Sancti Michaelis Henricus rex Anglorum habito concilio apud Wincestre, de conquirendo regno Hibernie et Guillermo fratri suo dando, cum obtimatibus suis tractavit. Quod quia matri eius imperatrici non placuit, intermissa est ad tempus'.
[138] *Annales Monasterii de Wintonia*, ed. H. R. Luard, in *Annales Monastici*, II, London 1865, 55: '1156. Hoc anno obiit Johannes cardinalis. Quo mortuo audierunt nautae sub Ethna vocem dicentem, "Accendite focum". Obiit Johannes cardinalis. Simile factum est de Ebrono praefecto in barbarorum insula'. Who was 'Ebronus praefectus'?

Aspects of the Continental Education of Irish Students in the Reign of Queen Elizabeth I

Helga Hammerstein

There is no knowledge of God or of their duties to their prince in the hearts of this people that should teach or move them to their dutiful obedience; only the scare of the sword . . . Learning, understanding and the knowledge of God grounded in their hearts would breed in them good liking and love of civility, honesty and true obedience . . .

With this expostulation the Protestant lord chancellor of Ireland, Robert Weston, prefaced an urgent appeal in 1570 to the English queen and her ministers for the erection of grammar schools and a university in Ireland.[1] The contemporary Irish public records contain an overwhelming number of statements which point with the same insistence to the crucial significance of schools and universities, rating the promotion of state controlled education as the *conditio sine qua non* for the preservation of English rule and for a thorough religious conquest.

The educational policies of other European countries under the impact of the reformation and the counter-reformation show that these English officials in Ireland were not simply airing vague philanthropic views. In the Holy Roman Empire, for example, where the spread of the reformation had chequered the mosaic of self-asserting states with rival religious allegiances, the significance of local grammar schools and state universities was clearly recognised.[2] Philip Melanchthon, the highly acclaimed universal scholar, called

[1] 12 March 1570 (P.R.O., *S.P. Ire., Eliz.-Geo. III*, xxx, no. 29; *Cal. S.P., Ire., 1509–73*, 428).

[2] F. Paulsen, *Geschichte des Gelehrten Unterrichts an den deutschen Schulen und Universitäten vom Ausgang des Mittelalters bis zur Gegenwart*, Leipzig 3rd ed. 1919, I, 10, 128.

into being numerous famous grammar schools in Protestant states and worked out or supervised no less than six statutes for state universities, firmly committing them to humanistic studies.[3] The Jesuits, who were invited to take up teaching in schools and universities in Catholic territories, also insisted on preparatory training in the classical languages.[4]

In Catholic Spain, where the number of progressive educational institutions increased steadily throughout the century,[5] the traditional close connection between the crown and universities[6] was utilised to keep a strict watch on them in the interest of Philip II's rigidly symmetrical state and Church.[7]

In Protestant England the number of grammar schools and colleges, often privately sponsored, increased substantially after 1550.[8] They came under close state control through visitations and new statutes, in the cause of uniformity of state religion.[9] In both England and Spain the character and scope of education had been influenced by pre-reformation humanistic studies, often integrated into the medieval curricula, in a stimulating exchange with other countries.[10] However, when conflicting religious allegiances divided Europe foreign studies were viewed with intense suspicion. In Philip's Spain protestantism had reared its head as an academic movement to which the contributory channels had to be stopped.[11] The English queen wished to prevent the infiltration of Catholic scholars; but her experience of Marian exiles returned as rebellious Calvinists in the House of Commons and as innovating preachers in the established Church must also have influenced her against foreign studies. Progressive education, considered crucial for the preservation of the state, had to be subordinated to it, for the sake of the principle of uniformity in the state Church.

[3] K. Hartfelder, *Philipp Melanchthon als Praeceptor Germaniae*, Berlin 1889, 401 ff. (Monumenta Germaniae Paedagogica, VII) and R. Stupperich, *Philip Melanchthon*, transl. R. H. Fischer, London 1966, 70.

[4] Ignatius Loyola in a letter to the Duke of Bavaria with regard to the Academy of Ingolstadt, quoted in P. Van Dyke, *Ignatius Loyola*, London 1926, 252–3: '. . . no Jesuits will teach there unless "according to the methods of our other colleges, provision is made for teachers of humane letters to give the preparatory training in Latin, Greek and Hebrew literature"'. On the first Jesuit schools in Germany see also: L. von Ranke, *History of the Popes*, ed. G. R. Dennis, London 1908, I, 432–40.

[5] R. Trevor Davies, *The Golden Century of Spain, 1501–1621*, London 1967, 280 f.

[6] H. Rashdall, *The Universities of Europe in the Middle Ages*, London 1936, re-issue, II, 64.

[7] J. Lynch, 'Philip II and the papacy' in *Transactions of the Royal Historical Society*, fifth series, ii (1961), 23–42.

[8] W. K. Jordan, *Philanthropy in England, 1480–1660*, London 1959, 284.

[9] Joan Simon, *Education and Society in Tudor England*, London 1966, 284–5, 311–12.

[10] P. S. Allen, 'The trilingual colleges in the early sixteenth century' in *Erasmus Lectures and Wayfaring Sketches*, Oxford 1934, 138–63.

[11] Trevor Davies, *The Golden Century of Spain*, 139 ff.

Viewed against this background, an investigation of education with regard to Ireland is no mere exercise in antiquarian curiosity.

There was no shortage of comprehensive schemes and policy measures on the part of the English government. Simultaneous with the legal introduction of the Henrician reformation into Ireland, an act of parliament envisaged the establishment of schools in every parish to promote knowledge of the English language, and through this medium the acceptance of religious changes.[12] The Elizabethan government tried to tackle the problem by stipulating in an act of parliament the foundation of free schools in every diocese.[13] The first detailed university plan was developed in 1547, by George Browne, Protestant archbishop of Dublin. It was followed by several other equally abortive schemes, and significantly all of them were put forward after rebellions.[14] Browne pressed the government for the establishment of an institution of higher education based on humanistic studies, on a par with Oxford and Cambridge, to train good citizens and learned ministers of the word.[15]

The reasons for which such comprehensive programmes were not put into practice need not be analysed here. What was most significant was the fact that whatever education in Ireland was available outside of Dublin was not controlled by the Protestant authorities.

The effect of the dissolution of the monasteries was less harmful to the education of Irish youths than one might be led to believe, considering that they had provided a more complete educational system than in England. Among the secular and regular clergy, made redundant by the reformation changes, because they did not wish to be incorporated into the new state Church, there were a few excellent scholars who found useful substitute occupations as teachers in the Anglo-Norman towns of the south which, in other respects, had distinctly English affiliations. Protestant teachers sometimes strove in unequal competition with them. John Shearman, M.A., reported from Waterford in 1585 that his original thirty pupils had all left him to go over to the 'papist schoolmaster'.[16]

The small number of these teachers, some of whose names are mentioned in the oaths of Irish students at Salamanca,[17] shows that a few determined and able men provided a sufficiently

[12] *Stat. Ire.*, 28 Hen. VIII, c. 15, printed in T. Corcoran (ed.), *State Policy in Irish Education*, London 1916, 42–3.

[13] *Stat. Ire.*, 12 Eliz., c. 1, printed in T. Corcoran (ed.) *op. cit.*, 47–8.

[14] C. Maxwell, *A History of Trinity College, Dublin*, Dublin 1946, 3–4.

[15] E. P. Shirley (ed.), *Original Letters and Papers*, London 1851, No. II.

[16] *Cal. S.P. Ire., 1574–85*, 573, a letter to the archbishop of Armagh who had sent him there.

[17] D. J. O'Doherty (ed.), 'Students of the Irish College Salamanca (1595–1619)', *Archivium Hibernicum* ii (1913), 1–36.

advanced grammar education to make their pupils eligible for studies at leading universities on the continent.

Peter White's school at Kilkenny is the most prominent example. After a promising career at Oxford, White had become Dean of Waterford. He had refused the oath of supremacy and opened a school at Kilkenny in 1565. In the manner of a true humanist he supplemented his teaching with the writing of learned treatises; he concerned himself with Erasmus and the problem of rhetoric.[18] Richard Stanihurst, one of his numerous former pupils, approvingly compared the properties of White's institution with those of the Trojan horse, implying that its teaching fashioned the weapons to save catholicism in Ireland. The pupils of White's school were in fact identical with the leading missionaries who returned from continental studies at the turn of the century: Archer, Quemerford, Strong, Walsh and Lombard.[19]

For the basic instruction in grammar this type of Catholic education relied on books sent over from England; but, at least in the school in Cork, as Bishop William Lyons lamented in 1596, all her Majesty's titles were torn out, 'although the books came new from the merchants' shop'.[20]

As far as Protestant influence in education was concerned, private sponsorship, the decisive factor in England, was lacking in Ireland.[21] Some timid attempts were made by Anglican bishops, usually labouring under the extreme scarcity of adequate means, but these could not redress the balance and prepare students for college education in England. The only successful and sufficiently advanced Protestant school in Tudor Ireland was that opened in 1587 in Great Ship Street, Dublin, by James Fullerton and James Hamilton. Ironically, it simply provided them with a congenial cover occupation; they were secret agents of James VI. Both had probably studied at St Andrews and later became closely associated with Trinity College Dublin. Their most famous pupil was Archbishop James Ussher who gratefully acknowledged the thorough grounding he had received in their school.[22]

The belated foundation of Trinity College Dublin in 1592 was the most significant indication of the English government's inability to capture education and implant its Protestant order in the country.

In the absence of a university and with the available grammar

[18] Anthony A. Wood, *Athenae Oxoniensis*, two vols., Oxford 1692, reprinted in T. Corcoran (ed.), *op. cit.*, 45–6.

[19] Richard Stanihurst, *De rebus in Hibernis gestis*, printed in T. Corcoran (ed.), *op. cit.*, 45.

[20] *Cal. S.P. Ire., 1596–7*, 7 July 1596, 'A view of certain enormities . . .'.

[21] Jordan, *Philanthropy in England, 1480–1660*, 279 ff.

[22] C. R. Elrington, *The Life of James Ussher*, Dublin 1847, 2–4; and John Lodge, ed. by M. Archdall, *The Peerage of Ireland*, Dublin 1789, III, 1–2.

education firmly in the hands of Catholic teachers, it was virtually impossible to prevent Irish students leaving the country in the pursuit of further education or to direct them towards institutions favoured by the authorities. In the Middle Ages Irish students had traditionally gone to England or the continent. Oxford had been the 'Gymnasium Hibernorum' for about two hundred years until Henry V shut the Irish out in an attempt to stop riots. Since the imposition of a restrictive policy had coincided with an increase in Irish commerce with north-west Europe and Spain, the inducement to seek education in continental universities was all the more strong.[23] Students were almost exclusively the sons of merchants. The migration to the continent in the second half of the sixteenth century was thus in the first instance an increase in a well-established trend. Towards the end of the century, however, under the influence of the counter-reformation, proper educational institutions were established on the continent with papal and Spanish help to prepare Irish students for missionary activity.

At the beginning of Elizabeth's reign Pope Paul IV had devised a plan for Catholic reconstruction in Ireland by encouraging local education. A bull issued to the papal nuncio, David Wolfe, and to the titular Catholic archbishop of Armagh, Richard Creagh, directed them to confirm princes and gentlemen in their faith, to visit bishops and clergy and to erect colleges out of the endowments of suitable monasteries. The prime object in founding these colleges was to provide diocesan seminaries (as envisaged by the Council of Trent in 1562) to enable future and already ordained priests to study theology and canon law and receive thorough grounding in the holy languages. The proposed colleges—which in administration and academic scope were to be modelled on Louvain and Paris—should also furnish citizens and gentlemen with education in arts and medicine, philosophy and other canonically allowed sciences.[24]

As far as Wolfe's and Creagh's own academic training was concerned this need not have been an educational Utopia, for they were well equipped for the task. Wolfe, born in Limerick, spent seven formative years in Rome under the guidance of Ignatius Loyola and Francis Borgia. As rector of Cardinal Morone's college at Modena he was responsible for the overall material, spiritual and academic care of that famous institution. Before being sent on his Irish mission he

[23] Alice Stopford Green, *The Making of Modern Ireland and its Undoing*, London 1909, 273; also a list of Irish students at Oxford and Cambridge in the sixteenth century, 289–302.

[24] Papal bull dated 31 May 1564 in P. F. Moran (ed.), *Spicilegium Ossoriense*, Dublin 1874, I, 32–8; also E. Hogan (ed.), *Ibernia Ignatiana*, Dublin 1880, 14–15.

successfully tried his hand as an educational organiser by erecting a new Jesuit college in the Valtelline in 1559.[25]

Richard Creagh's academic record was even more impressive. A Limerick merchant's son, he obtained a free bourse from the almoner of Charles V and received a most progressive training at Standonck College, Louvain. Afterwards he studied at Louvain's Pontifical College where he became a bachelor of divinity in 1555. He returned to Limerick and, in order to fight the corruption of the Catholic faith, opened a grammar school in the house from which the Dominicans had been expelled soon after Queen Elizabeth's accession. David Wolfe recommended him to the Vatican where he presented himself in 1562. Although he was sent back to Ireland much against his initial intention—he wanted to enter the Theatines in order to lead a more contemplative life—he approached the task in the true spirit of the counter-reformation. He supported his mission by writing books on the Irish language and devised an Irish catechism.[26] Throughout his hazardous life as a missionary he held to the view that catholicism in Ireland was not a question of mere survival, but of revival and reconstruction by thoroughly trained religious teachers.[27]

The political situation at the time of this mission, as assessed by the Vatican, formed the background to its basic purpose. No disloyalty to English rule in Ireland was intended. In fact, the pope still hoped that Elizabeth might return to the fold. The measures devised in the bull of 1564 thus reveal an interesting plan of Catholic 'reform from within' for the country and its Church through education. This could, however, only have succeeded if Elizabeth as head of state had given her energetic co-operation; but she was not prepared to do anything of the sort. Different ways had to be found by the Vatican.

There is an interesting parallel with the development of counter-reformation educational policy in Sweden. In 1578, the Jesuit, Antonio Possevin, was sent to make strenuous efforts for the conversion of King John, who had already shown an inclination to return to catholicism by entrusting some important educational institutions to Jesuits from the Low Countries. But the Vasa king changed his mind and Possevin was forced to leave the country. The Jesuit's alternative plan was the establishment of colleges in Pomerania. In addition to the already flourishing seminary at Braunsberg, a further one was envisaged for young Swedes in order that afterwards

[25] *Ibernia Ignatiana*, 10; also E. Hogan, 'Irish worthies of the sixteenth century' in *The Month*, lxviii (1890), 352–69.

[26] *Spicil. Ossor.*, I, 38–58; also P. F. Moran (ed.), *The Analecta of David Rothe*, Dublin 1884, XLVIII and 395 ff.

[27] Henry Fitzsimon, *On the Masse*, 1611, in *Irish Ecclesiastical Record*, ix (1872–3), 266–7.

they might influence their countrymen. Possevin pointed out that, in the circumstances, Catholic education of the young was the only means of saving Sweden for the Catholic faith.[28]

Not surprisingly, the systematic education of Irish students abroad was delayed rather than furthered by the increasingly military tenor of the counter-reformation.

There were three distinct categories of these Irish students:—

1. Individual, unattached students at most European Catholic universities who followed the old tradition of scholarly migration.
2. Students who entered newly established Jesuit colleges or the secular English college at Douai.
3. Students who followed courses at Irish colleges proper.

In the first category some regional preferences existed which seem to have originated from trading connections. The ancient university of Louvain, for example, was attended by Waterford students 'at the charge of their parents and friends'.[29] Some of the thirty-four students registered as paupers in the matriculation lists between 1548 and 1569 were received into one of the four local colleges; others lived in the town. They all participated in general university activities.[30] Most of these individual students did not remain all the time at the same university or even finish their university education. They were all too often forced to interrupt their studies and seek paid occupations to earn a living.[31] There were, however, several Irishmen whose scholarly distinctions qualified them for influential academic positions in continental universities. Some were spotted by the vigilance of missionary organisers in search of suitably trained scholars to go to Ireland and preach reformed catholicism there.

One of these was David Delahide who had been fellow of Merton College Oxford in 1549 (M.A. 1553). He had been imprisoned in London for not swearing the oath of supremacy, but escaped and went to Douai.[32] He was learned in mathematics and languages, became a doctor of divinity and appeared in a list of prominent

[28] Possevinus, *Brundbergensis seminarii historia*, reprinted in appendix of documents in: L. von Ranke, *History of the Popes*, London 1908, I, 465 and 482.

[29] W. M. Brady (ed.), *State Papers concerning the Irish Church in the time of Queen Elizabeth*, London 1868, No. XV, 14 April 1577. Much valuable information is contained in: J. Brady, 'The Irish colleges in Europe and the counter-reformation', in: *Proc. Ir. Cath. Hist. Comm.*, 1957, 1–8.

[30] B. Jennings (ed.), 'Irish students in the University of Louvain', in S. O'Brien (ed.), *Measgra i gcuimhne Mhichíl Uí Chléirigh*, Dublin 1944, 74–97. (There is a hiatus in the list from 1569–1616.)

[31] William P. Treacy, *Irish scholars of the penal days: glimpses of their labours on the continent of Europe*, 2nd ed., New York 1887; and *Cal. S.P. Ire., 1588–92*, 455–6.

[32] J. Brady, 'Some Irish scholars of the sixteenth century', in *Studies*, xxxvii (1948), 226–31.

prospective ecclesiastics for the Irish mission in 1580.[33] Stephen White, who studied and remained in several teaching capacities at the university of Salamanca, was another example. He wrote an Irish history outlining the great contributions Ireland had made to the development of Europe from the seventh to the tenth centuries, an attempt to redeem the Irish cultural and educational debts of his own generation.[34] Father Richard Fleming became the first chancellor of Pont-à-Mousson, established in 1573 in Lorraine. He was the Jesuit theologian who refuted the attacks on the Order published by the renowned bishop of Ypres, Cornelius Jansen. Significantly, the Irish missionaries kept in touch with such scholars. James Archer, Richard Field and Christopher Holiwood visited Fleming in 1593.[35] Even if they did not actively participate in the Irish mission, the scholars who remained on the continent gave it their advice and an academic orientation.

In the second category of students, those who entered the new Jesuit colleges or the college at Douai, the earliest groups developed along two lines. Irish students became associated with such institutions as William Allen's English college at Douai, or were readily absorbed into general Jesuit colleges, for example in Paris or the German college in Rome.[36]

The Irish association with the English secular college is of special interest because of the limitations of Douai in its educational scope and its missionary intention. Apart from Leonard Fitzsimon, a former Oxford scholar, several Irishmen are named in the college diaries.[37] The pope had recognised the college as one of the first diocesan seminaries. But gentlemen's sons also studied there, imbibing a Catholic education in the humanities, philosophy and jurisprudence. The teaching of the future clergy was intended to familiarise them with the texts of Scripture in their most approved meaning for the defence of the faith. A little Greek and Hebrew were thought necessary to avoid being trapped by Protestant sophisms, but no high 'theological science' was taught since the students were simply intended for the home harvest.[38] John Bossy has shown that William Allen had started the college in 1568 'as a sort of dissident university' created by Oxford clerks who wanted to preserve their

[33] Dermot O'Hurley's list is reprinted in *Archiv. Hib.*, v (1916), 157 ff.

[34] W. Burke, *History of Clonmel*, Waterford 1907, 457–64.

[35] E. Hogan, 'Irish worthies of the sixteenth century', in *The Month*, lxviii (1890), 366–69.

[36] Appendix of documents in: A. Bellesheim, *Geschichte der Katholischen Kirche in Irland*, Mainz 1890, II, 714 ff.

[37] T. F. Knox (ed.), *The 1st and 2nd diaries of the English College, Douay*, London 1878 (*Records of the English Catholics under the penal laws*, I).

[38] *Ibid.*, XXXVIII–XLIII.

courses of study. He points out that it 'became the spring of a missionary venture' only under the impact of the continental counter-reformation.[39] In the early years questions relating to the deposition of Elizabeth as a heretical sovereign were avoided at Douai. But, from 1581 onwards, Allen himself considered military support for the establishment of the renewed faith by backing the Duke of Lennox. It was surely significant to the Irish students of his college that Allen's great missionary schemes treated Ireland as a mere side line.

After the wars in Flanders had forced the English college to move to Rheims in 1578–9, six Irish students together with several of their compatriots from Louvain went to Paris and were received into the Jesuit college there. According to a petition placed by the papal nuncio in Paris before Gregory XIII, these Irish students would have preferred 'a little house of their own' so that they could instruct themselves in a Catholic manner more particularly orientated towards the Irish mission.[40]

The foundation of separate Irish colleges with the exclusive purposes of mission and Catholic education of gentlemen's sons did not materialise before the 1590s. The two colleges selected here for closer scrutiny, Douai (1594) and Salamanca (1592), are typical examples of the earliest foundations.[41] Each was started by the determined efforts, unrelenting over years of hardship, of individual Irish scholars. Their final success depended to a great extent on a decisive reorientation of counter-reformation policy. As Frederick M. Jones has pointed out with regard to Ireland,[42] Clement VIII abandoned the military policy as anachronistic in order to explore the possibilities of diplomacy as a means of promoting spiritual renewal. The vigorous promotion and protection of education was clearly a manifestation of this new spirit. There was also the additional challenge—as the Irish students on the continent saw it—of the newly erected Protestant Trinity College in Dublin. In a petition to the pope they argued that other countries had their colleges, and that Ireland alone was left helplessly exposed to the onslaught of protestantism.[43]

[39] J. Bossy, 'The character of Elizabethan catholicism', in T. Aston (ed.), *Crisis in Europe 1560–1660*, London 1965, 232.
[40] Appendix of documents in A. Bellesheim, *op. cit.*, 718.
[41] Another Jesuit college was founded at Lisbon by John Houling of Wexford in 1593; it became closely linked with Salamanca through White's simultaneous rectorship; for its early history cf. *Ibernia Ignatiana*, 32–3. Cf. generally: J. F. Kenney, *The Sources for the Early History of Ireland*, New York 1929, I, 29.
[42] F. M. Jones, 'The Counter-Reformation', in Patrick J. Corish (ed.), *A History of Irish Catholicism*, III, ch. 3, Dublin and Melbourne 1967, 42.
[43] *Ibernia Ignatiana*, 36–7.

The university of Douai had been erected by Philip II as a counter-reformation measure in 1562. Colleges of the new diocesan seminary type, the English college for example, had soon been founded in connection with the university. But lack of funds and of encouragement as well as the unsettled state of Flanders delayed the organisation of an Irish college until 1594. Extant records testify to how enduring was the struggle to maintain the college.[44]

For some time, its early organiser, Christopher Cusack, kept students on his own funds.[45] We know very little of Cusack's academic qualifications. Henry Fitzsimon, a near kinsman and himself a seminarian, referred to him as a 'zealous rather than learned guide . . . meanly languaged . . . unexperienced in foreign countries'.[46] Cusack's main asset was his reputation, and the high connections of his family in the Pale. He was the son of Sir Robert Cusack, one of the few lawyers favourable to the reformation, and a grandson of the lord chancellor, Sir Thomas Cusack.[47] His actions and Catholic re-orientation emphasise a well-known pattern in the fortunes of protestantism in Ireland: the failure of the English government to organise and control education in order to retain the religious allegiance of local officials, who in other respects were quite loyal. Cusack's main achievement was to bring together students who had been dispersed and to provide an institution specifically designed for Catholic education.

A well-informed spy report sent to Cecil in 1600[48] referred to these students as sixty young gentlemen, eldest sons of the principal families of the Pale, the Plunketts, Barnewells, Warrens and Rochefords. The report suggested that there was a systematic rescue scheme in operation, with merchants from Drogheda and Dublin conveying students from Ireland to the college on the continent. The informer therefore advocated the closing down of this seditious institution. He maintained that this could be achieved by sending a commission into Ireland, whose members should be given the power to stop the treasonable practices which the merchants carried on. The Douai college was considered dangerous because it was purported to be the missing link between the Pale and the rebel O'Neill of Tyrone. O'Neill was certainly anxious to reinforce this impression in order to establish himself in the eyes of the pope as the true *pater*

[44] B. Jennings (ed.), 'Documents of the Irish College at Douai', in *Archiv. Hib.*, x (1943), 163–210.
[45] J. Brady, 'Father Christopher Cusack and the Irish College of Douai, 1594–1623', S. O'Brien (ed.), *op. cit.*, 98–117.
[46] Fitzsimon, *On the Masse*, in *Ir. Eccl. Rec.*, lx, 262–3.
[47] J. Brady has established his wide family connections in his article on Christopher Cusack, in S. O'Brien (ed.), *op. cit.*, 99–100.
[48] *Cal. S.P. dom., 1598–1601*, 496–7.

patriae, who supported the education of the young since the Catholic commonwealth needed educated men.[49]

Papal encouragement and financial support of Douai were indications of the prominent place it had won in the spiritual revival of the country, owing to the great learning of its students.[50] According to the testimony of Henry Fitzsimon, the Jesuit whose treatise *On the Masse* was sponsored by the college, it firmly adhered to the principle that the best and most perfect clergy were those who were most learned.[51] The training of the students comprised the holy languages, dictations of biblical interpretations, controversies, sermons and cases of conscience, as well as the Irish language. The teaching of Irish to students from the English-speaking parts of Ireland is evidence of the college's comprehensive missionary intent. It was in fact, as Henry Fitzsimon pointed out, the realisation of what Richard Creagh had hoped to set up in Ireland.[52] Yet, because of the college's loose organisation—much depended on Cusack himself—we catch only occasional glimpses of its operation during the first decade of its existence.

The early history of the first Irish college in Spain is more fully recorded.[53] The medieval curriculum of Salamanca university, which eventually became the *alma mater* of the organised Irish students, proved singularly elastic. Humanist teaching became a natural part of the rhetoric and philosophy course, and, what was particularly valuable to the community's Irish students, the best traditions of scholasticism were combined with modern mysticism in theological studies.[54]

The collected petitions of Irish students who attended Salamanca university between 1574 and 1591[55] show that they were the sons of leading families in self-governing Munster towns. The stated purpose of their presence in Salamanca was to obtain a Catholic education and

[49] *Cal. S.P. Ire., 1599–1600*, 337–8, 21 Dec. 1599.
[50] A letter dated 20 Sept. 1597 in *Archiv. Hib.*, x (1943), 165–6.
[51] Fitzsimon, *On the Masse*, in *Ir. Eccl. Rec.*, ix, 266.
[52] *Ibid.*, 266–7.
[53] The Salamanca archives, now in St Patrick's College, Maynooth, have not been systematically catalogued as yet; the main bulk of the material dates from the seventeenth century to the early nineteenth century, including early diaries. Of special interest for this period is a seventeenth-century alphabetical list of students from the foundation to about 1640. (National Library of Ireland photostat MS 4840, wrongly described as list of students at Salamanca, 1597). D. J. O'Doherty (ed.), 'Students of the Irish College, Salamanca, 1595–1619', in *Archiv. Hib.*, v (1913), 1–36, prints the oaths of entering students. J. Corboy, 'The Irish College at Salamanca' in *Ir. Eccl. Rec.*, lxiii (1944), 247–53, is a useful survey of the early development.
[54] T. M. Parker, 'The Papacy, Catholic reform and Christian mission', in *The New Cambridge Modern History*, London, Cambridge 1968, 71.
[55] A. Huarte (ed.), 'Petitions of Irish students in the university of Salamanca, 1574–91', in *Archiv. Hib.*, iv (1915), 96–130.

to return to Ireland as missionaries. It is possible that this single-mindedness was not always genuine, since a display of religious zeal was obviously the best means of securing Spanish and papal support. But there can be no doubt that the missionary direction was well established before Thomas White[56] began to organise Irish students in Spain and to give them the benefit and stricter discipline of collegiate life. He had for ten years entertained a number of Irish students at Valladolid before finally securing Philip II's support and recommendation to the university authorities of Salamanca in 1592.[57] The college which was set up there, Real Colegio de San Patricio de Nobles Irlandeses, Salamanca,[58] was for all practical purposes under the control of Thomas White, with James Archer and Richard Conway as his helpers and eventual successors.[59]

Thomas White of Clonmel was born in 1560 or 1558 and after obtaining his theological training at Valladolid entered the Society of Jesus. He had the same advantages as Cusack because of his influential and well-placed Munster family.[60] The Jesuit, James Archer of Kilkenny, received his basic education at Peter White's famous school and further training at Paris and Louvain.[61] Richard Conway of New Ross entered the Society of Jesus in 1573 and after completing a philosophy course at Monterey in Spain went to Salamanca to study theology. His own contribution to education for the mission was a history of the persecution in Ireland. This was, however, confiscated by the Jesuit authorities at the time on the grounds that it might unnecessarily provoke English fury.[62]

The regulations of St Patrick's College, Salamanca, finalised after a process of adjustment in 1604, are evidence of its true Jesuit character.[63] Good health in mind and body were considered essential; even in the most heated disputations the students had to control themselves; the time for recreation had to be well balanced against the time for study. Before a student entered the college he had to set aside eight to ten days for spiritual exercises and deliberate on a

56 *Ibernia Ignatiana*, 31; also T. Corcoran, 'Early Irish Jesuit educators', in *Studies*, xxix (1940), 545 ff.

57 Royal letter dated 20 August 1592, printed in translation in T. Corcoran *op. cit.*, 546. Besides Philip's private subsidy there may also occasionally have been alms received by the Irish college from Irish bishops. See the episcopal petition asking to commute fast obligations accordingly, reprinted in F. M. Jones (ed.), 'Canonical faculties on the Irish mission in the reign of Queen Elizabeth 1558–1603', *Irish Theological Quarterly*, xx (1953), 170.

58 Inscription above the door of the new house given to the college by Philip III in 1610.

59 J. Corboy, 'The Irish College at Salamanca', in *Ir. Eccl. Rec.*, lxiii (1944), 248–9.

60 W. Burke, *History of Clonmel*, 464–9, traces his family connections.

61 *Ibernia Ignatiana*, 36, and article in *D.N.B.*

62 Corboy, 'The Irish College at Salamanca', *art. cit.*, 249.

63 Extracts printed in: Hist. MSS. Comm. Report 10, Appendix 5, 1885, 368–71, compared with E. Fitzpatrick (ed.), *St Ignatius and the ratio studiorum*, New York 1933.

decision which would be irrevocable; afterwards the superior must be obeyed in everything. Only students of Irish parents were eligible for entry; they had to be between 18 and 25 years of age and must have obtained the basic training in grammar. Latin had to be spoken at all times except during recreation, to enable the students to take up a course in logic, which included also cases of conscience and controversy, for at least three years. This was the lesser of two streams of studies for those who, in the judgement of the superior, were not gifted enough to undergo a three year philosophy course followed by four years of theology. The students had to consent to keep only their set books and had punctually to follow their courses of study, which consisted of university lectures, repetition and disputations. Hebrew, Greek and music were to be studied daily for some time. William Bathe's famous *Janua Linguarum* was sponsored by the college.[64]

The single purpose of mission is attested by the extant oaths taken by entering students. A student who stated medicine as his preferential choice was not admitted. The oaths prescribed obedience to the superior and to the college statutes; the students had to promise to refund the college if they failed to go on mission.[65]

We know the names of twenty-two students who attended the college before the death of Queen Elizabeth. They were, with one exception, all from Munster.[66] In the early days of the college's existence the concentration on Munster led to allegations of provincialism and a quarrel which threatened to undermine all the efforts of Irish Jesuits. White's bias towards his native province can, however, be accounted for by missionary requirements. He had to prepare students for mission; it is obvious that he tried to make this venture as safe as possible in an area where he and they had personal connections. The allegations of partiality have to be seen as an attempt by Hugh O'Donnell and Hugh O'Neill, assisted by the O'Donnell's spiritual director, the Franciscan Florence Conry,[67] to gain greater influence on the college's mission and to politicise it. In a letter, dated 22 May 1602, they maintained that White could not be regarded as a true Catholic since he had been born in a schismatic province and showed no affection for Ulstermen and Connaughtmen, who were the only professed Catholics and had for many years defended the Catholic faith. They suggested that he should be replaced by a

[64] T. Corcoran, 'Early Irish Jesuit educators', in *Studies*, xxx (1941), 65.
[65] 'Juramentos' ed. by D. J. O'Doherty in *Archiv. Hib.*, ii (1913), 1–36.
[66] *Ibid.*, compared with list of students in National Library of Ireland MS. 4840 (photostat).
[67] He was for some time provincial of the Franciscans in Ireland. See: *Brevis Synopsis Provinciae Hiberniae FF. minorum* in: *Analecta Hibernica*, v (1943), 171.

Spanish Jesuit who would promptly carry out whatever orders he should receive.[68]

Florence Conry was one of the most constant promoters of schemes of confederacy to overthrow the Elizabethan government in Ireland. He was a widely acclaimed scholar, devoted to the study of St Augustine. He had received his education in the Netherlands and in Spain, where he had become a Franciscan of the strict observance at Salamanca. Conjectures that he might have been one of the first students of the Irish college at Salamanca cannot be substantiated. At Conry's motion, Philip III founded the famous college of Irish Franciscans at Louvain in 1616.[69] Conry had evidently absorbed his continental training into the well-established social tradition of the Franciscans: co-operation with the Irish chiefs. Possibly, the allegations arose out of a basic disagreement between the traditional, practical, political orientation of the Franciscan and the more theoretical, unconventional approach to Irish problems adopted by the Irish Jesuits. The latter were mostly sons of merchant families in the towns of the south, who had had been in no hurry to participate in O'Neill's war. Professors of theology and canon law had waited until March 1602 before they issued a resolution of encouragement, which stated that the Irish might lawfully assist O'Neill and his confederates since they were no rebels but true Christians engaged in a *bellum justissimum* for the orthodox faith.[70] It is generally accepted that the Jesuits working in the Pale were highly critical of the religious motivation of O'Neill's campaign.[71]

The activities of some continentally trained Irish students can be traced in Ireland before the end of Queen Elizabeth's reign. Reports of English officials in Ireland leave the impression that, around 1580, there was a tremendous influx of seditious and traitorous priests from the continent who co-operated with local priests in knitting the country together in rebellion. Barnaby Rich, self-appointed Protestant arbiter, wrote that the whole country 'does swarm with Jesuits, seminaries and massing priests, yea, and friars and these do keep such

[68] *Ibernia Ignatiana*, 106–8. It should be noted that O'Neill's son, Henry, was at that time kept hostage at Salamanca under the care of a Spaniard. This is mentioned in the correspondence of Ludovico Mansoni, S.J., papal nuncio to Ireland, in: *Archiv. Hib.*, xvii (1953), 7–8, 16. Significantly, Hugh O'Neill petitioned Clement VIII to appoint the Franciscan Matthew Oviedo instead of the Italian Jesuit Mansoni as papal nuncio to Ireland. See: *Archiv. Hib.*, xvii (1953), 18–19.

[69] Among his works is a 'compendium doctrinae S. Augusti circa gratium', published in Paris in 1644. See: Thomas D'Arcy Magee, *Gallery of Irish Writers: The Irish writers of the Seventeenth Century*, Dublin 1843. Also: article in *D.N.B.*

[70] Resolution dated 7 March 1602 (Oxford Bodleian Library MS. Laud Miscellany, No. 612; National Library of Ireland microfilm p. 3884: wrongly described as a disputation).

[71] F. M. Jones, *op. cit.*, 44.

continual and daily buzzing in the poor people's ears that they are not only led from all duty and obedience of their prince, but also drawn from God by superstitious idolatry and so brought headlong by heaps [*sic*] into hell'.[72]

In fact only a small number of students returned before 1603 and they were not always inclined to co-operate with the uneducated local priests. That candidates for the Irish mission were most carefully screened is suggested by a list compiled by Dermot O'Hurley in 1580: the necessary prerequisites were thorough academic training and, preferably, a knowledge of Irish.[73] The latter confirms the observation made in connection with the training in Douai, that the basic missionary concept must have been to work from the nuclei of the towns into the Irish-speaking countryside.

The students were to look on themselves as tools of the counter-reformation for the spiritual renewal of the country through teaching, preaching and hearing confessions. School teaching was an ideal start as well as a convenient disguise for their activities.[74]

The Jesuits by force of their training and organisations were in conspicuous command of these missionary enterprises. In 1603 five of them worked together in Ireland. Andrew Moloney and Nicholas Lynch were active in their native Munster, Richard Field and Patrick Lennon in Leinster and Henry Fitzsimon, very effectively, from his prison cell in Dublin castle.[75] They formed the spearhead of the third Jesuit mission under Christopher Holiwood of Artane, who had been captured and could not carry out his assignment of installing priests in Ireland until 1604.[76] Nicholas Lynch gives an impression of the ardous task undertaken by them when, as late as in 1605, he dates a despairing letter to the Jesuit general *ex desertis Iberniae*.[77]

As for the actual co-operation of the former continental students in the Catholic attempts to overthrow Elizabeth as sovereign of Ireland, the evidence is rather ambivalent. Richard Creagh had been highly critical of Shane O'Neill's championship of catholicism and had in fact excommunicated him.[78] When David Wolfe started to support James Fitzmaurice, it was in the hope that the spiritual renewal might succeed more fully through the military victory of this more con-

[72] Barnaby Rich, *Greenes Newes from Heaven and Hell*, 1593, reprinted by R. B. McKerrow, London 1911, 57.
[73] *Archiv. Hib.*, v (1916), 157 ff.
[74] Faculties for Jesuits in Ireland, Sept. 1601, Vat. Archives, Barberini Latini, No. 2693 (National Library of Ireland microfilm p. 871), and *Cal. S.P. Ire., 1592–96*, 484–8, esp. 487.
[75] Letter dated 25 Feb. 1630, in *Ibernia Ignatiana*, 108–11.
[76] *Ibernia Ignatiana*, 118.
[77] Letter dated 3 April 1605, in *Ibernia Ignatiana*, 161–2.
[78] R. D. Edwards, *Church and State in Tudor Ireland*, New York 1936, 204.

vincing defender of faith and freedom of conscience.[79] Fitzmaurice's major diplomatic agent was, however, very significantly, the Catholic archbishop of Cashel, Maurice MacGibbon, an ecclesiastic in the old tradition with useful connections but no university training at all.[80] Hugh O'Neill and the confederates were assured of the active co-operation of several continentally trained clerics: James Archer, S.J., and Peter Lombard, S.J., were the most prominent examples. But, again, another traditional churchman, the Catholic archbishop of Armagh, Edmund MacGauran, was more active in engineering the warlike confederation and putting pressure on the pope and the king of Spain to aid and abet O'Neill's 'crusade'.[81] Archer's, and more especially Lombard's, influence, as the latter's subsequent stand suggests, should be seen in the forceful insistence on 'liberty of conscience' as the sole purpose of the rebellion. This also manifested itself in the detailed stipulations for Catholic education in the peace negotiations with the English government in 1599. They were drawn up at a time when Archer was collecting alms for the Irish college of Salamanca in Ireland.[82]

In the Pale and the towns of the south the concept of freedom of conscience could be sure of genuine support. An interesting clue as to the new Catholic tactics is contained in one of Lord Chancellor Adam Loftus' reports in 1590.[83] A group of Catholics, clamouring for liberty of conscience, had mounted a concerted action at the time of Sir John Perrot's parliament in 1585–6. Sir Nicholas White had argued in the Irish Council that toleration of their faith would make Catholics willing to come to terms with the government over other urgent matters. Edward Nugent, a lawyer, had subsequently stressed the same point in the House of Commons, claiming that the English government had always been successful in Ireland while it upheld the Catholic faith. The co-ordinator of this campaign was Councillor Luke Dillon, who was influenced by his continentally trained relations, the Rochefords. Foreign Catholic education and legal training in the English Inns of Court were joined in a sophisticated defence of the Catholic faith, separating it from secular loyalty. This argument was diametrically opposed to the English concept of

[79] E. Hogan, 'Irish worthies in the sixteenth century', in *The Month*, lxviii (1890), 352–69.
[80] R. D. Edwards, *op. cit.*, 321, and F. M. Jones, *op. cit.*, 13, 18–19.
[81] F. M. Jones, *op. cit.*, 43–4. Edmund O'Donald, whom O'Neill wished to have appointed to the see of Armagh, had studied at the university of Alcala. See: *Archiv. Hib.*, xvii (1953), 18.
[82] *Cal. S.P. Ire., 1599–1600*, 279–80, Nov. 1599, for Archer. For Lombard see: J. J. Silke, 'Later relations between Primate Peter Lombard and Hugh O'Neill' in *Ir. Theol. Quart.*, xxii (1955), 15–30.
[83] *Cal. S.P. Ire., 1588–92*, 365–6, 22 Sept. 1590.

government, which upheld the unity of state and Church as a *sine qua non*.

The adoption of Bellarmine's principle of dual loyalty opened up great prospects for the missionaries in Ireland; but still they urgently pressed the colleges and Catholic authorities on the continent for more and better trained clerics to reinforce their efforts at counter-acting the influence of active protestantism. Andrew Moloney emphasised the need for learned, experienced Jesuit missionaries since they alone could solve the people's problems in what he significantly called 'this new plantation' of the Catholic faith.[84] When the Catholic army seemed near victory in 1600, the Jesuit Richard Field hailed this prospect as a great opportunity to set up colleges in Ireland at last. He proceeded to name former monasteries near Dublin, then in Protestant hands, as suitable for conversion into colleges, maintaining that only the more readily available local training could initiate the renewed Catholic faith in its fullest scope.[85] His hopes were not to materialise. But, for their part, Irish colleges on the continent had profited from the pioneering work of the early institutions and increased rapidly in numbers during the seventeenth century.

Only a few aspects of the continental education of Irish students have been briefly reviewed here. No categorical pronouncements can be made; but it may be safe to suggest that the energetic start and the academic orientation of these studies should be considered a crucial factor in determining the unique course of Irish history: Ireland is the only country in Europe where the counter-reformation succeeded against the will of the head of state.

[84] Letter to the General dated 3 April 1605, *Ibernia Ignatiana*, 161.
[85] Letter to the General dated 20 July 1600, *Ibernia Ignatiana*, 67–8.

The Counter-Reformation and the People of Catholic Ireland, 1596–1641

John Bossy

I have tried elsewhere to describe what happened to the popular catholicism of western Europe, and in particular of France and Italy, in the age of the counter-reformation, and to present an argument about the social implications and consequences of the transformation which it then underwent.[1] No evidence was brought in that paper about the popular catholicism of Ireland, and here I want to enquire how far the general argument may be supported by Irish experience, and whether it may help to explain any features of the history of Irish catholicism in this period.

The argument, stated baldly, runs as follows. The principal characteristic of the counter-reformation, in so far as it affected the ordinary population, particularly the rural population, of western Europe, lay in the enforcement of a code of religious observance—of Mass attendance and sacramental participation—in a frame of parochial uniformity. Whatever the state of legislation, this code was not actually in force in the pre-reformation Church; through the efforts of the counter-reformation episcopate it had become so by the later seventeenth century, by which time it would seem to have been almost universally observed in the Catholic regions of western Europe.

This ecclesiastical programme had to overcome a variety of social obstacles before it could be fulfilled in practice. The most general of

[1] The paper, entitled 'The Counter-reformation and the People of Catholic Europe,' was in fact given at the ninth Irish Conference of Historians; it will appear in *Past and Present*, no. 47.

I should like to express warmest thanks to Dr W. L. Warren for his comments on the present paper, which has not had the benefit of public exposure; and to those students of Queen's University with whom I have had the pleasure of exploring the territory into which it ventures.

these arose from the fact that the pre-reformation Church, in practice and at the popular level, was not a hierarchically-ordered structure but a 'conglomerate of autonomous communities'. Among these, the communities of natural kinship must be included: 'the internal articulations of a society in which kinship was a most important social bond and feud, in however conventionalised a form, a flourishing social activity' presented one of the larger obstacles to the progress of tridentine conformity. The code of religious practice of the counter-reformation Church came into conflict with kinship solidarity in questions of Mass attendance, where feud might be incompatible with uniformity; in matrimonial law, where the tridentine legislation against non-parochial marriage was an innovation of central importance, and in the practice of baptism, where ecclesiastical policy about godparents and other matters seemed to have been intended to weaken the bonds of extended kinship. The hierarchy also came into conflict with a most important organ of medieval popular religion, the artificial kinship of the fraternity, succeeded in subjecting it to various types of control and secured its disappearance in the eighteenth century. It also succeeded in its ambition to make the parish church a suitable and exclusive receptacle for the acts of religion which were being funnelled into it, and to expel from it the ritual celebrations of wake and beanfeast which had, if such a thing existed, expressed the collective solidarity of the parish, or helped to get rid of tensions accumulated between the jostling communities of the medieval popular scene.

The most positive aspects of the new regime lay in the fields of confession and catechism. In this period, and in popular practice, the sacrament of penance moved from being an act of social regulation for visible offences, retaining large elements of composition-theory in its emphasis on 'satisfaction' and not clearly envisaged as implying inward repentance, towards becoming a private act concerned with the reform of the individual. The counter-reformation hierarchy posed dilemmas for itself by including this act among the items of prescribed religious observance, and sought to solve them and other problems by compulsory and systematic religious instruction. By about 1700 it had succeeded in imposing almost universally the parochial catechising of children, and so set off a profound mutation in the popular understanding of religion. But formal understanding was achieved at a high cost, in the widespread detachment from catholicism among the rural population of western Europe which became evident at the fall of the *ancien régime*. I consider, at the end of the paper, why to this degree the popular counter-reformation in western Europe must be accounted a failure. It has been suggested that this was the outcome of a fatal sequence in which catechism led to secular primary education and this to detachment from religion. I express doubt about the form in which this argument has been put, and suggest that what particularly went wrong with the counter-reformation, as an educative process and in general, was that its hierarchical proponents were unwilling and perhaps unable to allow to the domestic community of the household the degree of autonomous participation which the medieval Church had allowed to the larger kinship association, natural and artificial.

Before investigating how far this argument may be relevant to the counter-reformation in Ireland, I should like to enter three caveats. The first is about dates: I have not felt equipped to pursue the subject beyond the crises of the mid-seventeenth century, by which time the counter-reformation, as here understood, was scarcely half a century old in Ireland. The second concerns the evidence available. For France and Italy there exists a large and growing body of work, based mainly on the records of ecclesiastical visitation, from which it is now possible to get a reasonable idea of the impact of legislation on popular practice during this period. For Ireland, I can support such understanding of popular religion as may be gleaned from the legislation itself only with a scratch collection of missionary reports and odd bits of literary evidence. Finally, I am not an expert in the history or society of Ireland, and especially not of Old Irish Ireland. I quite concede that this is a grave disqualification for discussing the subject I have chosen here, and can only say that, having constructed a hypothesis about the continental counter-reformation, I was too impatient to wait until more qualified people should have told me whether or not it would do for Ireland.

Popular religion in Ireland on the eve of the reformation seems in most respects to have been in much the same condition as it was on the continent, only more so. The Irish Church, too, clearly entered the sixteenth century as a 'conglomerate of autonomous communities', among which the communities of natural kinship were prominently represented; it possessed little in the way of a real parochial structure, and performed erratically in religious observance and sacramental practice. The reformation simply intensified these characteristics. The monk who, by Edmund Campion's account, found a 'grave gentleman' in Ulster who had never been to communion and was not aware that homicide was a sin; Sir Henry Sidney, the lord deputy, who 'doubt [ed] whether [the people of Munster] christen [ed] their children or no'; Captain Cuellar who remarked of the girl from Donegal who helped to rescue him from the wreck of the Armada that she was a 'Christian in like manner as Mahomet'—these seem reasonably accurate observers of the state of popular religious practice in post-reformation Ireland.[2] This is not to say that the sixteenth-century Irish were heathens, but that, whatever one calls their religion, it does not readily correspond to the criteria of modern catholicism.

It seems to be agreed that the origins of modern Irish catholicism are to be found in the activity of missionary clergy and bishops at the end of the sixteenth and in the early seventeenth century; it was one of the achievements of the counter-reformation.[3] This was of course in various ways unusually placed in Ireland, and one of these is of special importance here. Irish bishops might speak of themselves as engaged in setting up a parochial clergy, and of their subjects as parishioners, but this was a loose manner of speaking. As Professor Corish says, they 'had to apply the *ius novissimum* of the counter-reformation Church to a situation which it was not quite designed to fit'.[4] The 'new kind of parish' which emerged was not a watertight structure inside which a code of regular Mass attendance, of Easter confession and communion and the rest, could be enforced by authority. Nor does the information exist which would make it possible to estimate how much progress the Irish had, by 1641, made towards observing it.

Allowing for this, most of the social implications which I have claimed for the counter-reformation on the continent may to a greater or less degree be claimed for it in Ireland. There can surely be little doubt that the Ireland to which it came was a society dominated by kinship relations and articulated by feud. Anyone consulting the reports of the Jesuit mission in Ireland about 1600 will be impressed by the reporters' conviction of the prime importance of feud among the people they were dealing with, and of the antipathy which they felt to exist between a society so constituted and the form of Christian life they were seeking to diffuse. What above all, in the early days of the mission, seems to account for its enthusiastic reception, was that, by their prestige and relative detachment, Jesuits were in a position to act as universal arbitrators in a way impossible for branches of the clegry more deeply established in Irish society. Soon they were claiming the status of 'singulares pacis arbitri', of makers of law and order and restorers of the republic, and passing on appreciative comments from Protestants about their

[2] Canice Mooney, 'The first impact of the reformation', in Patrick J. Corish (ed.), *History of Irish Catholicism*, III, ch. 2, Dublin and Melbourne, 1967, especially 7 f; Edmund Campion, *Two Bokes of the Histories of Ireland*, ed. A. F. Vossen, Assen 1963, [21]; Sidney, in R. Bagwell, *Ireland under the Tudors*, II (1885), 113.

[3] Cf. Patrick Corish, 'The reorganisation of the Irish Church, 1603–41', *Proceedings of the Irish Catholic Historical Committee* (1957), 13 f.

[4] Corish, 'An Irish counter-reformation bishop: John Roche', *Irish Theological Quarterly*, xxv (1958), 14 f, 104–11, and 'The crisis in Ireland in 1648', *Ibid.*, xxii (1955), 252.

achievements in reconciling feud and instituting civility.[5] Jesuits were given to making large claims of this sort, but in this case I think one may take them with only a moderate pinch of salt, if only because the idea of devoting time and effort to peace-keeping operations aroused a good deal of distaste among the Jesuit missioners themselves. All the very few Jesuits then in Ireland were working either about Dublin or in north-east Munster; enthusiasm for social reform was understandably stronger among the latter, and Christopher Holywood, superior of the mission and very much a Palesman himself, told them to stop it and get on with their strictly spiritual work. This was a most respectable but perhaps rather unrealistic reaction: however much he groaned, Holywood could not avoid being cast in the same role by the Old English gentry among whom he worked, and he was, while telling his southern colleagues to keep out of arbitration, complaining to Acquaviva that he had just spent a whole year sorting out a dispute which had arisen between two gentry families.[6] By the time of its first surviving annual letter, which dates from 1609, the public view of the *Missio Hibernica* seems to have been that conflict-settling was an unavoidable incident to the general reform of Irish manners without which the spiritual mission could not go forward.

It is at first sight very odd that there is no evidence of this kind from the secular clergy. David Rothe, bishop of Ossory and patriarch of the Irish seminary clergy of the seventeenth century, believed as strongly as the Jesuits that religion and civility must advance hand in hand. In his *Analecta sacra*, published in 1617, he was concerned to show that 'civil prudence, urbanity, industry' and other social virtues were the natural accompaniments of the Catholic faith; that it 'eliminate[d] barbarous customs, abolishe[d] bestial rites, and convert[ed] the detestable intercourse of savages into polite manners and a care for maintaining the commonwealth'; and that the Catholic clergy was both a gentler and a more efficient instrument of public order than the common law.[7] But neither here nor in the clerical assemblies which legislated under Rothe's guidance was there any reference to conflict-settling as a responsibility of the clergy. By the standards of the continental episcopate this silence is extraordinary; what I think explains it is the anxiety of loyalist Old English bishops to avoid giving offence to the government by

[5] E. Hogan (ed.), *Ibernia Ignatiana*, I (only volume published), Dublin 1880, 150, 162 f; also 44, 109, 199, and the Annual Letter of 1609, in P. F. Moran (ed.), *Spicilegium Ossoriense*, series I, Dublin 1874, 116. The mission was effectively launched in 1596 which explains the *terminus a quo* of this paper.

[6] *Ibernia Ignatiana*, 164 f.

[7] P. F. Moran (ed.), *The Analecta of David Rothe, bishop of Ossory*, Dublin 1884, 100, 309.

appearing to condone interference in matters not wholly 'spiritual'. It would seem to follow from the principle, handed down to Rothe by his master Peter Lombard, emigré archbishop of Armagh, and incorporated by Rothe in all the legislation which he inspired,[8] that the Catholic clergy should not make themselves objectionable to the king or temporal authorities in any way other than by performing their spiritual office towards God and the people.[9] It is hard to believe that an interpretation which would extend this principle to cover all forms of conflict-settling really corresponded with the facts of Irish life, and that the secular clergy did not often act in the same way as the Jesuits had done. But it was not until the erection of the Confederation of Kilkenny that the formal doctrine was abandoned, and the bishops issued a decree which, optimistically, prohibited feud among members of the confederacy and required the clergy to intervene so as to maintain peace and charity among them.[10]

Many of the cases of dispute in which the Jesuit mission got involved were disputes about marriage:[11] an argument that the marriage legislation of the Council of Trent ought to be regarded as of peculiar importance in the popular reception of the counter-reformation receives embarrassingly strong support from an Irish experience which is no doubt in some degree *sui generis*. To anyone brought up with normal European expectations, Irish marriage-habits in the sixteenth century appeared unconventional in the extreme. 'Where the clergy is faint', wrote Campion in his *History of Ireland* in 1571, when this meant more or less everywhere, 'they can be content to marry for a year and a day of probation, and at the year's end to return her home again upon any light quarrel, if the gentlewoman's friends be weak and unable to avenge the injury'. Where the parochial structure was so tenuous, and kinship relations so strong, contractual marriage had the field to itself; given their lead, Irish inclinations obviously ran to polygamy as well as to divorce.[12] Campion may have been talking about the upper classes, and it is true that much of the evidence concerns the aristocracy, Old

[8] These were: (1) at Drogheda, 19 February 1614, for the province of Armagh, in L. F. Renehan, *Collections on Irish Church history* (ed. D. McCarthy), Dublin 1861, 116 ff, 427 ff; (2) at Kilkenny, 22–27 June 1614, for the province of Dublin, in P. F. Moran, *History of the Catholic archbishops of Dublin*, I, Dublin 1864, 440 ff; (3) 1618, province of Armagh, *ibid.*, 427 ff; (4) 1624, province of Cashel, in B. Jennings (ed.), *Wadding Papers*, Irish Manuscripts Commission 1953, 83 ff. To these one may add (5) those of Malachy O'Queeley, archbishop of Tuam, 1631, in Renehan, *op. cit.*, 491 ff. They will be referred to here as (1) *Armagh, 1614*; (2) *Dublin, 1614*; (3) *Armagh, 1618*; (4) *Cashel, 1624*; (5) *Tuam, 1631*, with page references.

[9] J. Silke, 'Primate Peter Lombard and James I', *Ir. Theol. Quart.*, xxii (1955), 128, 137, 146; *Armagh, 1614*, 118 f; *Dublin, 1614*, 454 f; *Armagh, 1618*, 431.

[10] *Spicil. Ossor.*, I, 263, 265.

[11] E.g. *Ibernia Ignatiana*, 39, 165.

[12] Campion, *Two Bokes*, [22], [25].

English and Old Irish alike. But there seems little reason to believe that the attitude he described was not universal. Strafford thought it was; like the Council of Trent he thought clandestinity the root of the trouble. The Jesuit reports suggest the same. In the case of the bigamous baron, whom they had persuaded to put away his second wife, public feeling seems to have been against them. Holywood remarked particularly of the 'incultior populus' that they seemed not to understand the impediment of affinity, which implies insensitivity to the social effect of sexual relations, in marriage or out of it.[13]

Most accredited missionaries arrived upon this scene with powers to dispense for marriage within the prohibited degrees as part of their missionary faculties; the Jesuits, who were not sure they had them, found these in great demand.[14] One wonders, though, whether anything which made marriage easier quite met the needs of the situation; it came to be alleged that couples were keen to get a dispensation of this kind because later, by denying that it had existed in circumstances where no one could prove the contrary, they could secure themselves a convenient divorce. There was probably justice in the bishops' complaint that, by granting matrimonial authority to missionaries outside episcopal control, Rome was simply helping to maintain the old regime.[15] A complete remedy, in the form of the full tridentine legislation, was out of the question; but Rothe's matrimonial statute, which is the longest article in the decrees of the 'synod' of the province of Dublin held in 1614, approximated as nearly to this as circumstances might seem to permit.[16] It began by deploring, as a matter of general knowledge, the calamities which were befalling the commonwealth through the present matrimonial disorder, and by forbidding all private or clandestine betrothal and marriage. It required all marriages to be contracted, where parishes existed, before the parish priest, another priest with his licence, or the Ordinary; where parishes did not exist, before a priest of some kind; and in either case before two or three witnesses. It excommunicated *ipso facto* anyone contracting or inducing to contract, and any priest present at, a marriage in any other conditions. It required priests to publish banns in all places where the Ordinary did not judge this to be too dangerous; there, the priest was not to solemnise marriage

[13] Strafford, in [Winifred Gardner], Lady Burghclere, *Life of James, first duke of Ormonde, 1610–88*, 2 vols., London 1912, I, 78; *Spicil. Ossor.*, I, 118; *Ibernia Ignatiana*, 165: 'Inveniunt nostri, dum incultiori populo tractant, conjuges, qui contraxerunt cum impedimento affinitatis in 2°. gradu nato ex peccato alterius'—i.e., 'I think, marriage with a woman with whom, e.g., one's father or brother had had sexual relations'. Also *Ibid.*, 175, 187, 191 f, 211.

[14] *Ibid.*, 165, 175, 191, etc.; F. M. Jones, 'Canonical faculties on the Irish Mission in the reign of Queen Elizabeth', *Ir. Theol. Quart.*, xx (1953), 153–9.

[15] *Dublin, 1614*, 453; *Wadding Papers*, 85, 628, 639.

[16] *Dublin, 1614*, 451–4.

before he was satisfied, of his own knowledge and that of four or five reliable and informed witnesses, that there existed no impediment to the contract. Many people, it went on, did not understand exactly how marriage was contracted, and in particular what was the difference between a marriage *de praesenti* and a betrothal *de futuro*; some priests clearly did not understand it either since, it alleged, they allowed couples intending a betrothal to pronounce the words of matrimony. Priests were therefore to enquire carefully of the parties which of these steps they were proposing to take, and whichever it was to record it, with details, in a register. Those betrothed *de futuro* were told that until they were properly married they must avoid excessive familiarity and in no case have carnal relations; nor were couples contracted *de praesenti* to cohabit or consummate until they had received the nuptial blessing at Mass. The Armagh legislation of the same year was to much the same effect, though briefer, and more clearly concerned, like Trent itself, to ensure that marriage should represent the free individual choice of adult partners.[17]

Had this legislation entered immediately into effect, it would have meant something like a social revolution. Obviously enough it did not. The married clergy who apparently still flourished in Ulster in the 1620s were hardly the people to enforce it;[18] independent missionary faculties continued to interfere with its reception; and the law in the provinces of Cashel and Tuam was not very clear. Clandestine marriage flourished in Ireland well after the mid-seventeenth century. Nevertheless, for what it is worth, my impression is that by this time some progress had been made at a point which was crucial to any advance in other directions.[19]

Of the acts which, with marriage, define the borders of a Christian kinship, Irish instinct seems to have differed from that of most continentals in raising more enthusiasm for funerals than for baptisms. Despite pessimistic comments about the sixteenth century, baptism seems to have presented remarkably few problems for the Irish counter-reformation. There are signs of popular error or peculiarity, like the comment of Patrick Comerford, bishop of Waterford, that Irishwomen thought churching more important than baptism; the prohibition of baptism by immersion may imply that popular preference ran in this direction.[20] But aspects of baptismal practice which caused grave trouble on the continent do not

[17] *Armagh, 1614*, 128.
[18] Corish, 'John Roche', *Ir. Theol. Quart.*, xxvi, 102; cf. Canice Mooney, 'The Irish Church in the sixteenth century', *Irish Ecclesiastical Record*, fifth series, xcix (1963), 105–7.
[19] For later phases of the question, see K. H. Connell, *Irish peasant society*, Oxford 1968, 51 ff, 113 ff.
[20] *Wadding Papers*, 617; *Dublin, 1614*, 444.

seem to have done so in Ireland. The legislation against excess at baptismal feasts is very sparse,[21] and there does not even seem to have been much difficulty about godparents. The Kilkenny assembly of 1614 repeated the tridentine restriction to one godparent or one of each sex, and specified that spiritual kinship did not extend beyond them, the natural father and mother, the baptiser and the child. In Ulster, where godparenthood was perhaps a graver matter, the reformers must have anticipated stronger resistance, for the clergy assembled at Drogheda allowed further for two male godparents, presumably to represent the kin of father and mother, and warned people against admitting more 'for the sake of forming a friendship or for any other cause'.[22] There is no sign that this legislation was objected to.

Funerals and wakes were a different matter: it certainly looks as if the funeral wake, though customary in most parts of Europe, flourished in Ireland with peculiar intensity. Ecclesiastical legislation against it seems to go back to this period, though there may well have been medieval precedents; from the beginning of the seventeenth century it continues in a steady stream which gives the impression that, seen from the popular end, the wake and funeral were something like the principal acts of religion.[23] At this time it was concerned with two sets of problems, one about funerals and another about wakes. The problem about funerals was that techniques of parochial control were here more than usually inappropriate, because parochial burial was voluntary by the general law of the Church and inapposite in Irish conditions. In any case, as Boetius Egan, bishop of Elphin, remarked in 1637, it was against Irish tradition, which preferred interment in monastic burial-grounds and similar places. This gave rise to a lot of bad blood between the secular clergy and the religious orders about burial rights, which is only relevant here in so far as the friars, especially the Franciscans, were in close touch with popular burial practice.[24] Early in the seventeenth century the Franciscan Donagh Mooney explained the relative persistence of his order in Ireland as being principally due to this. 'Most of the leading men of the whole kingdom', he wrote, 'had monasteries of our order founded by their forefathers, where their own tombs and those of

[21] Only a brief mention in *Armagh, 1618*, 430.
[22] *Dublin, 1614*, 444 f; *Armagh, 1614*, 122—'Nemo praeterea amicitiae ineundae, aut alia ex causa, plures admittat patrinos ad levandum de sacro fonte, quam unum et unam, aut duos, eosque duos ad iis assignatos ad quos pertinuerit.' Perhaps this last phrase means something different from what I have taken it to mean in the text. For godparenthood in Ulster, cf. the incident in Bagwell, *Ireland under the Tudors* III (1890), 394. and perhaps Campion, *Two Bokes*, 22, on 'Godseptes'.
[23] Seán Ó Súilleabháin, *Irish wake amusements*, Cork 1967, especially 146–57.
[24] *Spicil. Ossor.*, I, 216; Corish, 'The reorganisation of the Irish Church', *Proc. Ir. Cath. Hist. Comm.* (1957), 13; etc.

their families were'; in consequence they 'intimately loved the brethren (friars) and believed that without them they could not survive at all'.[25] There are plenty of examples, both Old Irish and Old English, to bear him out, and while again the particular circumstances would only apply to the aristocracy, the feeling seems to have been widely shared by Irishmen at large. The influence of the friars thus protected private enterprise in funerals, and this in turn made it more difficult than it would in any case have been to make a real impression on popular instinct about wakes.

The main legislation about wakes does not appear in the original counter-reformation 'synods' of 1614, but as part of a series of supplementary ordinances for the province of Armagh issued four years later and reproduced for the province of Cashel in 1624.[26] The two features of funeral behaviour which it reprehends in some detail are conspicuous consumption and sexual license. On the first point, and referring to the upper classes, it attacks excessive feasting at funeral banquets and excessive expenditure on mourning clothes, as ruining the expectations of heirs, depriving creditors of their money, and excluding the relief of the poor; the less well-endowed, it says, are driven into grave sin and run their children into debt trying to keep up with them. The other complaint concerns 'idlers and buffoons'[27] who introduce into the wake 'improper songs, obscene gesticulations, and often enough, with the coming of darkness, the works of darkness'; 'with the failing of light there fails also the fear of death which, as its image in the corpse is present to the sight, so the thought of it should be present to the mind'. The statute requires the clergy to take all possible steps to deter from this behaviour those under their charge, and to root out 'the offence to God, spending of the commonwealth, damnation of souls, scandal of the weak and other evils which are known to arise from these excesses and defects in the conduct of funerals'. It is clear that a variety of motives are present here, prominent among them a counter-reformation puritanism which demanded of Catholics a regular and continuous discipline of life. It is probably unwise for an outsider to venture into the anthropology of wakes, but it seems obvious that one of the issues between a predominantly Old English clerical assembly and a predominantly Old Irish population was a difference of opinion about the social obligations of kinship. On the sexual side the clergy seems to have been confronted by a sense that family potency and continu-

[25] *Analecta Hibernica*, VI (1934), 17—'nec sine eis se ullo modo posse esse putarunt'; cf. 45, 92, etc. For Mooney, see Canice Mooney 'The golden age of the Irish Franciscans', in S. O'Brien (ed.), *Measgra i gCuimhne Mhichíl Uí Chléirigh*, Dublin 1944, 22 f.

[26] *Armagh, 1618*, 429 f; *Cashel, 1624*, 85.

[27] 'Nebulorum (*sic*; i.e. nebulonum) et joculatorum.'

ity must be asserted in the face of what finally threatened them;[28] on the social side, by competitive ostentation as a form of aggression not unlike the drinking-competitions which also caused them concern at this time. It may well have been a sound popular instinct which sought to formalise feud into non-lethal competition of various kinds;[29] but the counter-reformation hierarchy did not appreciate this point, and the mention of heirs and children suggests that it saw the progress of civility as requiring the supersession of one idea of the family by another.

The funeral wake was not the only popular festivity to be condemned: the ordinance against wake activities included a prohibition of similar goings-on at baptismal and marriage-feasts and 'other profane and excessive junketings'.[30] But the first two of these were clearly a lesser problem, and Irish bishops found little or nothing to say about the wider collectivities whose festal activity dismayed their continental colleagues. Fraternities were fairly common in Old English towns, and were probably, as elsewhere, of some importance as funeral societies; the 'synods' of 1614 applied to them the continental law of episcopal visitation, supervision and examination of accounts, but do not sound very worried.[31] Irish tradition, and the circumstances of the time, united to ensure that parochial assemblies should present no problem at all. In so far as anything filled their place, it was the clerical feast, and particularly the patronal feasts of the older religious orders: it seems proper to treat them as part of the field of popular religious behaviour. The ordinance about wakes also prohibited the patronal feast where, it alleged, vast quantities of food and drink were consumed, numbers of both sexes attended, and the laity in general were laid under contribution for anything from cattle to whiskey;[32] and this was one of the numerous problems brought up during a lively dispute between the Franciscans of Drogheda, led by Donagh Mooney, and the local vicar-general, Balthasar Delahoid, which went on in the town during the 1620s. Delahoid complained that Mooney held feasts in the convent, to which laymen and women were invited; Mooney replied that it was the custom of the country to give hospitality to one's kindred and benefactors and that it was unreasonable to prevent women from partaking of a feast for which they had provided the victuals. He could not see why he should eject them when Delahoid had in his house two gentlewomen who looked after his own domestic

[28] Ó Súilleabháin, *op. cit.*, 94 f (on 'Frumsy Framsy', etc.), 160.
[29] *Spicil. Ossor.*, I, 118; *Armagh, 1614*, 130; Ó Súilleabháin, *op. cit.*, 38 ff, 71 ff.
[30] *Armagh, 1618*, 430.
[31] *Dublin, 1614*, 458; *Armagh, 1614*, 135; *Cashel, 1624*, 86.
[32] *Armagh, 1618*, 430.

arrangements.[33] They, too, were at odds about what were necessary social bonds; it is fair to remember that an order of friars was by definition an artificial kin-group, and this may do something to explain the popularity of the Franciscans in Ireland. Bishops might require that these occasions be transmuted into the 'sacred and salutary banquets of sacramental confession and holy communion', but it seems unlikely that they were.

Indeed it is very difficult to see, in general, how much success attended these first efforts of the counter-reformation to reconstruct the religious behaviour of the people or peoples of Ireland. Like everything else in the history of Irish catholicism in the early seventeenth century, they were mixed up in the antagonism of Old Irish and Old English; Rothe was an eminent representative of Old English Ireland, and the 'counter-reformation', as he understood it, was evidently associated with an attempt to diffuse Old English 'civility' throughout the island. This in its turn provoked the Old Irish reaction which, with assistance from the Spaniards, succeeded in recapturing control in the later 1620s by filling the hierarchy with Old Irish and pro-regular bishops;[34] from this time the tone of legislation about popular religious practice becomes a lot milder. The efforts of an Old English episcopate which was effectively in the saddle for little more than a decade were unlikely to have achieved profound results; for such success as it had it was probably indebted to the automatic effects of English government.

Like their counterparts on the continent, Irish counter-reformation bishops sought to reform confession and institute catechism. Except for innovations like the confessional-box, which were obviously not relevant to Irish conditions, the practice of the sacrament of penance seems to have evolved in Ireland in much the same way as on the continent, if with some delay. Confession may well have been uncommon in sixteenth-century Ireland: the Jesuits claimed to have been besieged by people who had not confessed themselves for forty years.[35] Irish evidence would in any case support the view that the sacrament was felt by medieval Christians to be primarily a social act, mediating between overt offences and overt acts of 'satisfaction', and owing more to composition-theory than to a recognised need for repentance. It emerges from the dispute at Drogheda that it was accepted practice in Ulster to impose money-penances on people confessing at Easter, and that these would commonly be handed over to the friars, who were alleged to retain collectors for the purpose. Though the Franciscans objected to many of Delahoid's complaints

[33] *Wadding Papers*, 639, 39 f.
[34] H. F. Kearney, 'Ecclesiastical politics and the counter-reformation in Ireland', *Journal of Ecclesiastical History*, xi (1960), 202–12.
[35] *Spicil. Ossor.*, I, 118.

about Ulster religion as exposing the ignorance of a man who had never been north of Dundalk in his life, they did not deny the substance of this charge. The Tuam statutes of Archbishop O'Queeley in 1631 imply that the practice was also common in Connaught, and that here the priest might be expected to pocket the proceeds himself.[36]

Against this background it is easy to understand the exceptionally sharp tone of Rothe's legislation.[37] It is noticeable that this assumed that the laity were wholly ignorant of any form of confession which modern Catholics would recognise. Priests, in so far as they could be supposed to understand these things themselves, were required to explain to their penitents that they must detail the types of sin they were confessing, the number of times they had committed them, and any circumstances which might aggravate guilt; some difficulty seems to have been anticipated in getting them to confess their own sins without mentioning those of other people. Priests were also to point out the need for true sorrow and a firm purpose of amendment; where the matter concerned slander or theft, they were not to give absolution before a plausible promise of restitution had been made. They were to go easy with 'penances', enjoining such as should be reformative as well as 'satisfactory'; and they were never to expose the confessional secret by enjoining a public penance for a sin which was private or only known in confession. 'These instructions', the statute continued, 'are sufficiently obvious that they ought to be known of themselves to everyone, but what with the backwardness of the people and the ignorance of some priests we have found it practically impossible to get them into people's heads.' Priests who in future proved incapable of grasping them were to have their faculties for hearing confession withdrawn; parochial clergy were to teach them to the children of their parish before the age of seven or eight, when they would be expected to make their first confession. The statute then went on to denounce people and clergy, in a spirit not unworthy of the young Luther, for wholesale resort to indulgences as an alternative to sacramental confession and a general licence for sin. I wonder whether one could find, even in the legislation of Charles Borromeo, a pithier or more comprehensive account of the difference between counter-reformation ideals and traditional popular practice in this critical matter.

Rothe and his fellow-legislators understood very clearly that a drastic alteration in the practice of confession depended on a drastic improvement in the state of popular instruction. Priests were not to

[36] *Wadding Papers*, 639 f; *Tuam, 1631*, appendix, 494.
[37] *Dublin, 1614*, 449–51; *Armagh, 1614*, 124 (confession: in general more abstract, but to the same effect), and 131 (indulgences).

admit to confession anyone who did not know the principal articles of faith and could not recite the Lord's Prayer, Hail Mary, Apostles' Creed and Ten Commandments in the vernacular.[38] Elsewhere the 1614 statutes required parish priests to possess a catechism of some kind, and to give an instruction from it before or after every Sunday or feast-day Mass. Here the legislators were simply reproducing tridentine decrees, but they showed that they were not blindly applying to Ireland legislation designed for an entirely different environment. Parish priests, they said, were to see 'that those children of their parish who are more apt to learn should be exercised in Christian doctrine by the method of question and answer; and when they go round their parish, or stay the night in the house of one of their parishioners, they should, in the presence of the others, teach one person in the house or place the Apostles' Creed or the Lord's Prayer, or something else pertaining to Christian doctrine, as time and opportunity permit'.[39]

Here again one must ask how much impression had been made on popular practice by 1641. The trouble at Drogheda in the 1620s, and O'Queeley's statutes of 1631, imply that the legislation about confession was not entirely a dead letter, but also that there were large areas of the country where it had scarcely penetrated. Much the same seems true of catechism. Twenty years after 1614, Rothe's friend and disciple, John Roche, bishop of Ferns, was still making the same complaints about popular ignorance and urging the need for catechism. Of the several diocesan reports to Rome which date from the 1630s, I have found only one, that of Egan of Elphin, which reports activity on this front: all his parish priests, he says, teach their parishioners Christian doctrine on Sundays in secret places in the woods. Perhaps they did. Yet Florence Conry's Irish catechism, apparently brought to Ireland in manuscript in 1598, was never put into print, although there was an Irish press in the Franciscan college at Louvain which he had founded in 1609; this does not suggest much enthusiasm on the Old Irish side. The Irish Jesuits certainly did a good deal of catechising, but their impact, however intensive, must have been confined to rather small areas, and by 1641 they had come to concentrate practically all their educational effort on secondary schools in the Old English towns.[40] Altogether it looks as if by this time popular

[38] *Dublin, 1614*, 449.

[39] *Ibid.*, 442; likewise *Tuam, 1631*, 492—'Quoties Parochus a loco in locum suam intra parochiam transmigret, catechizet tota coram familia aliquos illius domus in qua pernoctabit in oratione dominica, ecclesiae praeceptis ac decalogi, et symbolo fidei; quod similiter diebus dominicis et festivis coram populo facere tenentur (sic).'

[40] Corish, 'John Roche', *Ir. Theol. Quart.*, xxvi, 327; *Spicil. Ossor.*, I, 215, 356; L. Ceyssens, 'Florence Conry, Hugh de Burgo, Luke Wadding and Jansenism', in *Father Luke Wadding Commemorative Volume*, Dublin 1957, 330–1; Canice Mooney, 'The golden age of the Irish Franciscans', 29.

catholicism in Ireland was only beginning to struggle towards the change of life which came with systematic religious instruction.

In this respect the Irish counter-reformation was probably in a backward state compared with Germany, Italy or France though, all things considered, not remarkably so. But perhaps, at one point, one can detect that it might have prospects which apparently more favoured regions of the counter-reformation would turn out to lack. Rothe's idyllic picture of the rural priest circulating around his parish giving instruction in the family circle was hardly realistic in 1614. Like others features of his legislation, it could not achieve real embodiment in practice until the continental colleges could supply priests to the whole of Ireland, which was not the case before 1641. It was also, probably, for men brought up in tridentine expectations, something of a poor alternative to universal, public parochial instruction. Yet what, by instinct or force of circumstances, the bishops of the Irish counter-reformation had here stumbled on was surely the real answer to their problems. If their vision of a civil Ireland was genuine, that was what it meant; and if those among them who chose English government had chosen without passion, that was just what they had chosen it for. When Rinuccini arrived on his mission in 1645, he reported that many of the Catholic Irish had come to associate the acts of their religion with the environment of their private lives to such a degree that they thought ecclesiastical buildings a not very attractive luxury.[41] These sentiments inspired in a tridentine bishop, despatched in mint condition from Italy, a reaction of intense disgust, and he did all he could to suppress them. I should think it was just as well for Irish catholicism that he did not succeed.

[41] M. J. Hynes, *The Mission of Rinuccini, nuncio extraordinary to Ireland, 1645–9*, Louvain 1932, 57 f, 60, 61 n.

James Anthony Froude and Ireland: a Historiographical Controversy of the Nineteenth Century

Donal McCartney

Few Victorian politicians or intellectuals knew Ireland at first hand as well as James Anthony Froude. Yet, none were denounced more bitterly for ignorance of things Irish than he. His associations with Ireland began in 1840 when fresh from Oxford he accepted a post as tutor in the family of an Irish clergyman. The Rev. William Cleaver of Delgany, co. Wicklow, son of a former archbishop of Dublin was an evangelical whom the young tutor described as 'nearer to the type of christian saint' than any other person of any creed that he had ever met. Froude later claimed that this first contact with Ireland, together with his reading of Carlyle, had helped him to break away from the spell of Newman and the Oxford Movement. It had brought home to him a realisation of all that was best in protestantism, and the experience contributed to the formation of Froude's views on Ireland and on Irish history.[1]

In 1845 Froude was back in Ireland having agreed to do research on a life of St Patrick for Newman's series, *English and Irish saints*. He found, however, that it was impossible to separate the truth from 'the wilderness of nonsense', and became convinced that the Patrick of legend was not a single star or a double star, or even a quadruple star. 'Patricius was a title, not an individual, and the glory of converting the island to Christianity was the work not of one saint but of many.' 'St Patrick might be a myth', he wrote, 'the living Ireland was a reality'.[2] And Froude's antiquarian researches lost their interest

[1] Froude's autobiographical notes dealing with his first visit to Ireland are given in W. H. Dunn, *James Anthony Froude: a biography 1818–1856*, Oxford 1961, 63–71.
[2] Dunn, *op. cit.*, 86.

in the problems of contemporary Ireland. He offered himself without success for a professorship in one of the Queen's Colleges, and in 1848 he was again in Ireland during the insurrection. As a '48 intellectual and liberal he wrote: 'I have hopes of these young Paddies after all. I think they will have a fight for it . . .' (meaning, however, against the landlords).[3]

During the time he was working on his twelve-volume history of Tudor England (1856–70) Froude spent many months on holiday in Kerry, as a tenant on the Lansdowne estate at Dereen, Kenmare. These visits resulted in two articles on Kerry for *Fraser's Magazine* of which he was editor.[4] In the first of these which appeared while Gladstone's first Land Bill was under discussion in the House of Commons it was evident how much Froude enjoyed Ireland. He described it as 'the most beautiful country in the world', and 'the Paddies' as 'still among the most interesting of peoples'. References in the first article to the influence of the local clergy and to Daniel O'Connell and the Irish generally annoyed the parish priest, members of the O'Connell family and the American Fenian paper, *The Irish Republic,* which denounced him as 'a representative of the hereditary enemies of Ireland'.[5] To the parish priest he explained what he had meant by his references to the clergy, and they made it up; he assured the O'Connells that he had meant no dishonour to the past or present owners of Derrynane, but stood by what he had said about the Liberator who had become 'public property'. He offered no apology whatever to *The Irish Republic.*

Again, in certain respects, these articles were a foreshadowing of his *English in Ireland*. Commenting on them, the liberal *Spectator* wrote:

> It may not be unfairly said that Mr Froude simply loathes the Irish people; not consciously perhaps, for he professes the reverse. But a certain bitter grudge breaks out despite his will now and then. It colours all his tropes. It adds a bitter sting to the casual allusions of his language. When he wants a figure of speech to express the relations between the two islands, he compares the Irish to a kennel of fox-hounds, and the English to their master, and declares that what the Irish want is a master who knows that he is master and means to continue master.[6]

The Times in a leading article stated that what Froude had written on Kerry would not promote friendship between the two peoples. *The*

[3] *Ibid.*, 123.

[4] *Fraser's Magazine*, new series iii, no. 13 (Jan. 1871), 28–45. These articles were reprinted in J. A. Froude, *Short studies on great subjects*, II, The silver library, Longman's, Green & Co., 1911.

[5] Froude, *Short studies*, II, 262.

[6] Quoted by Justin McCarthy in 'Mr John (sic) Anthony Froude', in *Galaxy*, xiv, no. 3 (Sept. 1872), 298.

Times also held that Froude's allegation that Ireland was as disloyal as ever she was, and that she would never be otherwise, was simply a profession of utter disbelief in all remedial measures. It was therefore a poor consolation to be told by Froude that the islands were inseparably linked. *The Times* referred to Froude's historical speculation as unsound and delusive, and regretted this all the more since 'historical delusions have exercised a very mischievous influence on Irish character'.[7]

Froude's interest in Ireland's past, his long visits to the country, and the contemporary pre-occupation of Gladstone. the politicians and the press in England with Fenianism, Disestablishment and the land problem involved Froude all the more in the study of Ireland. What should not be overlooked is that Froude's concern with Ireland was also intimately related to his involvement at this time with the question of England's colonies.

In January 1870 Froude contributed a long article to *Fraser's Magazine* entitled 'England and her colonies' and he returned to the subject with 'The colonies once more' in September.[8] With these articles Froude placed himself at the head of a small school of literary men who advocated the retention of the colonies and who reacted to those who had been warning England to prepare for their ultimate separation from the mother country. To the Manchester school, wrote Froude, the colonies had seemed merely an economic burden. Intellectually the idea of a separation had been supported by men like Mill, Bright and Goldwin Smith. The government of Gladstone, Lowe and Granville was regarded as either resigned to an inevitable dissolution of the Empire, or as even favouring the views of the separatists.

Central to Froude's views about the colonies was the fact which had greatly impressed him, namely, that millions of Irish fleeing from famine to America had been allowed to colonise unsystematically when England should have taken responsibility for them, and these emigrants had carried with them the belief that it was England which was the cause of their misery. The result was that 'the Irish in America were our bitterest enemies', and their presence there was 'the immediate cause of the present humour in Ireland itself'. England ought to have settled them in Canada and Australia. He attacked the ideas of the little Englanders:

These are not days for small states . . . The German states gravitate into Prussia, the Italians into Piedmont. While we are talking of dismembering

[7] *The Times*, 21 Jan., 1871. For the section especially complained of by *The Times* see Froude, *Short Studies*, II, 299.

[8] These articles were republished in Froude, *Short Studies*, II, 180–216, 397–438.

our empire, the Americans have made enormous sacrifices to preserve the unity of theirs.[9]

Froude was not in the van of the imperial unity movement, and for him the problem of the colonies and the Empire could not be solved except against the background created by the Irish problem and vice-versa.

Early in 1870 and while he was very much concerned with the question of the empire and the colonies, Froude began his history of the English in Ireland. I believe that this book was written not primarily to tell the story of Anglo-Irish relations in the past at all, but to state his views and to preach his solutions to the contemporary problems of Empire and Ireland, and responsible self-government and democracy. Historical narrative was merely the form which Froude naturally chose to present his case. My argument is that Froude's *English in Ireland* is more closely paralleled with, for example, Lecky's *Democracy and Liberty* than with Lecky's *History of Ireland*—the book with which it is normally associated and compared. *The English in Ireland* was Froude's protest against the movement for Irish self-government and its threat of disruption of the Empire. It was also a protest against Gladstonian liberalism and emerging democracy and as such it had certain things in common with Maine's *Popular Government*, or J. F. Stephen's *Liberty, Equality, Fraternity*. Froude acknowledged so much himself when he wrote to Lady Derby:

The meaning of the book as a whole is to show what comes of forcing uncongenial institutions on a country to which they are unsuited. If we had governed Ireland as we govern India, there would have been no confiscation, no persecution of religion and consequently none of the reasons for disloyalty.[10]

He had only been a short time working on his book when, in the summer of 1870, the Home Government Association was founded. It was not, however, until its first victory in the by-election for Meath in January 1871 that there was any sign that Butt's new movement would have to be taken seriously.[11] By July 1871, when as yet only three home rulers had been returned, Froude sniffed the dangers inherent in the movement for the imperial cause he advocated. The July number of *Fraser's Magazine*, which Froude was editing, carried an article entitled 'Home government for Ireland', which argued that home rule would only be disastrous.[12] A further article, written

[9] Froude, *Short Studies*, II, 212–3.
[10] Herbert Paul, *Life of Froude*, 244; W. H. Dunn, *James Anthony Froude*, 370.
[11] D. A. Thornley, *Isaac Butt and Home Rule*, London 1964, 114.
[12] 'Home government for Ireland', in *Fraser's Magazine*, July 1871. This article was signed: 'By an Irish Liberal'.

undoubtedly by Froude himself, entitled 'Irish experiences of home rule', treated the question historically, and argued that every form of separate government for Ireland had been and must be a failure.[13] At the very time then that *Fraser's Magazine*, under Froude's guidance, was directing an early campaign against home rule, its editor was also preparing an extended offensive in his book.

And while he was still engaged in completing volume one he accepted an invitation to give a series of lectures in American cities on Anglo-Irish relations in the past, in order to counter the damage being done to England's good name there by the lectures of the recently released Fenian, O'Donovan Rossa.

Froude's lectures, like his book—volume one of which he had just finished—were based on the assumption that God had left the Irish, as a race, unfinished. Froude regarded them as children who could never be given their own way, but must be treated firmly for their own good. He denied the dictum of democrats and liberals which claimed that all men were equal and should be free. Men, he said, are not equal but infinitely unequal, and man became free only by submission.

Superior men and nations, he wrote, had a natural right to govern: the inferior had a natural right to be governed. An adequate test of superiority was strength. The rights of man and of nations were not to liberty, but to wise direction and control. The rights of a people to self-government consisted in nothing but their power to win it and defend it. The English meant by liberty the right to govern themselves. An Asiatic meant by it the right to be governed. 'As the Asiatics are, so are the Irish.' Rule an Irishman resolutely and he will not rebel: rule him justly and he will follow you to the world's end. The greatest friend the Irish ever had was Oliver Cromwell. Ireland's worst enemies were the many weak, conciliatory, vacillating governments of England on the one hand, and the so-called Irish patriots and heroes on the other. The Floods and the Grattans and the O'Connells were all bag and wind (like Gladstone in England). For Froude, like his master, Carlyle, despised 'stump oratory' and claimed that great orators were always wrong even when they were on opposite sides. The brilliance of oratory was always in inverse ratio to the truth contained in it. Nations were not born on the floors of debating societies. Freedom must be won on the battlefield or it is perishable as the breath that boasts it. This did not mean that Froude approved of Tone, '48 and the Fenians. On the contrary, he sneered

[13] 'Irish experiences of home rule', in *Fraser's Magazine*, Feb. 1872. This article was unsigned, but from the style and from the similarities between the views expressed and the 'experiences' chosen to illustrate the argument and those in *The English in Ireland* it is highly probable that the author was Froude.

at their ineffectiveness and said that if the Irish had been in earnest they could like men, and like other small countries even more unfavourably situated, have defended their independence. The truth was the Irish never meant to fight but only to threaten to fight, and when the hard truth was spoken to them they screamed like hysterical girls.

In any situation where two Irishmen were gathered together in the name of national liberty, one was certain to be a traitor. Irish rebellions were made of loud promises and vain performances—they blazed up like straw and went out in dust and ashes.

With Carlyle, he believed that it was a holy thing to hate evil while extending sympathy to the sinner. So, he said, he loved the Irish but not their faults. And the faults of the Irish in his opinion were Roman priests and superstitions, demagogues and orators, cowardice, idleness, unruliness, military weakness and political failure.

These views of the Irish character which Froude held progressively informed his articles, his American lectures and his history of eighteenth century Ireland.[14] They were also the inspiration of his novel, *The two chiefs of Dunboy or an Irish romance of the last century*, published in 1889, and which used the art-form of the novel explicitly to preach a homily on the Irish problems of his own time. The novel enabled him to use an even greater amount of poetic licence in dealing with historical documents than he had allowed himself in his historical narrative.

While Froude was delivering his lectures on Irish history in the United States, the first volume of his *English in Ireland* was published in London. The reactions among the Irish in America and at home are perhaps best summarised in the words of the *Nation*:

> At both sides of the Atlantic simultaneously the Irish race find themselves attacked by the tongue and pen of Mr James Anthony Froude. He has managed this matter with skill.[15]

Together, the five lectures and the book created a fantastic stir in America, England and Ireland. Never, perhaps, was a lecture series on Irish history so widely reported, nor a book on Irish history so widely discussed.[16] For two months each weekly issue of the *Nation*

[14] The best synopsis of Froude's argument is to be found in the preliminary chapter to *The English in Ireland in the Eighteenth Century*, 3 vols. London 1872–4.

[15] *Nation*, 9 Nov. 1872.

[16] The following American papers and journals were quoted in the Dublin press on the controversy: *New York Times*, *New York Tribune*, *New York Commercial Advertiser*, *New York Freeman's Journal*, *Sun*, *Herald*, *Chicago Tribune*, *Philadelphia Evening Telegraph*, *Boston Pilot*, *Boston Traveller*, *Galaxy*, *Irish American*, *Metropolitan Record*, *Nation* (New York), *Daily Advertiser* (Boston), *Evening Telegram* (New York). Also taking part in the controversy were the following American papers and

devoted an average of three full pages to the Froude controversy, and for a further two months an average of one-and-a-half pages.

One of the reasons for all this hullabaloo and for the swelling of the controversy to such proportions arose from the fact that, at the precise moment of Froude's visit to the U.S.A., the most famous Irish orator and controversialist of the period, Fr Tom Burke O.P., also happened to be in America.[17] And Fr Burke was persuaded to reply formally to Froude. Burke announced that the issues between Froude and himself must be discussed calmly and historically, like antiquarians prying into the past and not with the warm feelings of boiling blood. Having made his genuflection to the science of history, however, Burke got down to the real business of vindicating Ireland and refuting Froude. *Laudabiliter* (the papal grant of Ireland to Henry II), which Froude had made much of, was dismissed by Burke as a 'thumping English lie'. He said of Cambrensis, whom Froude had quoted, that the only time Cambrensis had ever told the truth was when he said the Confiteor and came to the part, 'I have sinned exceedingly, in thought, word and deed'. So long as Froude used Cambrensis as his source 'he might as well be whistling jigs to a milestone'. And Burke made short work of Froude's hero, Henry VIII. In life, said Burke, Henry was a 'bloodthirsty, licentious tyrant'; when he died a requiem was said over his 'inflated corpse', but, said the Dominican, some other poor soul got the benefit of that Mass.[18]

Burke, who claimed it was better to laugh at Froude than frown on him, faulted Froude's logic, noted prejudices and inconsistencies, detected exaggerations and in this way scored a number of oratorical points off his opponent, for Froude had left himself open to this line of attack.[19] If the controversy had been merely one about historical fact and accuracy Froude had one great advantage over Burke: he was better versed in the original documents for the Tudor and eighteenth century periods. But Froude never confined himself to pure history and he had gone to America specifically to argue a political case, namely, that the Irish were not fit for self-government

journals: *Appleton's Journal*, *New York World*, *Commercial Gazette* (Cincinnati), *Harper's Weekly*, *Harper's Monthly*, *New Englander*, *Evening Star* (Washington).

[17] On Burke see W. J. Fitzpatrick, *The Life of the Very Rev. Father Thomas N. Burke, O.P.*, 2 vols. London 1885. See also Wayne C. Minnick, 'The Froude-Burke controversy', in *Speech Monographs*, xviii, no. 1 (March 1951), 31–36.

[18] T. N. Burke, *Ireland's Vindication*, Glasgow, n.d., 192, 122, 170, 151; also Fitzpatrick, *op. cit.*, II, 71–2.

[19] W. H. Dunn in his biography of Froude holds that Froude was masterly in his reply to Burke, and that his 'rapier-like thrusts' 'infuriated Burke only the more' (383, 377). To be fair to Burke, Dunn should have given as much attention to Burke's 'Last words on Mr Froude'. There was less fury and more gentlemanly respect for each other between the antagonists than Dunn allows.

and never had been, and to persuade America to tell the Irish 'that they have no longer a grievance which legislation can redress, and that they must depend for their future prosperity on their own industry'.[20]

After delivering his lectures in New York, Boston, Philadelphia and Ithaca, Froude had to cut short the rest of his tour, although halls had been hired for him in Washington, Chicago and Brooklyn. He had been insulted at railway stations. His life was threatened and a special guard had been provided for him. Irish servants in hotels and homes where Froude stayed staged what was known as the strike of the Noras and Biddys. Not to upset his friends further, and claiming that he had done the work for which he had come to the States, Froude decided to return to England to complete his work on volumes two and three of *The English in Ireland*.

Fr Burke, on the other hand, was indeed hailed by the Irish as their champion, and a chorus of congratulations rang out in his favour. Typical of the hero's welcome Burke received on his return to Ireland was the ballad 'Céad Míle Fáilte', which appeared in the *Nation* (22 Mar. 1873):

> On the instant, thy hand the green banner unfurled,
> On the instant, thy voice with its thunders rang loud,
> When our still-bleeding wound was laid bare to the world
> In the foulness and falseness that festered in Froude.

Froude's lectures and his book were immediately subjected to a barrage of attacks from Irish newspapers, journals and writers of all shades of political and religious opinion. Indeed for the rest of the nineteenth century Froude continued to be the whipping-dog of Irish historical writers, and to such an extent that there was much truth in Standish O'Grady's remark that:

> It is like bringing coals to Newcastle to point out the inaccuracies of this historian, but I must furnish my contribution.

Perhaps the Irish historian who came nearest to bursting a blood vessel because of Froude's treatment of Irish history was J. P. Prendergast, the author of the valuable and scholarly book, *The Cromwellian Settlement*. Prendergast's immediate reaction to Froude's lectures was a long letter to the *Freeman's Journal*, in which he described Froude as a 'cold-blooded hypocrite', a 'viper' with 'poison under that tongue', 'out-slandering indeed all our former maligners' and 'possessed of a devil'. In a further full-page letter Prendergast claimed that no one had shown such antipathy to the Irish since 1641; that Froude's hatred amounted to madness; that he reminded him of

[20] *Nation*, 2 Nov. 1872 quoting *New York Tribune*; W. H. Dunn, *James Anthony Froude*, 377.

Shaftesbury, who, on being offered food before being committed to the Tower of London, said that he had no appetite unless he could get a roasted Irishman.[21]

A few days later Prendergast had read an elaboration of the American lectures in Froude's book, and he again wrote to the press commenting on his own original letter:

Since I have read his book I would wish to alter one phrase. I would withdraw the term cold-blooded hypocrite, and substitute blood-thirsty fanatic.[22]

He now described Froude as being 'filled with demoniac hate', and thought there was 'nothing in the world like his present effort except Peter the Hermit's preaching the Crusade'; 'his book smells of blood'; 'ferocious Froude'; 'fraudulent knave'; 'does he take us for dogs?'; 'libeller of our name and nation'.

Part of Prendergast's chagrin might be explained by the fact that he had assisted Froude while the latter was doing research for his book. This assistance was duly acknowledged by Froude. But the manner in which Froude had quoted from Prendergast's book only increased Prendergast's rage.[23]

Although Prendergast, when reviewing the book, admitted that *The English in Ireland* 'is a work full or original matter, derived from a most laborious investigation of the government correspondence', nevertheless he asked:

is there a nation in Europe . . . except the English (I do not except Russia) able to produce such a monster of cruelty and bigotry as this cynical and insolent author?[24]

It is well to remember, however, that Prendergast's lack of decorous language was no different from that which had been used by Freeman (afterwards Regius Professor of History at Oxford) about Froude (who was Freeman's successor as Regius Professor). Freeman had

[21] *Freeman's Journal*, 11 Nov. 1872; *Nation*, 16 Nov. 1872.
[22] *Freeman's Journal*, 19 Nov. 1872; *Nation*, 23 Nov. 1872.
[23] In the *Nation* (30 Nov. 1872), Prendergast bitterly complained of a misquotation in *The English in Ireland* I, 135. Prendergast had some grounds for complaint, but he was much too severe on Froude. A better substantiated charge of misquotation from Prendergast was brought against Froude in the *New York Metropolitan Record* (7 Dec. 1872), and reprinted in the *Nation* (21 Dec. 1872). Froude quoted Prendergast as writing about the Irish that no wonder they destroyed or betrayed each other when they had no longer 'any public cause to maintain', (Froude in *Fraser's Magazine*, January 1873, 20; *The English in Ireland* I, 136). But in the context, Prendergast (*Cromwellian Settlement*, London 1875, 344–5) was denying the general validity of this statement. Words included in quotation marks and attributed by Froude to Prendergast were not Prendergast's but a compressed misstatement. This misquotation and misstatement of Prendergast's words also appeared in the second edition of *The English in Ireland*, London 1881, I, 150.
[24] *Nation*, 30 Nov., 7 Dec. 1872.

written: 'Froude is certainly the vilest brute that ever wrote a book'.[25] The kind of reference which one Oxford historian wrote for another had now been adopted by Froude's Irish critics in reviewing his book.

None of the Irish critics had provided a full or cool-headed historian's answer to Froude. This was precisely what Lecky who was, as Herbert Paul said 'curiously unlike the typical Irishman of Froude's imagination',[26] now set out to do. From the modern historian's standpoint, Lecky, in his review as well as in his history, provided the most satisfactory retort.

The full title of Froude's three volume book on Ireland was *The English in Ireland in the Eighteenth Century*. And apart from the first three chapters in volume one, the rest of the book dealt with the eighteenth century. It was not so much his narrative of eighteenth century Ireland, however, as the preliminary comments on Irish character and his chapter on the 1641 rebellion which attracted the most extensive and bitter criticisms. John Mitchel's book written in refutation of Froude's was entitled *The Crusade of the Period: 1641*. Edmund Hogan S.J., as he said himself, 'in the interests of truth and humanity' edited *The History of the Wars of Ireland from 1641–53*, an account by an English soldier giving instances of humanity among the Irish which had been ignored in Froude's charge of a general massacre. Dr John McDonnell, although in his 83rd year, was also moved to reply to Froude's chapter on 1641, and his book, *The Ulster Civil War of 1641 and its Consequences* was offered 'in vindication of the calumniated Ulster Irish'. Fr Burke, J. P. Prendergast and Lecky also devoted considerable space to a criticism of Froude's treatment of 1641.

The amount of print which Froude's Irish critics devoted to his account of the 1641 episode was not altogether misplaced. The essence of his historical methods, and his political attitudes to the Irish and the Catholic Church, were highlighted in this chapter. Besides, Froude himself had described the rebellion of 1641 as 'the gravest event in Irish history, the turning point on which all later controversies between England and Ireland hinge'. When Froude began his study, 1641 had not yet passed out of politics into history. Froude, indeed, followed the more traditional melodramatic Protestant line, especially as laid down by Temple and Borlase in the seventeenth century, and he described 1641 primarily as an unprovoked general massacre of Protestants by Catholics, placing it in the same category as the Sicilian Vespers and St Bartholomew's Day.

[25] Quoted in H. Paul, *The life of Froude*, 152–3; W. H. Dunn, *James Anthony Froude*, 464.

[26] Paul, *op. cit.*, 245.

Extracts from the depositions in Trinity College, Dublin, concerning murders and spoliations by the 1641 rebels, which were given in Temple's account of the affair, formed Froude's chief source for the massacre story. Here, for Froude was what he as historian liked, the high dramatic content and the story told in the words of frightened participants. His vivid account recaptures some of the panic of the period.

The shock of Froude's vivid retelling of the massacre story at the height of Gladstonian liberalism acted as a catharsis on the historiography of 1641. Or to change the metaphor, his book was a catalyst which by a series of chain reactions served to release 1641 from politics into history. Apart from the refutations and apologies that were offered immediately by Irish writers, Prendergast, and more especially Lecky, questioned Froude's whole approach to the problem of historical evidence. In Lecky's opinion, Froude's method was neither 'philosophic' nor 'judicial'. And Lecky's counsel of perfection was that in dealing with the kind of evidence such as the depositions afforded, one should follow Voltaire's maxim and believe only the evil which a party writer tells of his own side, and the good that he recognises in his enemy. For this reason Lecky condemned Froude's reliance on one-sided evidence for the atrocities of 1641 and 1798, and his method of elaborating 'in ghastly pictures the crimes that were committed on one side while concealing those that were committed on the other'.[27]

Froude's account of 1641 and Lecky's criticisms of Froude helped to open up the problem to a more scholarly discussion. Mary Hickson's *Ireland in the Seventeenth Century, or the Massacres of 1641–2*, in the preparation of which Lecky's advice was sought and given and for which Froude wrote an introduction, marked an important advance in so far as, unlike either Froude or Lecky before her, she personally examined the T.C.D. depositions and edited some of the more credible ones. Her book when published was anything but satisfactory to Lecky, Prendergast, Robert Dunlop or S. R. Gardiner, but it was a step towards the critical assessment of the 1641 depositions as historical evidence. And after this step forward it was no longer acceptable to follow either the tradition that had existed from Temple to Froude, of selecting the most extravagant of the stories of massacre in the depositions, or the other tradition that existed among Irish Catholic apologists of tending to write off the thirty-three volumes of depositions as a massive English and Protestant lie.

Thomas Fitzpatrick's critical examination of some half dozen

[27] W. E. H. Lecky, *History of Ireland in the Eighteenth Century*, cabinet edition, I, 82; see also the review of Froude by Lecky in *Macmillan's Magazine*, xxvii (Jan. 1873), 246–64; xxx (June 1894), 166–84.

depositions dealing with one particular episode in the massacre alleged by Froude proved to be more acceptable than Miss Hickson's. His book *The Bloody Bridge* won from Dunlop the comment that this was the only method of arriving at a satisfactory conclusion about the worth of these depositions.

The argument about the depositions, however, was never resolved. Hickson, Froude and to a lesser extent Bagwell tended to accept at least some of the evidence in them. Prendergast, Gilbert, Lecky, Fitzpatrick and Dunlop minimised their historical value. Both Froude and Dunlop called for the publication of an authoritative Calendar of the depositions in the manner of the State Papers. This has never been done and Gilbert in fact reported adversely on them to the Historical Manuscripts Commission. One of the reasons why they were not published is undoubtedly because Froude had urged these depositions as an 'eternal witness' of Irish barbarity. Since, as Fitzpatrick said the 'eternal witness' was urged against a nation and a creed, not simply against those who were suspected of a crime, Froude's point about publication was not well received. The present generation of historians might profitably reopen the problem.

Froude's contribution to the historiography of eighteenth century Ireland was more direct than his effect on 1641. Sir Bernard Burke had only recently arranged the Irish State Papers in Dublin Castle which greatly facilitated the researches of both Froude and Lecky into the eighteenth century. Froude, in fact, had been to the Castle first. And it was precisely because he had been there first, and had interpreted his discoveries in such an anti-Irish and anti-Catholic way, that Lecky felt obliged to go over the same material and more besides.

What Froude had written hung like a shadow over Lecky's pages. Froude had to be refuted by him even when not actually named. He had to be followed into the manuscript repositories and his sources checked and verified. His partial evidence needed counterbalance; his generalisations measured against particulars; his assumptions queried; his theories rejected; his prejudices condemned; his whole claim to be regarded as a historian of Ireland examined under a searching light. At places in Lecky's work the shadow cast by Froude's book became something of an obsession with the Irishman. But because of Froude, Lecky's work on Irish history was all the better for having to be the more thorough and the more 'scientific'.

Between them Lecky and Froude who had released 1641 into history, by the sheer weight of solid achievement, imposed a pattern on the history of eighteenth century Ireland that has not been broken to this day. Most of the valuable and specialist studies done on eighteenth century Ireland since their time have tended to be additional or supplementary and within a framework constructed and sanctioned, not to say sanctified, first by Froude and then by Lecky following on his heels.

Apart from the effects which Froude had on the historiography of 1641 and eighteenth century Ireland, his political impact was also remarkable. In America he had at least succeeded in giving the other side of the picture of Anglo-Irish relations and there were those like the *New York Times* (2 Dec. 1872) who were willing to believe that the Irish were 'intractable', 'shiftless', 'credulous' and finally betrayed by their own demagogues. Even these had it on Froude's authority that for Irish discontent, as the *New York Times* also noted, England shared much of the responsibility. And the reports of Froude's lectures under headlines such as 'British Monarchs Condemned' (quoted by *The Times* in an editorial of 8 Nov. 1872) were welcomed by the friends of Irish independence in the U.S.A. Americans with no particular affection for Britain made the most of the opportunity afforded by the Froude controversy to condemn his lectures as partisan, and to declare in the words of the well-known American liberal orator, Wendell Phillips, who also replied to Froude, that Ireland had summoned England before the bar of the civilised world to pass judgement on her legislation.

A sceptical English press, on first learning of Froude's American mission, had expressed fears that he would only succeed in raking up the past before a popular tribunal. His lecture-tour and his book, indeed, went a long way towards creating just such a situation. And one thing his services helped to ensure was that from the very start of the home rule controversy the argument was going to be about history, or at least about the past politics of Anglo-Irish relations.

The attitude of many British and some American critics was that perhaps Froude should have let sleeping Celts lie. The Irish, they said, suffered from too much history and were too retrospective. Froude's sharpness of tongue and pen only prodded the bitter folk memory of an excitable race. The nineteenth century Irish romantics, however, were obsessed with the love of the 700 years of misery and of English oppression. They liked to picture themselves in Augustin Thierry's sympathetic description of them as 'victims of history'. The national poet, Tom Moore, the political Moses, Daniel O'Connell, the national preachers, Fathers Mathew or Tom Burke, the nation's propagandists and historians all wallowed in the 700 years of oppression, and throughout the nineteenth century the theme was prominent in song, sermon, school-text and story. And precisely because the theme was so widespread, the Irish resented all the more Froude's picture of them, not as one of history's victims, but as one of its fossils—survivals from a past that was antiquated and barbarous rather than ancient, glorious and sad.

As soon as they recovered, however, from the original shock of Froude's vigorous attack they began to realise, in the words of John Martin, that 'the affair of Mr Froude is doing valuable service to the national cause'.[28] He had certainly helped to publicise the Irish question, and nationalist propagandists were soon to appreciate the value of Froude's work for their own ends. There is no scarcity of evidence regarding the widespread use they made of it. Moderate home rulers preferred to bolster up their case with quotations from the historical work of the more judicious Lecky. The more extreme nationalists, in the tradition that sprang from Tone and led up to Pearse, and who regarded the holy-hatred of English rule in Ireland as one of the cardinal virtues of Irish nationalism, seemed to have had a strong preference for Froude. Indeed, in his condemnation of English rule, Froude displayed the very temperament of a holy-hater that must surely have qualified him for high Fenian rank had he only been Irish.

I know no reason whatever to suppose that that other holy-hater of England, Parnell, was addicted to reading, and Fenianism was one of the few things in Irish history that he seemed to know anything about. R. B. Haldane has recorded that, at a dinner party, Parnell once said to him that he had been reading a most remarkable book which threw more light on the Irish question than any book he had ever seen. When asked what the new source of knowledge was, Parnell replied that it was a book called *The English in Ireland* by a Mr Froude.[29] It has even been suggested that this was Parnell's favourite book because it exposed the iniquities of the English government of Ireland.[30] And at least on one important occasion, when addressing the U.S. Congress, Parnell cited Froude against Irish landlordism. So too did the Irish Press Agency in its propaganda leaflets, and one of these leaflets entitled 'Why Ireland has hated English rule' provided generous excerpts from Froude's work.

In his review of *The English in Ireland*, Lecky had claimed that it was hardly possible for any Irish Catholic to read the book without being driven into the ranks of home rule and more or less alienated from Great Britain. He also forecast as one of the 'mischievous' effects of Froude's book, that it would be quoted by Fenians at home and by England's enemies abroad in order to prove the selfishness of English rule. The forecast proved correct when people like Rossa, Mitchel and Tynan of the Invincibles did in fact quote Froude for

[28] *Nation*, 25 Jan. 1873.
[29] R. B. Haldane, *Autobiography*, 89; Sir Frederick Maurice, *Haldane 1856–1915*, 41–2.
[30] H. Paul, *op. cit.*, 241.

their own purposes.[31] And the *Irishman*, a paper sympathetic to Fenianism, in an editorial entitled 'Our Friend, Froude' reported that the Fenians in America had voted Froude a congratulatory address on being *the* representative man of English rule. It was stated that his work vindicated their efforts and that 'chosen extracts shall be conspicuously displayed in every Fenian lodge in America, to stimulate the memory of wrong and strengthen the soul with the consideration of an inflexible policy'.[32] The *New York Herald* believed that Froude had damaged the cause of England more than ten thousand Fenians could do.[33]

Froude might even be credited with helping to inspire the philosophy behind the dynamite raids on Britain during the 1880s. O'Donovan Rossa said that he had heard Froude quote Macaulay during the lectures in America, to the effect that England would only allow Ireland go free when the artist from the antipodes stood on the broken arch of London Bridge sketching the ruins of St Paul's. Accepting the challenge on behalf of his dynamitards, Rossa replied that if that was the way Froude and the people he represented wanted it, then so be it![34]

In Britain Froude's *English in Ireland* became something of a touchstone. The reactions to it in the numerous contemporary reviews and comments reveal not only conflicting British attitudes to the Irish question, but also the even wider political and intellectual fissures in Victorian society. Froude's English critics, those who praised him and agreed substantially with his ideas about Ireland, as well as those who regarded his work unfavourably, were all more or less in agreement that his *English in Ireland* was to a considerable extent a piece of political as distinct from historical writing. Professor A. V. Dicey writing in the New York *Nation* said: 'It is not history . . . His work must be judged as a piece of advocacy'.[35] And *The Times*, the *Edinburgh Review*, the *Saturday Review*, *Macmillan's Magazine*, the *Spectator*, the *Fortnightly Review*, all specifically agreed. Amongst the more serious journals Froude's staunchest champion was the tory *Quarterly Review*. But on this point it confessed:

Impartial the work certainly is not, and scarcely pretends to be. Sometimes it more resembles the speech of an accusing counsel, or the pamphlet

[31] See the references to Froude in P. J. Tynan, *The Irish National Invincibles and their times* (1894), 150, 423, 424.
[32] *Irishman*, 13 June 1874.
[33] Quoted in an editorial in the *Nation*, 7 Dec. 1872.
[34] J. O'Donovan Rossa, *Irish rebels in English prisons: a record of prison life*, see 'Supplementary chapter—1884', iii. For similar sentiments see J. Mitchel, *The Crusade of the Period*, 14; and P. J. Tynan, *The Irish National Invincibles*, 423–4.
[35] *Nation* (New York), xvi, no. 412 (22 May 1873), 355–7. For the attribution see Poole's *Index to periodical literature*, London 1891, I, 655.

of a political partisan, than a dispassionate narrative of past events; and in certain passages it is rather an indictment than a history.[36]

Froude, then, in writing history too obviously for the purpose of preaching political doctrines was regarded by British critics generally as swimming against the main current of contemporary developments in historiography. And Lord Acton no doubt had the *English in Ireland* in mind as well as Froude's *History of England* when he pronounced Froude's master, Carlyle, to be 'the most detestable of historians' only if one excepted Froude himself.[37]

Of all the political ideas expressed in Froude's *English in Ireland*, significantly his theory of race superiority got a large amount of support, either explicit or implicit, from the British reviewers. His whole argument, said the *Quarterly* was 'curiously in harmony with its own views of Irish character'. No other writer had depicted so clearly as Froude the 'incompleteness' and 'illogical unfinishedness' which pervade their nature and had spoiled their history.[38] An 'admirable portraiture of the Irish character' was how the *Edinburgh Review* reacted. *The Times* agreed that the Irish lacked the capacity for union, order and discipline. Even the *Saturday Review*, normally a bitter critic of Froude, expressed the general feeling when it claimed that 'at no time have there been any Irish fit to govern themselves'. It did imply, however, that it would not have been so grudging as Froude in allowing, as it said, 'some human traits' to the Irish.[39]

Faced with Froude's explicit racialism the Irish intellectuals were, naturally enough, the protesters. The unionist *Irish Times* as well as the nationalist press, the Protestant *Dublin University Magazine* as well as the Catholic *Dublin Review* resented Froude's comments on Irish character and regarded them as an insult.[40] Justin McCarthy reminded his readers that Froude settled every question easily and off-hand by reference to what Stuart Mill had called the resource of the lazy—namely, the theory of race. 'Celts are all wrong and Anglo-Saxons are all right, and there is an end of it'.[41] It is significant that on this question of race the Irish intellectuals preferred to take their political philosophy from the 'old liberal' authorities, such as Mill, Hallam and Macaulay.

[36] *Quarterly Review*, cxxiv, no. 267 (Jan. 1873), 170.
[37] Herbert Paul (ed.), *Letters of Lord Acton to Mary Gladstone* (1904), 70.
[38] *Quarterly Review*, cxxiv, no. 267 (Jan. 1873), 174.
[39] *Edinburgh Review*, cxxxvii, no. 279 (Jan. 1873), 128; *The Times*, 8 Nov. 1872; *Saturday Review*, xxxiv, no. 888 (2 Nov. 1872), 553–4; *ibid.*, xxxiv. no. 893 (7 Dec. 1872), 735–7.
[40] *Irish Times*, 7 Nov. 1872; *Dublin University Magazine*, lxxxi, no. 481 (Jan. 1873), 79–85; *Dublin Review*, new series, xx, no. 40 (April 1873), 421–48.
[41] *Galaxy*, xiv. no. 3 (Sept. 1872), 298.

The Irish critics of Froude's racialism got a certain measure of support from some English reviews—notably from the *Athenaeum*, the *British Quarterly*, and the *Spectator* which disliked Froude's habit of denouncing 'every statesman who . . . held Irishmen to be "a two legged race" '.[42] Gladstone was later to sum up the British liberal rejection of Froude's race theories in his satirical comment that Froude had assumed that the Irish suffered from a double dose of original sin.

The notion propagated in *The English in Ireland* that the English were among 'the nobler and wiser sorts of men', and as such justified in acting as a governing nation was, however, fairly widespread in Britain if we are to judge by the non-Irish reactions to Froude's book. It was fertile soil upon which British imperialism might thrive. But in so far as it looked upon the 'Celts' as inferior, and had not yet learned to think of the Irish as integrated in the Empire, it won no support from Ireland.

Froude's work on Irish history indeed contained matter which was a foretaste of what British imperialism, in its more extreme and repulsive forms, was about to become. In his writing he was an evangelical missionary who believed that the English were the chosen people with a duty to rule Ireland well, as these poor souls could not do so for themselves. For him the Irish were simply the whiteman's burden nearer home. The significance of Froude's *English in Ireland* as an imperialist tract, however, has been overlooked. But properly understood, the first edition, 1872–4, and the second edition, 1881, with its additional concluding chapter, should take a prominent place beside such works as Dilke's *Greater Britain* (1869) and Seeley's *Expansion of England* (1883), which are usually regarded by modern commentators as having carved out an intellectual pathway for the emerging British imperialism of the late nineteenth century.

The English in Ireland illustrates that Froude believed at least as strongly as Dilke in the superiority and destiny of the Anglo-Saxon race. And in several ways Froude's book was a closer anticipation of Seeley's imperialist influence than Dilke's was. It has been said that Seeley's account of England's wars of the eighteenth century encouraged the view that the Empire had been founded on war and conquest. But Froude had already, and in the same spirit as Seeley, outlined the various rebellions and the subsequent wars of reconquest in Ireland. Like Seeley a decade after him, Froude held it to be unthinkable that the colonies should be permitted to separate from England. Some of Froude's greatest scorn, therefore, was reserved for those Anglo-Irish colonists who had demanded legislative

[42] *Spectator*, xlvii, no. 2390 (18 April 1874), 501–2.

independence in the eighteenth century. For Seeley, withdrawal from India would have been the most inexcusable of all conceivable crimes. Froude told his American audience: 'You need not tell us to come out of Ireland, for we cannot and will not'.[43] The essence of British rule in India, according to Seeley, was moral. The essence of British rule in Ireland, according to Froude, was also moral—the duties of a civilised state towards a backward one, the duties of a people born to rule towards a people who were born to be ruled.

Closely related to his racialist assumptions, Froude's hard-line imperialist ideas received varying degrees of support in England. Carlyle, of course, backed his disciple. So too did James Fitzjames Stephen (recently returned from his experiences of the Empire at work in India) and the *Pall Mall Gazette*. Others, like the *Edinburgh Review*, *The Times* and the *British Quarterly*, although not prepared to accept what they regarded as Froude's 'might is right' dogma, nevertheless saw plenty of sense in his insistence on the 'claims of Empire'. With him they held that the conquest of Ireland was no crime, and that its compulsory retention could be justified on the grounds that Ireland was indispensable to Britain's imperial existence.[44]

Apart, however, from questions of race and Empire, the reviews illustrated that democratic and liberal principles found many defenders against Froude's onslaughts. Most of his reviewers thought him needlessly alarmed by the spectre of democracy and they disliked his apology for the penal laws, his abuse of Roman catholicism, his partiality for strong and even one-man government and his close linking together of might and right.

> No *sansculotte* of the first French Revolution ever talked so glibly of cutting brave men's throats and extirpating a whole nation as this cultured, lettered, middle-aged English gentleman

said the *Evening Telegraph*.[45]

The controversy sparked off by Froude's book pointed to the fact that most British intellectuals in the early 1870s belonged to the liberal tradition. But the Froude debate was a foreshadowing of the crisis which was produced by the troubles in Ireland and Gladstone's policies on Irish land and home rule in the 1880s. In one sense, Froude was a prophet who had forecast this crisis of the democratic and liberal conscience. In another sense, however, his book had

[43] *The Times*, 5 Nov. 1872; Colonel James E. McGee (ed.), '*Thumping English lies*': *Froude's slanders on Ireland and Irishmen*, New York, n.d., 29–30.

[44] *Pall Mall Gazette*, 27 April 1874; 8 May 1874; *Edinburgh Review*, cxxxvii, no. 279 (Jan. 1873), 122–153; *The Times*, 4 April 1874; *British Quarterly*, lvii, no. 94 (April 1873), 484–511.

[45] Quoted in *Freeman's Journal*, 7 Nov. 1872.

helped to prepare the ground for just such a crisis. He was, therefore, as much abettor as prophet. The *English in Ireland* confirmed the liberal view of which Gladstone became the chief representative, namely, that the Irish were victims of history who had been oppressed for 700 years by English misrule. And in the words of Goldwin Smith the 'burden of historical guilt' affecting the national conscience of Gladstonian England began to 'sit heavy on the spirit of the nation'. Froude, although not quite in the manner he intended, helped to foster that sense of historical guilt. And he did this in two conflicting ways—firstly by his candid and eloquent condemnation of the misgovernment of Ireland in the past, and secondly by exhibiting in his own writing the most extreme forms of racialism, imperialism, religious intolerance and anti-democratic feeling.

On the other hand, a number of critics who had condemned Froude in the 1870s hastened to adopt his ideas and almost his very language during the land and home rule agitations of the 1880s. And not the least of these were his Irish critics, unionists like Lecky and Prendergast, who, in the altered circumstances, were prepared to reread Froude with more sympathy, with less of the earlier castigation and even with some respect for his analysis of Anglo-Irish relations, his diagnosis of Irish ills and his solutions to the Irish question.

In the late 1880s and 1890s it was even possible to reread the *English in Ireland* as a remarkable blueprint for the Balfourian policy of killing home rule with kindness and twenty years of resolute government. And the message of Froude's book could be said to be most neatly wrapped up in Arthur Balfour's phrase when he declared that English governments had failed in Ireland in the past because they had been either all for repression or all for reform. Balfour added: 'I am for both; repression as stern as Cromwell; reform as thorough as Mr Parnell or anyone else can desire'.[46] And it was really not surprising that when Lecky declined to accept the Regius Professorship of Modern History at Oxford, Salisbury, partly at least as a reward for services rendered to the cause of unionism and the conservative policy in Ireland, extended the invitation to the 74-year-old Froude, who accepted it.

With Froude's appointment to the Oxford chair *The English in Ireland* had risen well above the storms that had first greeted it. And it seemed that Froude's ideas had at last earned a kind of official sanction from the conservative government.

His critics, of course, and especially his Irish ones, were far from silenced. Yet with all his faults Froude was, with the possible excep-

[46] Quoted in L. P. Curtis, *Coercion and conciliation in Ireland 1880–1892: a study in conservative unionism*, Princeton and London 1963, 179.

tion of Gladstone, the Englishman who had helped most to publicise what were called Ireland's historic wrongs. Directly and indirectly he had made a very real impact on the political controversy surrounding the Irish question, as well as on Irish historiography. And much had come out of his contributions in both fields.

He may not have been what he himself had claimed for his hero, Oliver Cromwell, the very best friend that Ireland ever had. But he was most certainly not what his first Irish critics believed him to be—Ireland's worst enemy.

The Dual Economy in Ireland, 1800–50

Joseph Lee

It is fifty years since the publication of Dr O'Brien's *Economic History of Ireland, from the Union to the Famine*.[1] This encyclopaedic work remains an indispensable guide to the period, but, written at the height of Ireland's struggle for independence, it is essentially a study in political determinism, attributing Ireland's economic misfortunes after the Union primarily to the obtuseness and malevolence of English policy. Despite important subsequent research into the fateful pre-famine decades, Lynch and Vaizey are the first to provide an explicit alternative to O'Brien's interpretation.[2] According to their model, a monetary economy along the east coast and in the towns of Limerick and Galway was sharply separated from a subsistence economy in the rest of the country. The monetary zone extended its frontiers during the war inflation from 1797 to 1815, only to contract again with the adoption of a deflationary policy by the Bank of Ireland in 1815. This disastrous post-war deflation, culminating in 'the suppression of paper money in 1826', by which 'the tragic effects of the great famine twenty years later were made inevitable', was 'of the greatest political and economic significance'.[3] In consequence of the Bank of Ireland's folly, the barter economy was finally monetised, not by injections of inflation, but by the brutal catharsis of the great famine, which was followed by a spectacular increase in monetisation.[4]

Irish historians, while insisting on the need for further research, immediately recognised that this approach offered an exciting alternative to accepted views.[5] More recently, however, the model has

[1] London 1921.

[2] P. Lynch and J. Vaizey, *Guinness's Brewery in the Irish Economy 1759–1876*, Cambridge 1960.

[3] *Ibid*., 9, 34, 26, 35.

[4] *Ibid*., 7, 247.

[5] See the detailed reviews by R. B. McDowell, *Irish Banking Review*, December 1960, 12–18; T. D. Williams, *Studia Hibernica*, II (1962), 245–8; F. S. L. Lyons, *Irish Historical Studies*, xiii (1963), 371–4.

been severely criticised for grossly underrating the market orientation of the whole economy.[6] This paper examines some of the evidence used in support of the three central concepts—the sharply dualistic nature of the economy, the decisive importance of monetary policy in determining the degree of dualism, and the crucial change in Bank of Ireland policy after 1815.[7]

Though Lynch and Vaizey nowhere precisely define the boundaries of the monetary zone, they insist that the two economies were geographically distinct: 'there were links between the two, but they were slight and tenuous as the division between the economies was fairly sharp . . . the cash economy extended tentacles into subsistence Ireland, but the penetration was neither broad nor deep'.[8] However, there is abundant evidence that the penetration, though growing increasingly shallow as one moved west, was broad, and that a money economy lay superimposed on a non-money economy throughout the country. In 1835, the 1,600 replies to the query: 'Are wages of labour paid in money, or provisions, or by conacres, or in any other way?' indicate that a monetary stratum spread over 'subsistence' Ireland, just as a subsistence stratum spread under 'monetary' Ireland.[9] Over most of the country, barter and cash zones alike, farmers paid their rent in money, cottiers in labour. In the barony of Lecale, in 'monetary' Down, 'small farmers pay their rent in money; labourers generally pay it in labour',[10] while at the opposite end of the country, in the barony of Trughenackmy, in 'subsistence' Kerry, 'the small farmers pay their rent almost universally in money'. In Middlethird, Waterford, 'small tenantry, or those who hold above two or three acres, pay their rents in money, as other farmers'; in Gowran, Kilkenny, 'the rent of small holdings is always paid in money'; in Maryborough, Queen's County, 'the cottiers pay the rents of their small holdings in labour; other small tenants more generally pay them in money'; in Mohill, Leitrim, 'the rents of the small farmers, as distinguished from the holdings of the cottiers, were always paid in money'; in Omagh, Tyrone, 'the small farmers pay their rent in money, the cottiers mostly in labour'.[11]

[6] L. M. Cullen, 'Problems in the interpretation and revision of eighteenth century Irish economic history', *Transactions of the Royal Historical Society*, 5th series, xvii (1967), 20; R. Crotty, *Irish Agricultural Production*, Cork 1966, 306–7.

[7] In addition to evidence concerning general economic conditions, Lynch and Vaizey believe that Guinness's sales closely reflect changes in the nature of the economy. I have argued elsewhere that fluctuations in sales of Guinness do not always support the authors' conclusions (see the discussion in the *Economic History Review*, 2nd ser., xix (1966), 183–194). This essay is confined solely to evidence of a more general economic nature.

[8] Lynch and Vaizey, *op. cit.*, 25.

[9] *Poor Inquiry* (*Ireland*), H.C. 1836 (36), xxxi, supplement to app. D. 2–393, Q. 11.

[10] *Ibid.*, H.C. 1836 (38), xxxiii, app. F, 75.

[11] *Ibid.*, 63, 77, 46, 54, 38, 78.

The subsistence stratum was undoubtedly deeper in the west than in the east, partly because of poorer soil, partly because transport costs generally placed markets beyond the reach of whatever meagre surpluses might have existed. But by including farmers with cottiers and labourers under the conceptually useless terms 'peasantry' or 'country folk', the model seriously underestimates the depth of the rural monetary stratum and the size of the domestic market. The maritime zone is allotted a population of only 2 million in 1845.[12] Even a crude calculation suggests that this estimate must be doubled. The famine left 6·7 million survivors by 1851. The maximum number on public relief had slightly exceeded 3 million, indicating that about 3·5 million survived entirely on their own resources—the truly hidden Ireland of these years. When allowance is made for the substantial proportion of monetised emigrants, and for double counting of those on relief who died or emigrated, the monetary economy had a minimum population of 4 million. It now becomes possible to understand why 170 bank branches were established in the twenty years before the famine, compared with only 79 in the following twenty.[13] The authors cite the establishment of bank branches as evidence of growing monetisation,[14] but on this criterion the advance of the money economy actually slowed down sharply after the famine! What seems an anomaly in the context of geographical dualism can be explained on the basis of strata dualism. Bank branches certainly facilitated commercial transactions among the members of the monetary stratum throughout the country before the famine—but what did the cottier know of the inside of a bank?

The rigorous application of the dualistic hypothesis conveys as misleading a picture of the maritime as of the subsistence economy. The description of the advanced techniques and the high capital/output ratio characteristic of the monetary zone belongs to theory rather than history:

In the growth of a country with two economies, one capitalist and the other subsistence, the primacy of the maritime capitalist economy with a heavy bias towards exports is a well established historical phenomenon. The problem is to explain the lack of contact between the two. Where contact is limited, the main exporting industries in the maritime zone tend to be those with a high capital/output ratio, often using relatively advanced techniques. Indeed there is usually a gap in the hierarchy of techniques corresponding to the boundary between the zones—in the maritime the level of technique is high: in the subsistence it is very elementary. In Ireland brewing—situated in the maritime economy—was an industry

[12] Lynch and Vaizey, *op. cit.*, 10.
[13] *Thom's Directory, 1847*, 213; *Thom's Directory, 1867*, 780.
[14] Lynch and Vaizey, *op. cit.*, 169–70.

with a high capital/output ratio, using relatively advanced techniques, and Ireland is, to this extent, one of a generality of cases.[15]

But Guinness's was no more typical of maritime than of subsistence Ireland. Brewing was not the principal industry in the monetary zone; even less was it the main export. As late as 1835 beer accounted for less than two per cent of Irish exports.[16] Lynch and Vaizey's statement that 'where contact is limited, the main exporting industries in the maritime zone tend to be those with a high capital/output ratio, often using relatively advanced techniques' overlooks the fact that agriculture, not brewing, was overwhelmingly the main export industry of monetary, no less than subsistence, southern Ireland.

Lynch and Vaizey believe that the famine confirms the concept of two geographically distinct economies. In fact it seriously weakens the argument. According to their analysis, 'the areas unaffected directly by the great famine were the maritime economy centred on Dublin, Cork and Belfast', and in so far as the maritime zone suffered from slump this was merely the downswing of the trade cycle, which indeed, 'may have been less severe in Ireland than in England'.[17] However, banking statistics support the contention of the chairman of the premier Irish railway, the Great Southern and Western, that 'every interest in the country was more or less affected by the failure of the potato crop'.[18] Bank deposits rose 60 per cent between 1840 and 1846, then fell 25 per cent by 1848, and did not surpass the 1846 figure until 1852.[19] Between September 1846 and September 1849, bank note circulation fell nearly 50 per cent—almost twice as sharply as in Britain.[20] Lynch and Vaizey attribute the failure of circulation to rise rapidly after 1848 to growing use of cheques.[21] Note circulation, however, remains a useful index of economic fluctuations long after 1850—the depressions of the early 1860s and the late 1870s were faithfully reflected in the 22 and 24 per cent declines in circulation from 1860 to 1863 and 1876 to 1880, respectively.[22] It may be hazarded that the steep fall in circulation in the later 1840s tells a grimmer tale than greater familiarity with the cheque system.

If these statistics cannot be easily reconciled with the claim that the monetary economy was little affected by the great famine, it seems

[15] Lynch and Vaizey, *op. cit.*, 17.
[16] *Second report . . . on . . . a general system of railways for Ireland*, H.C. 1837–8 (145), xxxv, app. B, no. 10, 91.
[17] Lynch and Vaizey, *op. cit.*, 165, 166.
[18] *Irish Railway Gazette*, 8 Feb. 1847, 132.
[19] *Thom's Directory, 1865*, 847.
[20] *Thom's Directory, 1850*, 192; B. R. Mitchell and P. Deane, *British Historical Statistics*, Cambridge 1962, 450.
[21] Lynch and Vaizey, *op. cit.*, 170.
[22] Mitchell and Deane, *op. cit.*, 450.

even more difficult to sustain the assertion that:

> Dublin soon recovered from the depression; by late 1848 the boom had resumed . . . and it may be doubted whether the distress among the working class was prolonged or widespread. The great famine had taken place as though it were a war in a neighbouring country, while Dublin was a brightly lit, comparatively well fed, slightly anxious neutral territory.[23]

Dublin undoubtedly suffered from the downswing of the British trade cycle in 1847, but, far from the boom having resumed 'by late 1848', 1849 began in a state of 'extreme depression', with 'the stagnation of trade' continuing into the autumn.[24] Dublin's recovery, instead of preceding, lagged behind that of England and Belfast, precisely because of the severe impact of the famine on the southern economy.[25] Indeed, some of the evidence in *Guinness's Brewery* itself casts doubt on the picture of a safely insulated Dublin. We are told, for instance, that in 1847 A. L. Guinness of Stillorgan, co. Dublin, received a presentation 'to mark the veneration of his faithful labourers, who in a period of dire distress were protected by his generous liberality from the prevailing destitution'. Guinness's gave gratuities to their clerks in February and September 1847 to relieve them 'from any remaining pressure which may have arisen out of the late awful famine' and again in March 1849 as an 'expression of the thankfulness we feel for the mercies we have (as a firm) enjoyed for some years past amidst so much mercantile distress'.[26]

Thus the pure theory of geographical dualism greatly exaggerates the lack of contact between the two sectors. Lynch and Vaizey make a contribution of critical importance to our understanding of the period by isolating the use of money as the crucial distinction between the two economies, but the contrast was less between a healthy east and a sickly west than between an east and a west suffering in different degrees from the same sickness. Can this diseased condition of Irish society be traced primarily to monetary policy?

Lynch and Vaizey nowhere seek the origins of dualism. They take the existence of two economies in 1797 as given,[27] and then explain subsequent changes in their frontiers in terms of monetary policy, without inquiring how or when dualism originated. This failure to

[23] Lynch and Vaizey, *op. cit.*, 167.
[24] *Advocate*, 24 Jan., 1 Aug. 1849.
[25] *Memo. on the state of Ireland, drawn up for Lord Clarendon by Mr Murray of the Provincial Bank*, 1 Jan. 1850, p. 3; 1 Jan. 1851, p. 12 (NLI Ms. 7562).
[26] Lynch and Vaizey, *op. cit.*, 116, 146.
[27] Lynch and Vaizey, *op. cit.*, 4.

incorporate monetary aspects adequately into their structural context is the major conceptual weakness of the model. The emphasis on monetary as distinct from structural factors finds striking expression in their assertion that:

> From 1815 to 1825 the revaluation of the Irish pound depressed exports, and it took a decade to readjust trade to the new currency conditions. Maritime Ireland in the years after Waterloo experienced what Britain was to experience in the twentieth century after the return to the gold standard in 1925.[28]

Can the same monetary explanation serve equally convincingly for such contrasting economies as the highly industrialised Britain of the 1920s and the agrarian Ireland of a century earlier? For Britain 'the immediate source of her relatively poor showing before 1930 ... was mainly the exceptional decline of the old staple industries, in nearly every case as a result of a heavy fall in exports ...'.[29] But Irish exports did not fall heavily between 1815 and 1825. On the contrary, despite temporary falls in some agricultural exports due to bad harvests, the volume of Irish exports in the decade after Waterloo surpassed that of the preceding decade.[30] On the other hand, British terms of trade improved considerably in the 1920s;[31] Ireland's probably worsened after 1815, as did those of the primary producing countries exporting to Britain in the 1920s. If one seeks a twentieth century analogy, the experience of these countries—including Ireland itself after the first world war—is likely to prove more instructive. The assertion that post-1815 Ireland and post-1925 England faced identical problems wrenches both economies out of their historical contexts.

Indeed, if production for export automatically ensured monetisation, then the growth in the volume of exports in the pre-famine decades should have occasioned a marked increase in the absolute size of the monetary economy. But while it is probable that its absolute, as distinct from its proportionate, size did increase between 1815 and 1845, production for the market did not guarantee membership of the monetary club. The *Drummond Report* pointed out in 1838 that 'from north to south indications of improvement are everywhere visible ... but these signs of growing prosperity are unhappily not so discernible in the condition of the labouring people,

[28] *Ibid.*, 33.
[29] W. Ashworth, *An economic history of England, 1870–1939*, London 1960, 413.
[30] Cf. *Imports and exports of Ireland, from 25th March 1771 to 5th January 1811*, H.C. 1823 (472), xvi; *Exports and imports: official value of all Ireland, 1811–1822*, H.C. 1823 (318), xvi; *Second report ... on ... a general system of railways for Ireland*, H.C. 1837–8 (145), xxxv, app. B, no. 10, 91.
[31] Ashworth, *op. cit.*, 415.

as in the amount of the produce of their labour'.[32] The profits did not wind up in labourers' pockets; they were siphoned off by traders and farmers—a phenomenon typical of 'export economies' where expanding trade occasions few 'spread effects' among the poor.

This seems to have been generally the case after 1815. It is crucial for Lynch and Vaizey's case that it should not have been the case before 1815, for if the monetary fruits of the war inflation did not percolate through to the cottiers and labourers, but simply swelled farmers' incomes, little progress would have been recorded in reducing the size of the subsistence stratum. If Wakefield is correct in arguing that the condition of the poor had not improved proportionately with the growth of foreign trade during the war,[33] pre-1815 Ireland may not have been so different from post-1815 Ireland. It is probable that the war years saw an actual deepening of the subsistence stratum, not only absolutely but even relatively, simply because the rate of increase in the numbers of cottiers and labourers may have been outstripping the rate of expansion of the monetary economy. In so far as this was the case, the post-war depression merely accentuated, rather than reversed, existing tendencies, and the emphasis which has come to be laid, from this point of view, on the Napoleonic wars as a sharply distinct period in Irish economic history may appear in retrospect almost as excessive as the once fashionable, and now, largely thanks to Lynch and Vaizey's demolition work, happily discredited emphasis on the Union.

The failure to incorporate structural factors into the model also vitiates the discussion of economic conditions in Ulster. Though including Belfast as a city of the same maritime genus as Dublin, Cork and Galway, the authors concede that Ulster's exemption from the most extreme ravages of the famine was 'a variation in local circumstances'. They partly attribute this 'variation' to Ulster's superior land system, but maintain the internal consistency of the monetary thesis by also arguing that 'in Ulster gold was the sole circulating medium, and there were hardly any banks until after the inflation in the Napoleonic wars. Ulster suffered less from the inflation, and from the subsequent deflation, than the rest of the country'.[34] How convincing is this monetary interpretation of Ulster's position?

Ulster, it is true, experienced less inflation between 1797 and 1803 than the south. But it is far less certain that she escaped the post-war slump. The three banks in Belfast were founded between 1806 and

[32] *Second report . . . on . . . a general system of railways for Ireland*, H.C. 1837–8 (145), xxxv, 9.
[33] E. Wakefield, *An Account of Ireland, Statistical and Political*, London 1812, II, 233–4.
[34] Lynch and Vaizey, *op. cit.*, 26.

1809, and the change-over to paper from gold was already well under way by 1810.[35] The circulation of the Belfast Bank plunged nearly 40 per cent between 1814 and 1816, recovered in 1818 and 1819, only to fall sharply once more in 1822, suggesting that Ulster suffered severely from the post-war fluctuations.[36] East Ulster got the worst of both monetary worlds—missing the best of the inflation, and catching the deflation—but this did not prevent it becoming the sole industrialised corner of Ireland. By lumping Belfast indiscriminately with Dublin, Cork and Galway, the authors severely limit the value of the model. For the 'variation' in Belfast was nothing less than the industrial revolution. Earlier historians believed that the real dualism in Ireland lay in the contrast between east Ulster and the rest of the country. The monetary interpretation does not even hint that such a contrast existed.

That the post-1815 (or, rather, 1814) depression caused serious short-term distress in Ireland, as all over western Europe, has long been recognised. Lynch and Vaizey's innovation consists in attributing this depression primarily to the folly of the doctrinaire deflationists in the Bank of Ireland, and in seeing the suppression of paper money in 1826 as sealing the fate of the subsistence economy twenty years later. However conceivable it may be that the Bank of Ireland held unenlightened views on monetary matters after, as distinct from before, 1815, the evidence adduced is not conclusive in this respect.

The authors contrast the deflationary solution to the payments crisis of 1819 with the capital import solution to the crisis of 1811–1815, explaining the favourable exchanges in the earlier years 'by heavy payments into the Irish economy arising from capital imports because the recorded balance-of-trade figures show a substantial deficit which would have been magnified in the balance-of-payments figures by payments for invisible imports'.[37] As this assertion is undocumented, it is not clear what is meant by the 'recorded balance of trade figures'. If these represent real values—exports and imports at current prices—the authors will perform an inestimable service by making them available to other historians, who have been unable to locate real import values for this period. If the reference is to official figures, these are worthless, as they value exports and imports at prices current in 1790. Butter exports, for instance, were

[35] E. R. R. Green, *The Lagan Valley, 1800–1850*, London 1949, 68; Wakefield, *op. cit.*, II, 176, 187, 190, 193.
[36] *Report . . . into . . . the circulation of promissory notes under the value of £5 in Scotland and Ireland*, H.C. 1826–7 (245), vi, 25.
[37] Lynch and Vaizey, *op. cit.*, 34, 30.

officially valued at only 42/6 per cwt,[38] whereas between 1810 and 1815 they fetched from 110/- to 138/- per cwt.[39]

The official balance of trade figures do show a substantial deficit from 1812 to 1815, but if the terms of trade moved markedly in Ireland's favour after 1790, then an 'official' deficit could well conceal a real surplus. This was the case between 1790 and 1802, when export prices rose 69 per cent compared with a rise of only 32 per cent in import prices, turning an official deficit of nearly £1 million into a real surplus of almost £1 million in 1802.[40] Real export values reveal how misleading the official figures are. In 1807, for instance, official imports amounted to £6·4 million, compared with official exports of only £5·3 million. Real exports, however, were valued at £10·1 million.[41] Unless the real value of imports was 60 per cent greater than the recorded value, the balance of trade was in fact favourable. Even a substantial surplus on trade, may, of course, have been still offset by an adverse invisible balance, but until more acceptable estimates become available, it seems premature to generalise on the basis of such hypothetical data.

Exchange rates provide little direct evidence of a change in Bank of Ireland policy after 1815. The Irish pound was virtually at par from 1808, falling appreciably below par only in 1815–16 and in 1819, and rising above par in 1812–14—quite the contrary of what one might a priori expect.[42] After 1805 it is the stability, not the instability, of exchange rates that is remarkable, and no evidence is adduced to refute Fetter's belief that the Bank of Ireland pursued a conscious stabilisation policy from that date.[43] If this was the case, the Bank should be condemned, not for changing, but for continuing, its policy in altered economic circumstances after 1815, though in view of the little amelioration brought about by the marked fall below par in late 1815 and early 1816 one may be sceptical of the relevance of devaluation to Irish circumstances. It seems probable that the elasticities of demand for Irish exports and imports after 1815 were such that devaluation would have been of doubtful effectiveness.

Can then the Bank of Ireland be exonerated from a major share of the blame for the post-war depression? Even if it may not have been

[38] *Exports and imports: official value of all Ireland, 1811–1822*, H.C. 1823 (318), xvi, 8.
[39] Lynch and Vaizey, *op. cit.*, 34.
[40] *Report from the committee on the circulating paper, the specie and the current coin of Ireland; and also on the exchange between that part of the United Kingdom and Great Britain*, H.C. 1803–4 (86), iii, 99, reprinted in H.C. 1826 (407), v.
[41] *Real value of exports from Ireland*, H.C. 1808 (214), xi. On the issue of real and official values cf. A. H. Imlah, *Economic Elements in the Pax Britannica*, Cambridge, Mass. 1958, 20 ff. 'Real' export values may themselves be far from accurate, but they are certainly much closer to the truth than 'official' values.
[42] Fetter, *op. cit.*, 20.
[43] *Ibid.*, 51.

primarily responsible for the immediate depression, did not the influence of its directors, Arthur Guinness and W. P. Lunnell, drive the last nail into the subsistence coffin by leading to the prohibition of paper money? For the crowning indictment of Bank of Ireland policy is that 'by the suppression of paper money in 1826 the tragic effects of the great famine twenty years later were made inevitable'.[44] The basic published evidence certainly indicates that Lunnell and Guinness opposed paper money.[45] But Guinness denied that the Bank had adopted an anti-paper policy:

Q. Can you state what was the general opinion of the directors of the Bank of Ireland?

A. I really cannot say that there has been any general conclusion formed upon the subject and therefore I feel myself hardly warranted to state what the opinion of the court may be upon it.[46]

What seem to have been differences of opinion among the Bank's directors would be irrelevant if the anti-paper faction eventually won their case. But in fact paper money was not suppressed in 1826 or subsequently. Notes under £5 were suppressed in England, but not in Scotland or Ireland. In 1845 these notes accounted for 60 per cent of the paper in circulation in Ireland.[47] The famine must be partly attributed to the dearth of purchasing power among the poor—but this dearth cannot be traced to the suppression of paper money in 1826.

This essay, though limited to a few of the fascinating issues raised by the dualistic model, has referred, at greater breadth than depth, to several features of the pre-famine economy. It has argued that geographical dualism existed only to a very limited extent, that Bank of Ireland policy after 1815 probably did not depart from the principles which had guided it during the preceding decade, and, whether it did or not, monetary policy was of relatively minor importance compared with structural factors in influencing the development of the Irish economy in the first half of the nineteenth century. By so stimulatingly pioneering the application of modern economic theory to the study of Irish economic history, Lynch and Vaizey's work is assured of a permanent place in Irish historiography. The enduring value of their approach cannot be doubted, but it seems to me that the particular model adopted, while allowing many fruitful insights, does not always fit the facts.

[44] Lynch and Vaizey, *op. cit.*, 26.
[45] *Report from the select committee of the House of Lords to inquire into the state of the circulation of promissory notes under the value of £5 in Scotland and Ireland*, H.C. 1826–7 (245), vi, 69–70.
[46] *Ibid.*, 67.
[47] *Thom's Directory, 1850*, 192.

Joseph Lee

Addendum

Since submitting the above paper, I have located real external trade figures for 1814 and 1815, which confirm the suspicion voiced in the text that the balance of trade, contrary to the official figures, was in substantial surplus, with exports valued at 14·6 and 12·7 million pounds respectively, compared with imports at only 10·4 and 9·4 million.[48] Though it remains not entirely inconceivable that an adverse invisible balance may have more than compensated for these very marked surpluses, the figures cast grave doubt on the assumption of a 'payments crisis' from 1811 to 1815 and on the interpretation of Bank of Ireland policy based on that assumption.

[48] P.R.O., Customs 15, 118, 119.

LIST OF ARTICLES IN *HISTORICAL STUDIES*, VOLUMES I TO VIII, INCLUSIVE

The articles in this and previous volumes of *Historical Studies* are listed here under the following headings:

(i) Irish History—Early and Medieval; Modern
(ii) British History—Early and Medieval; Modern
(iii) European and World History—Early and Medieval; Modern
(iv) Historiographical and Other Articles.

Some articles are listed under more than one heading.

(i) IRISH HISTORY

Early and Medieval

Liam de Paor: 'The Aggrandisement of Armagh', VIII, 95.
Francis J. Byrne: 'The Ireland of St Columba', V, 37.
Marjorie O. Anderson: 'Columba and other Irish Saints in Scotland', V, 26.
Denis Bethell: 'English Monks and Irish Reform in the Eleventh and Twelfth Centuries', VIII, 111.
W. L. Warren: 'The Interpretation of Twelfth-Century Irish History', VII, 1.
Jocelyn Otway-Ruthven: 'The Character of Norman Settlement in Ireland', V, 75.
E. St John Brooks: 'The Sources for Medieval Anglo-Irish History', I, 86.
Aubrey Gwynn, 'Bibliographical Note on Medieval Anglo-Irish History', I, 93.
R. H. M. Dolley: 'Anglo-Irish Monetary Policies, 1172–1637', VII, 45.
Urban Flanagan, O.P.: 'Papal Provisions in Ireland, 1305–78', III, 92.
J. F. Lydon: 'The Bruce Invasion of Ireland', IV, 111.

Modern

R. H. M. Dolley: 'Anglo-Irish Monetary Policies, 1172–1637', VII, 45.
R. Dudley Edwards: 'The Irish Reformation Parliament of Henry VIII, 1556–7', VI, 59.
D. B. Quinn: 'Ireland and Sixteenth-Century European Expansion', I, 20.
Helga Hammerstein: 'Aspects of the Continental Education of Irish Students in the Reign of Elizabeth I', VIII, 137.
G. A. Hayes-McCoy: 'Gaelic Society in Ireland in the Late Sixteenth Century', IV, 45.
John Bossy: 'The Counter-Reformation and the People of Catholic Ireland, 1596–1641', VIII, 155.
H. F. Kearney: 'Mercantalism and Ireland, 1620–40', I, 59.
Aidan Clarke: 'The Policies of the "Old English" in Parliament, 1640–41', V, 85.

J. C. Beckett: 'The Confederation of Kilkenny Reviewed', II, 29.
J. G. Simms: 'The Irish Parliament of 1713', IV, 82.
Michael Drake: 'The Irish Demographic Crisis of 1740–41', V, 101.
J. A. Murphy: 'The Support of the Catholic Clergy in Ireland, 1750–1850', V, 103.
Maureen Wall: 'The United Irish Movement', V, 122.
Kennedy F. Roche: 'The Relations of the Catholic Church and the State in England and Ireland, 1800–52', III, 9.
J. J. Lee: 'The Dual Economy in Ireland, 1800–50', VIII, 191.
K. H. Connell: 'Illicit Distillation: an Irish Peasant Industry', III, 58.
P. J. Jupp: 'Irish M.P.s at Westminster in the Early Nineteenth Century', VII, 65.
Kevin B. Nowlan: 'The Meaning of Repeal in Irish History', IV, 1.
O. O. MacDonagh: 'The Irish in Victoria, 1851–91: a Demographic Essay', VIII, 67.
Donal McCartney: 'James Anthony Froude and Ireland: a Historiographical Controversy of the Nineteenth Century', VIII, 171.
F. S. L. Lyons: 'The Economic Ideas of Parnell', II, 60.
T. W. Moody: '*The Times* versus Parnell and Co., 1887–90', VI, 147.

(ii) BRITISH HISTORY

Early and Medieval

Marjorie O. Anderson: 'Columba and other Irish Saints in Scotland', V, 26.
Denis Bethell: 'English Monks and Irish Reform in the Eleventh and Twelfth Centuries', VIII, 111.
G. W. S. Barow: 'The Reign of William the Lion, King of Scotland', VII, 21.
J. W. Gray: 'The Church and Magna Charta in the Century after Runnymede', VI, 23.

Modern

B. H. G. Wormald: 'The Historiography of the English Reformation', I, 50.
Charles Wilson: 'Government Policy and Private Interest in Modern English History', VI, 85.
Kennedy F. Roche: 'The Relations of the Catholic Church and the State in England and Ireland, 1800–52', III, 9.
P. J. Jupp: 'Irish M.P.s at Westminster in the Early Nineteenth Century', VII, 65.
Brian Inglis: 'The Influence of *The Times*', III, 32.
Maurice Cowling: 'The Use of Political Philosophy in Mill, Green and Bentham', V, 141.
Asa Briggs, 'Chartism Reconsidered', II, 42.
T. W. Moody: '*The Times* versus Parnell and Co., 1887–90', VI, 147.
C. L. Mowat: 'Social legislation in Britain and the U.S. in the Early Twentieth Century: a Problem in the History of Ideas', VII, 81.
Herbert Butterfield: 'Sir Edward Grey in July 1914', V, 1.

A3

List of Articles